# DATE DUE

| | | | |
|---|---|---|---|
| | | | |
| | | | |
| | | | |
| | | | |
| | | | |
| | | | |
| | | | |
| | | | |
| | | | |
| | | | |
| | | | |
| | | | |
| | | | |
| | | | |
| | | | |
| | | | |
| | | | |

DEMCO 38-296

# COURT-MARTIAL AT PARRIS ISLAND

# COURT-MARTIAL
## AT PARRIS ISLAND

# THE
# RIBBON CREEK
# INCIDENT

## JOHN C. STEVENS III

NAVAL INSTITUTE PRESS
*Annapolis, Maryland*

Library of Congress Cataloging-in-Publication Data
Stevens, John C., 1939–.
    Court-martial at Parris Island : the Ribbon Creek incident / John C. Stevens III.
       p.    cm.
    Includes bibliographical references and index.
    ISBN 1-55750-814-3 (alk. paper)
    1. McKeon, Matthew—Trials, litigation, etc. 2. Trials (Military offenses)—
South Carolina—Parris Island. 3. Courts-martial and courts of inquiry—
South Carolina—Parris Island. 4. Basic training (Military education)—United
States. 5. United States. Marine Corps. I. Title.
KF7654.5.M38S74  1999
343.73'0143—dc21                                 98-46368

Printed in the United States of America on acid-free paper ∞
06 05 04 03 02 01 00 99   9 8 7 6 5 4 3 2
First printing

To the young men who died on April 8, 1956, in Ribbon Creek

THOMAS HARDEMAN

DONALD FRANCIS O'SHEA

CHARLES FRANCIS REILLY

JERRY LAMONTE THOMAS

LEROY THOMPSON

NORMAN ALFRED WOOD

*Let's be damned sure no man's ghost will ever say, "If your training program had only done its job."*

Drill instructors' motto, 1956

# Contents

| | Preface | ix |
|---|---|---|
| | Acknowledgments | xi |
| | Introduction | xiii |
| 1 | Death in the Boondocks | 1 |
| 2 | Time and Place | 11 |
| 3 | Platoon 71 | 15 |
| 4 | Final Straws | 20 |
| 5 | "The Whole Marine Corps Has Had It, Too" | 27 |
| 6 | The Reaction | 35 |
| 7 | Inquiry | 40 |
| 8 | Media Feast | 59 |
| 9 | The Tide Turns | 66 |
| 10 | Trial Begins | 79 |
| 11 | Trial Continues—Week 2 | 97 |
| 12 | The Defendant's Version | 113 |
| 13 | Pulling Out All the Stops | 128 |
| 14 | Seven Courageous Men | 142 |
| 15 | Closing the Book | 155 |
| 16 | Retrospect | 162 |
| | Bibliography | 175 |
| | Index | 179 |

# Preface

The Ribbon Creek drownings and the fate of Matthew McKeon have been at the back of my mind since the news of the incident first broke in 1956 while I was a junior in high school. In 1989 my curiosity in this long-dormant subject was whetted by an article by Wil Haygood published in the *Boston Globe*. Haygood interviewed several of the survivors of the Ribbon Creek march, including McKeon, the drill instructor who led his platoon into the treacherous waters.

I mulled over the subject for several years after reading that article, thinking that more should be written about Ribbon Creek and Matthew McKeon. In the late 1980s, former marine Keith Fleming described the institutional response to the Ribbon Creek drownings in *The U.S. Marine Corps in Crisis*. Other publications have alluded to the affair in one form or another, but to my knowledge no one has attempted to examine the Ribbon Creek march and the ensuing events comprehensively from an objective perspective.

In late 1995, I decided to attempt to discover exactly what had occurred at Ribbon Creek in April 1956 and to tell the whole story. The full account really involves several stories: of a terrible training accident, of the consequent ripple of shock waves that imperiled the very foundation of the Marine Corps, of a brilliant trial lawyer who demanded only justice as his fee, and ultimately of the terribly flawed judgment, and yet simple nobility, of the man whose final sentence is to live with the memory of the six young men he led into waters that took their lives.

# Acknowledgments

Matthew McKeon, once he learned that I am a former marine, was more than gracious with his time and patiently recounted as many of the details of the still painful events as his memory could recall. His brother-in-law, Thomas Costello, willingly shared his insights into the case, particularly with regard to Emile Zola Berman's selection as defense counsel. Howard Lester, Fred Haden, Charles Sevier and his wife, Gwen, John DeBarr, and Jeremiah Collins offered firsthand information about the events surrounding the court-martial. Without the insights and information provided by Nicholas Sisak and Dr. Bentley Nelson I would never have known what prompted the court to disregard the recommendations of Generals Pate and Puller in making its decision.

Eugene Alvarez, Ph.D., a former history professor and former drill instructor, was a guiding hand throughout my research. I am sure he knows more about Parris Island, including the culture and practices of the drill instructors in the mid-1950s, than any other man alive. My questions to Gene Alvarez by e-mail always brought a detailed response by the next morning.

Duane Faw, the Parris Island Depot's legal officer in 1956, who ultimately rose to the rank of brigadier general, offered his insights, educated me regarding some of the relevant legal procedures under the Uniform Code of Military Justice, and was kind enough to review and critique my manuscript.

Former marines Vic Ditchkoff, Richard Hudson, Leland Blanding, and Hugh Jones described the life of a Parris Island drill instructor. All were on the drill field in the mid-1950s except Ditchkoff, whose more recent tours included instructing incoming DIs about the events that led to the Ribbon

Creek drownings. Meeting Hugh Jones, my own former drill instructor, was one of the most rewarding personal moments of this historical journey.

Dr. Stephen Wise, curator of the Parris Island museum, furnished invaluable background information and photographs. Major Ron Bernal, Dean Bradley, Jackie Loughery Schweitzer, Daniel Moyer, Louis Kane, William McCullough, Rose Bond, Plato Cacheris, the Hon. Paul Mullaney, Jim Fisher, Keith Fleming, Kay Mack, Kirsten Raymond, Susan Haas, David Raymond, and Wil Haygood all helped with one piece or another of the story.

I am particularly indebted to the former members of Platoon 71 who willingly answered my many questions and shared their memories of the night that will always be with them. David McPherson, Robert Dombo, Leonard (Banashefski) Bantel, and John Kochis were particularly helpful and receptive to my requests for information and written material. Interviews with Richard Acker, Eugene Ashby, Lew Ray Brewer, Marvin Blair, Willard Brooks, Mims Brower, Jerome Daszo, John Delahunty, Richard Drown, Richard Ferkel, Frederick Golden, Gerald Langone, Lawrence Mann, Stephen Mihalcsik, John Mitchell, Hugh Mulligan, Walter Nehrenz, Daniel Sulitka, Ted Stover, Walter Sygman, Ronald Tyre, Thomas Vaughn, and Robert Veney offered views of the Ribbon Creek march from various perspectives within the platoon.

Finally, my thanks to Kelly Gallant, as capable a secretary as one could ask for, and to my editor, Melinda Conner, who expertly polished many of the rough edges in my original manuscript. Most of all, thanks to my wife, Pamela, who supported this work throughout, encouraged me to keep going when I became discouraged, and suffered through periods of obsession with a quest that was of my choosing, not hers. Without her, I doubt that I would have had the staying power to see it through. When the writing was done and I often thought the finished product was not worthy of publication, she was ever the optimist. This book is a credit to her as much as anyone, and for that I add one more special place for her in my heart.

# Introduction

Parris Island—this famous, or, in the eyes of some, infamous Marine Corps training base is a heart-shaped body of land near the southern tip of the South Carolina coast. The island, about four miles across at its widest point, is surrounded on all sides by ocean, salt marsh, mud, and rivers, some small enough to be called creeks.

One of those creeks is Ribbon Creek. In earlier times, when the island was a cotton plantation, the creek abutted land of the Rippon family and was known as "Rippon Creek." The particulars of the evolution of "Rippon" to "Ribbon" are unknown. The latter is an apt name, however, for this tidal creek snakes ribbonlike behind the northwesterly boundary of the island less than one hundred yards beyond the ranges where all marine recruits receive intensive training in rifle marksmanship.

Parris Island in the summer is hot, humid, and infested with insects. In the winter it is only less warm and less buggy. But the heat and the bugs are only a small part of the island's ambiance. For year-round, Parris Island is the forge in which the base metals of adolescent youth are wrought into the refined steel of United States Marines. It is the place where the punk, the drugstore cowboy, the jock, the mama's boy, the college dropout, the arrogant, the insecure, and various other immature forms of the human species are deposited to face the shocking transformation that begins at the Marine Corps boot camp.

I was one of those adolescents in the summer of 1957. I had finished high school and had been accepted at a fine university. But the boys I admired were tougher than I was and were (or professed to be) more experienced with girls. Skinny and lacking in confidence, I decided a taste of the Marine Corps would do more to make a man of me than anything else that I could see in my future. So, at age seventeen, just two weeks out of high school, I enlisted. The summer of 1957, during the years between the end of the Korean War and the cultural upheaval that coincided with the Vietnam War, was a peaceful one. Elvis, Fats, and Pat Boone were popular. We danced to "Old Cape Cod" and "Bye, Bye Love" in the weeks before I left.

At 6:00 A.M. on June 27, 1957, I boarded a train at Fitchburg, a central Massachusetts city some forty miles west of my destination in Boston. My mother saw me off through tear-filled eyes. My father, himself a former marine, was stolid. I, too young and naive to be fearful, expected to experience an adventure that would be difficult but rewarding.

I have only stroboscopic memories of the next forty-eight hours. After a tedious processing in Boston, I recall being one of about fifteen patrons at a Scollay Square strip show (at a time when the women still wore pasties and G-strings). I have a fragmentary memory of riding a Pullman car to Washington, D.C., followed by an eighteen-hour ride in a seemingly pre–Civil War coach through the rural countryside from Washington to South Carolina. At 2:00 A.M., twenty-seven hours after leaving Boston, my companions and I arrived at our destination. Hot and tired, I longed only for a place to sleep.

The first shock of my new life occurred as I stepped down from the creaky relic that had delivered us. Several military police ordered us from the train at the desolate backwater of Yemassee, South Carolina. We were immediately instructed to stand at attention in the dirt lot adjacent to the station. Where was the bed I had been anticipating? Where had the friendly recruiting sergeant gone?

After what seemed like hours, two or three buses arrived and took us off into the night. I immediately fell asleep. When the bus stopped I was hit with shock number two—in this case two shocks in one. The first was the absolutely terrifying sight and sound of an enormous and fierce drill instructor, who bellowed at each of us as he ordered us from the bus. Simultaneously, my nostrils were assaulted by one of the foulest smells I had ever experienced. I later learned it was marsh gas. At the time the stench only exacerbated my fear and disorientation. Even the faintest hint of that foul odor today evokes the poignant memory of that frightening introduction to Parris Island. At about 4:00 A.M. on June 29, 1957, I began my military experience as one of the lowest forms of life—lower, my drill instructor often snarled, "than a pimple on a good marine's ass."

When I arrived at Parris Island I had no idea where Ribbon Creek was. I knew about but had only a passing interest in the tumultuous events that had occurred scarcely a mile from where I was standing. I had heard of the drowning of six recruits the preceding year, but it had not captured my interest. And the oblique warnings from the drill instructors not to write to our congressmen and their complaints that the training was soft and not like the "old Corps" were lost on me. I had no idea who my congressman was, much less any intention of writing to him. I was unaware that these warriors in their immaculate uniforms and broad-brimmed campaign hats who trained us from 5:00 A.M. until 10:00 P.M. were themselves just emerging from the aftermath of an incident that had threatened the very existence of the traditional Marine Corps and its methods of recruit training.

Today, forty years later, that incident still haunts the man who marched those recruits through the mud and into the chilly waters of Ribbon Creek— a march that began with seventy-five young men and ended less than an hour later with sixty-nine recruits straggling to shore, and six left forever behind.

This is the story of that fateful night of April 8, 1956. It is also the story of Matthew McKeon and the men of Platoon 71. In a larger sense, it is the story of the training that, for better or for worse, had made the Marine Corps the fighting force it has been since the first marines were recruited at Tun Tavern in Philadelphia in 1775.

# Court-Martial at Parris Island

# O N E

# Death in the Boondocks

At 8:15 P.M. on Sunday, April 8, 1956, seventy-five young men uniformly dressed in olive green herringbone trousers, jackets, and caps stood at attention on a serene South Carolina evening before a tall, wiry marine drill instructor. His name was Matthew McKeon. The men standing before him were the men of Platoon 71, Third Recruit Battalion, Parris Island, South Carolina. For five and a half weeks it had been McKeon's duty to teach and instill in his "boots" the discipline and pride necessary to become members of one of the elite fighting forces in the world: the United States Marine Corps. McKeon was failing, and he knew it.

Staff Sergeant McKeon was not a man normally given to anger. In fact, he was usually patient, friendly, and even garrulous. But as he faced his platoon that evening he was feeling anything but friendly. In fact, he was angry and troubled—angry because his recruits had embarrassed him earlier in the day before another drill instructor and again during evening chow; troubled for reasons both personal and professional. He had injured his back some weeks earlier and was experiencing shooting pain in his left leg when he walked. Professionally, he was even more concerned. Platoon 71 was his first assignment since graduating from drill instructor's school two months earlier. His career advancement hinged in part on his ability to mold these young men into good marines. While many were mastering the basic skills he taught, too large a number remained impervious to his efforts to break their civilian habits. As he later described it, "About three-fourths of the platoon was squared away, but the remainder were foul balls." On the verge of desperation, he had decided earlier in the day that the time had come to straighten out the "foul balls" and try to shock his men into working as a disciplined and cohesive unit.

Behind McKeon and before his men was Building 761, one of a uniform row of H-shaped white wooden buildings with four squad bays that housed recruit platoons while they were at the rifle range. Behind the platoon as it stood in formation was Wake Boulevard, the primary street connecting the rifle range area with Mainside on the island. Several other barracks similar to 761 lined Wake Boulevard. About a hundred yards farther down Wake Boulevard Capt. Charles E. Patrick, the officer of the day, had settled in to watch the 7:45 show at the movie theater. Directly across Wake Boulevard and extending perpendicular to it were rifle ranges B, C, and D, or, phonetically, "Baker," "Charlie," and "Dog." At the far end of the ranges, approximately six hundred yards from where McKeon stood, elevated earthen mounds known as "butts" shielded the target areas. Immediately beyond the butts were a narrow road and a small area of grassy fill that dropped off into a strip of marsh. Some fifty to seventy-five feet beyond the marsh was a meandering tidal stream known as Ribbon Creek.

The sun had set at 6:48 P.M., and the last rays of sunlight had descended over Ribbon Creek and Horse Island beyond it as Sergeant McKeon addressed his men. Relieved that he had decided on a course of action, McKeon declared jestingly that where they were going the nonswimmers would drown and the swimmers would be eaten by sharks. An anonymous recruit in the rear muttered, "Shoot." With just such a wise guy on his mind, the sergeant replied sardonically, "Shoot—we'll see."

Almost directly across from Building 761 and perpendicular to Wake Boulevard was a paved road that led to the butts between Baker and Charlie ranges. McKeon's intent was to march his men to the butts, but he had another route in mind. He barked, "Right face," followed immediately by "FOR-WARD, HUH." About twenty yards south of the point where the march began he ordered a column half-right. The platoon was now headed across Wake Boulevard and diagonally across Baker range. Sentries had been posted at ammunition sheds near the five-hundred-yard firing lines. The path Platoon 71 was following was approximately equidistant from the sentries and out of earshot of either. Had it followed the paved road, the platoon would have passed near the sentry at Charlie range.

Charles Francis "Chuck" Reilly was born in December 1937, in the midst of the Depression, in upstate New York. The Reilly family was poor, and Chuck's mother and father had both died by the time he was in his mid-teens. His older sister, Rose Bond, was already married at nineteen. With no other place to go, Chuck and his two younger brothers went to live with Rose and her husband, Frank.

With limited intelligence and without the luxury of parents to push and guide him in his studies, Reilly dropped out of school before the ninth grade. After drifting from job to job, he decided it was time for a steady paycheck and a place to live. In January 1956 he joined the Marines.

When he arrived at Parris Island he was tested and immediately classified as "illiterate." The low test score meant that Reilly would have to spend four weeks in what was colloquially known as the "slow learners" platoon, endeavoring to master the fundamentals of reading and writing before he could begin his actual recruit training. He was joined there by several other recruits, among them Richard Acker, Marvin Blair, Mims Brower, Thomas Hardeman, and Lester Hendrix. On February 29, 1956, Reilly, Acker, Blair, Brower, Hardeman, and Hendrix were transferred to Platoon 71, which was then in the first week of its training cycle.

Reilly wrote home to Rose Bond. He was not adapting well to the disciplined life of the military. He had a habit of laughing when nervous or anxious. Parris Island was not a place where such tendencies were tolerated. One day in early April he decided to sneak a Coke, thinking his drill instructor was otherwise occupied. He wasn't, as it turned out. Adapting the punishment to the crime, Reilly was ordered to keep on buying and drinking. Some stories have it that he drank nineteen more bottles of Coke; another witness claims it was twenty-five. Whatever the number, Chuck Reilly was learning the hard way that petty insubordination had its price.

On April 8, 1956, Platoon 71 was beginning the third of the three weeks the recruits spent in the Weapons Training Battalion, commonly known as the rifle range. Chuck wrote home to Rose that he was happier after moving from the drill field to the rifle range. Every moment from sunrise to sunset was devoted to mastering the art of firing the M-1 rifle from various positions and at various distances from two hundred to five hundred yards. Evenings were spent cleaning weapons and taking swimming lessons. Chuck Reilly was one of about fifteen men in the platoon who had never learned to swim. Whether in two weeks he had learned the basics of treading water is not clear. What is clear is that after two weeks of lessons he was no more a swimmer than he had ever been.

* * *

The platoon was subdivided into squads. Taller men in the lower-numbered squads marched near the front. As one of the shorter men in the platoon, Reilly was assigned to the tenth squad. Lewis Leake, Marvin Blair, Mims Brower, Richard Acker, and Thomas Hardeman all marched near him in formation. Blair and Reilly had formed a friendship in the "slow learners" platoon. In fact, Reilly was planning to visit Blair at his home in Georgia after boot camp rather than returning to his sister's home in New York.

The platoon marched two abreast through the spray of a water sprinkler and on into the darkness. Some of the lads in the rear of the column were laughing and talking; others moved slightly out of formation. A sense of apprehension hung in the night air as the word spread that they were going into the "boondocks"—the marshland that surrounded much of the island.

Sergeant McKeon set the pace at the head of the column. His back and leg pain continued to cause a slight limp. To relieve some of the pain in his leg, he had improvised a walking stick from a squeegee handle. However, his physical discomfort was not paramount in his mind as he strode forward.

Eugene Ervin, David McPherson, Norman Wood, and the larger men were at the front of the column. Many of the "foul balls" were farther back and out of McKeon's earshot. The big fellows he could control and reason with. He expected them to set the example and help straighten out the smaller men. Unfortunately, it did not always work out that way. Every approach he had used so far to instill discipline and cohesiveness seemed to have failed. Now, at wit's end, McKeon was about to try a different approach.

What thoughts were going through the minds of the dozen or so young recruits who were nonswimmers? Were they really going into the swamp? How deep was the water? Were there really sharks in there? Some relieved their anxiety by laughing and joking. Others were silent. What lay ahead? The recruits could see only the barest outlines of the men near them in the column as each step led them deeper into the ominous darkness and away from the security of the lights to the rear, where other young men prepared for another day of weapons training that would commence with the first rays of dawn.

At the far-left end of Baker range, the column turned ninety degrees to the right and followed a course behind the Baker range butts. After about two hundred yards they reached a target shed at the beginning of the Charlie range butts. At this point the grass to the left of the butts fanned out, having been cleared and filled many years earlier when the ranges were constructed. At the far end of the Charlie butts a small wooden pier extended across the marsh for fifty feet or so to the edge of Ribbon Creek. One day in the butts

Sergeant McKeon had seen a drill instructor march his platoon out that pier and off the end, right into the creek. The men had emerged chastened, muddy, and perhaps wiser for the experience. The incident had not been lost on Matt McKeon.

At the Charlie range target shed McKeon ordered the platoon to perform a column left, and thereby head straight for the marshes that descended into the dark waters of Ribbon Creek. Although tales of night swamp marches were legendary, no man in the platoon—including its drill instructor—had ever actually been in Ribbon Creek or the marshes around it. Unknown to McKeon, the creek bottom was covered with viscous ooze that some of the locals called "pluff mud." In the marsh, the mud was apt to be only a few inches deep and solidified by waist- to shoulder-high grass; but when the marsh dropped off into the creek, the mud was anywhere from several inches to more than a foot deep. Unlike McKeon, a lifelong New Englander, the southern boys who had grown up near such estuaries knew what that mud was like—and they wanted no part of it.

The grassy earth dropped off a few feet into the marsh, which was covered by two to three feet of cool water. McKeon led his men down the bank, from solid ground into the marsh. Pvt. Gerald Langone, a tough kid from New York City, was detailed to remain at the water's edge to ensure that the remainder of the men followed. Langone, who earlier in the evening had embarrassed himself by returning for seconds at chow in violation of McKeon's wishes, was eager to comply.

"Get your ass in there," prodded Langone, like a cowpuncher goading his herd. Seventy-four shadowy figures in loose columns of twos followed McKeon into the murky blackness.

As Langone drove the last squads of the platoon over the bank and into the flooded marsh, Chuck Reilly's anxiety and apprehension increased. Sergeant McKeon was far ahead out of sight. The rear of the column was a leaderless crowd slogging toward an unknown destination as black water gradually rose up their legs.

Richard Acker was next to Reilly. Acker was also from upstate New York, but he had learned to swim. Reilly gripped Acker's shoulders with both hands and pleaded with him to help him if anything happened.

Sergeant McKeon had already led the front of the column into the flooded marsh adjacent to Ribbon Creek. About ten to fifteen feet from the point of entry, he ordered the column to turn ninety degrees to the right so that it was now moving parallel to the bank in knee-deep to waist-deep water. McKeon advised the recruits within earshot that in combat it was important to stay near the bank of a stream and out of the moonlight to avoid detection by the enemy. At about the same time he asked where the nonswimmers were. Several voices responded from the invisible rear. As Langone urged the last of the recruits over the bank and into the marsh, McKeon continued the platoon on its course parallel to the water's edge for at least thirty feet. He then turned left toward the deeper waters for ten to fifteen feet, and then left again. The column now resembled a U-shaped snake as the men in the front were doubling back, again parallel to the water's edge but nearer to the center of the creek bed.

As the men moved out of the flooded marsh and into the creek proper, the water rose from below the waist to shoulder level. When the last of the men entered the marsh, Langone joined his squad near the middle of the column. The rear of the platoon was now leaderless and far out of McKeon's sight and hearing. The men near the rear began to fan out, some of them drifting toward the center of the stream. Perhaps through fear and apprehension, or perhaps because of the lack of discipline that had so frustrated their drill instructors, several of the young men began what in military terms would be deemed "grab-assing." Someone yelled, "Gator!" Others were slapping the water and pretending to be in trouble, behavior that ironically seemed to confirm the lack of discipline that had prompted the swamp march in the first place.

As the chilly water rose higher and higher, another and more ominous phenomenon was occurring. The men had left the stability of the grassy marsh and entered the actual creek bed. As they did, the mud that had been an inch or two deep in the marsh lapped over the tops of their low-cut marching boots, which were already filled with water. The deep, soft mud suctioned each of the fully clothed young men into the streambed as the water above lapped at their shoulders.

Amid the nervous banter arose a very different fear. One can only imagine the terror that must have gnawed at the thoughts of the nonswimmers on that dark and chilly night as they sank deeper into the mud on their journey into the unknown waters. Succumbing to fear and shrouded by darkness, some men simply refused to continue. Mims Brower crept back into the safety of the marshes and lay down in the shallower water. Lewis Leake, paralyzed by fear, was carried by Walter Sygman before retreating and joining Brower. Carl

Whitmore joined Leake and Brower. Robert Veney simply retreated until he was in waist-deep water and froze as the rest of the platoon continued on. Nearer the rear of the column, Willard Brooks stopped in his tracks when the mud reached his ankles and the water rose above his knees. Lester Hendrix, a small man marching near the rear, also chose not to continue forward. Melvin Barber quit when the water reached his chest.

In those fateful moments, Pvts. Donald O'Shea, Charles Reilly, Jerry Thomas, Leroy Thompson, and Norman Wood chose not to stop. They groped on through the darkness as ordered. Thompson and Wood were large men. Both were near the front of the column and only a few yards behind Sergeant McKeon. Thomas and O'Shea were about halfway between the front and rear of the platoon. Reilly was near the rear in the tenth squad. None of them knew how to swim.

The front of the column had now doubled back to a point nearly opposite the point of entry but nearer to the center of the stream. The taller men in the first squad near the front remained in loose formation behind McKeon. Farther to the rear the platoon was in greater disarray as in the darkness some of the young men continued drifting out toward the center of the stream.

Meanwhile, the tide, which had crested shortly after 6:34 P.M., was beginning to recede. Because of the creek's proximity to the ocean and its relative narrowness, the waters that had flooded the marshes less than two hours earlier were coursing strongly back to the sea in the same direction the platoon was moving. The swiftly moving waters acted like an undertow on the men already struggling with the deep mud as they fought to maintain their balance in the slippery ooze beneath their feet.

Suddenly and without warning the bottom of the creek seemed to fall off. Pvt. John Maloof, who was in the first squad and near McKeon, recalls, "The next thing I knew I was off whatever it was, this cliff, and in deep water, and I was floundering, and there was a strong current pulling me down." Earl Grabowski, who was in the second squad, recalls dropping "off the ledge." Forty years later, Richard Acker, who was in the tenth squad, near the rear, remembers struggling in water up to his neck when he noticed the tidal pull, and that the bottom dropped off abruptly, "almost as if a door opened" on the creek bed.

At that moment true panic broke out. From the darkness toward the rear and near midstream came yells, screams, and calls for help. Some of the recruits near the front thought it was just more horseplay. But in fact it was mass confusion.

Sergeant McKeon heard the first sounds of panic, which he estimated to be about twenty feet to his rear and off to his right, in the deeper water. He was able to see men splashing and began swimming toward them. Fighting the pull of the tide, McKeon dragged one man closer to shore. Suddenly Norman Wood, a large, strong recruit who had been near the front, latched onto him. Both went under as McKeon now fought to free himself. Wood let go, and McKeon did not see him after that. Earlier, moments after the panic began, John Martinez had tried to help Wood. As he described it shortly afterward:

> He was a few feet away from me. When I got to him he was practically finished already. He had so much water in his lungs he couldn't cry for help. All I heard was like when you gargle your throat. There was water in his lungs, sir. I latched onto him and started pulling him in. He grabbed the cord around my neck, sir, with the keys, and he pulled me down and I went down once. I had to let go and he came back up with me and I grabbed onto him again, and some of the boys that were drowning right next to him grabbed onto me also and I had to push him away and they took me down again. I had to let go of Private Wood, sir. I couldn't hold on because I had my boots on and all my clothes and I was going down. I don't think I would have come up if I went down again.

Joseph Moran, who was already in water over his head, fought his way to the surface and saw Leroy Thompson struggling to stay afloat. He and Donald Porter, a former lifeguard, pulled Thompson toward the creek's edge where the water was shoulder deep and left him standing there. Thompson said nothing, leading Moran and Porter to conclude that he would be able to make it to shore.

Stephen McGuire had been one of the young men fooling around in the water. When the commotion began he saw Donald O'Shea and Leroy Thompson fighting between themselves, trying to stay on top of the water. He was perhaps the first person to reach Thompson. The larger Thompson dragged McGuire toward the bottom. McGuire, now thinking only of his own survival, fought successfully to extricate himself from Thompson's frenzied grip. He did not see Thompson again.

Jerome Daszo had also spotted O'Shea, who was about fifteen feet away from him splashing in the water and yelling for help. Hugh Mulligan and Earl Grabowski were able to clutch a man they believe was O'Shea and drag him into waist-deep water. No one recalls seeing O'Shea thereafter.

Jerry Thomas was the first man in line in the eighth squad. He was next to Ronald Geckle. Neither man could swim. As the water rose on his body, Geckle slipped in the mud. At the same time a panicked Thomas dragged Geckle down toward the bottom. Geckle managed to resurface, only to have Thomas take him down a second time. Now fighting for his own life, Geckle freed himself of Thomas while under water and was able to reach shallower water. That was the last anyone saw of Thomas.

Thomas Hardeman had been a poor farm boy before joining the Marines. Small in stature but big in heart, he had fought to join the Marine Corps after failing his first entrance test. He had grown up near the creeks of rural Georgia and knew how to handle himself in the water. Hardeman was in the ninth squad with the shorter men. Mims Brower held onto Hardeman's belt as they entered the water. As the panic broke out and cries for help pierced the darkness, Brower let go and Hardeman swam out into the stream. Carl Whitmore also heard someone yell for good swimmers about then and saw Hardeman swim by him. Brower was just able to see a shadowy form grab Hardeman around the neck and jump on his back. Both disappeared beneath the surface. Hardeman never reappeared.

As the men reversed direction and found themselves in the deeper mud and water, Acker realized that Reilly was close to panic. Reilly grabbed frantically at Acker, clutching his belt and collar. Without warning the bottom disappeared as the tide sucked both men downstream and into water over their heads. The laughter and shouts of horseplay turned to cries of distress. Reilly's dread turned to terror as his precarious footing vanished. He climbed onto Acker's body in a desperate attempt to keep his head above the surface. Both men went under. Acker was able to wrestle his way to the top, only to be pushed below the water again. Finally, for his own survival, Acker was able to break Reilly's death grip and flounder to safety.

When McKeon realized the significance of the frantic commotion behind him, he ordered the platoon from the water. Human forms lurched and floundered toward the shallower water of the marsh. Eugene Ervin saw Clarence Bruner staggering alone in the water, weeping in frustration. Bruner's efforts to rescue one of the drowning men had failed when he lost his grip on the man. Lewis Leake, who was terrified of deep water, was vomiting repeatedly. A fatigued Matthew McKeon tottered through the muck toward the firm ground near the very spot where fifteen minutes earlier he had first stepped into the soft mud.

He was the last man out of the water. The screams of fear and terror that had pierced the night air only moments earlier had been replaced by eerie silence. As the flapping, gurgles, and screams of panic and struggle died out, he faced the realization that young men whose lives had been placed in his hands still lay beneath the murky waters of Ribbon Creek. Exhausted and in shock, McKeon said to himself, "Oh my God, what have I done?"

# T W O

# Time and Place

Although it is now connected to the mainland by a causeway and Archer's Creek Bridge, Parris Island is for every marine recruit as insular and remote as Devil's Island itself. Located just north of Hilton Head along the South Carolina coast, this former site of cotton plantations, a naval prison, and a naval station was designated "Marine Barracks, Port Royal" in 1915. Since that date, despite several changes in name, appearance, and style, the installation has had one mission: to transform raw civilian recruits into basic marines through a relentless and vigorous training program. To marines past and present it is known as "boot camp." All marine recruits from states east of the Mississippi River must pass through Parris Island.

In 1956, an integral part of boot camp involved rifle training at the Weapons Training Battalion, commonly known as the "rifle range." At that time recruit training began with approximately four weeks of physical and mental indoctrination during which fear, shock, and intense effort were used to convert civilian habits into military ways. This was followed by approximately three weeks at the rifle range; basic training concluded with several weeks of further training, inspections, and drill leading up to graduation. Men assigned to train the recruits were (and are) known as drill instructors, or DIs. A typical platoon consisted of seventy to eighty men led by a senior drill instructor and two junior DIs. A group of platoons was organized into a company, with several companies forming a battalion. In 1956 there were three male and one female recruit battalions at Parris Island. Most of the buildings, and the focal point for activity on the island, were at Mainside and in the nearby battalion areas where the recruits lived and drilled.

Wake Boulevard extends from Mainside for about a mile to the area collectively known as the rifle range. While at the rifle range the recruits focused on marksmanship training under the supervision of instructors assigned to the Weapons Training Battalion. During this three-week period there was apt to be a slackening in the rigorous discipline that had been instilled during the early weeks of training because the recruits were no longer under the thumb of their drill instructors except at the beginning and end of the day and on weekends. Drill instructors who sensed a loosening of their control during this time often used the evening hours and weekends for extra calisthenics or extra drill. But experienced DIs also knew that a relaxed recruit was likely to achieve a higher score. Thus arose a dilemma—how to maintain tight discipline while keeping the boot relaxed enough to score well on the firing line.

The mid-1950s was a relatively quiet time. The nation had been at peace since 1953. No American troops were anywhere engaged in combat. Public fear of communist attack or insurgency waned during the interlude between the censure and death of Sen. Joseph McCarthy and the launching of Sputnik. Americans were generally going about the business of having more babies, buying more goods, and enjoying the fruits of postwar prosperity. Newsworthy events in early 1956 included President Eisenhower's farm program, whether Richard Nixon would be replaced as Ike's running mate, and the myriad details of the impending marriage of Grace Kelly and Prince Rainier of Monaco. Most Americans, if asked, would not have known whether Vietnam was a person, a place, or a disease. Beatniks were a curiosity, and dissent was nearly unheard of in the home, neighborhood, or country. Rosa Parks's simple act of dignified defiance was yet to be recognized as one of the sparks that would finally stir the nation to eradicate the remaining vestiges of one of the greatest injustices in its history.

In contrast to the generally quiescent national mood, several forces were coming together at Parris Island to create considerable pressure on drill instructors and the recruits they commanded. Many recruits tended to have limited motivation, skills, and education. (For example, eight of the men in Platoon 71 were either illiterate or had General Classification Test scores—approximately equivalent to an IQ test—below 70.) Moreover, there was some question as to whether the overall quality of the youth coming to Parris Island was declining. There had been a substantial drop in the birth rate during the Depression years. By the mid-1950s, the number of available young men of enlistment age was smaller than it had been in years past. In fact, because of the limited manpower pool, in 1956 the Marine Corps was offering two-year enlistments to appeal to a broader range of potential applicants, particularly those with college experience or aspirations.

Although the Marine Corps had officially banned hazing and maltreatment of recruits, such practices were difficult to eliminate for a number of reasons. Courts-martial were infrequent because it was difficult to obtain sufficient evidence to convict. Whether through fear of retaliation or ill-placed personal shame, few recruits were prepared to testify under oath as to the brutality of their drill instructor. In fact, many techniques that might seem abusive to civilians were accepted by recruits as an integral part of their tough training.

At the same time, the prevailing culture that surrounded recruit training discouraged eradication of abuse except in the most severe cases. One of the most fundamental tenets of Marine Corps policy was that recruits, whose mission in the Corps would be to act as riflemen, were to be trained by noncommissioned officers rather than commissioned officers. The rationale for this policy was that the former would be their immediate superiors and would be leading them in combat. Commissioned officers were reluctant to intervene in a training regimen that had long been under the control of the drill instructors. One aspect of such noninterference was a reluctance to second-guess the drill instructor. Moreover, formal discipline arising from a court-martial would be damaging if not destructive to the future of a career enlisted man. A drill instructor might receive an informal reprimand, but unless the offense was sufficiently brutal and the evidence clear, he was unlikely to face a court-martial and even less likely to be convicted if he were brought to trial.

Maltreatment of recruits was still a problem at the beginning of 1956, when Platoon 71 was being formed. Brig. Gen. Wallace Greene reported that when he arrived at Parris Island to assume command in May 1956, "ten recruits were in the hospital with broken noses—broken by the fists of DIs!" General Greene also reported that "most of [the] old-time officers devoted their energies and time to golf, fishing, drinking, and womanizing—leaving training up principally to NCOs." As a result, drill instructors worked long hours with little supervision and under considerable stress and pressure to graduate highly qualified basic marines. A drill instructor's fitness reports and resulting career advancement hinged in large part on the performance of his platoon.

Hazing and corporal punishment, known as "thumping," were techniques DIs employed to varying degrees in their attempts to mold raw recruits into basic marines. At the time there was little impetus from the general public to change recruit training techniques and abolish the abuse. The same general attitude prevailed at the officer level from the commandant, Gen. Randolph McCall Pate, to Maj. Gen. Joseph C. Burger, the commanding officer at Parris Island, and on down through the officer ranks. The impressive and valorous performance of the Marines in combat was considered to be a testament to the rigorous training program that had been used for years, and essentially the DI was free to use whatever methods of discipline and punishment he chose. Better to leave well enough alone, was the attitude—but few people were asking if what was being left alone was really well enough.

# THREE

# Platoon 71

T hirty-five young men from backgrounds as diverse as the shabby tenements of Newark, New Jersey, and the tony New York suburb of Scarsdale boarded a B&O bus at 346 Broadway in Manhattan on February 21, 1956. They had enlisted in the United States Marine Corps earlier that day. Private Gerald C. Langone Jr., himself a raw recruit, had been ordered to take charge of the other thirty-four men and accompany them south by bus and rail. John Delahunty, Robert "Chip" Dombo, Hugh Mulligan, and Thomas Vaughn had been buddies since their days at Saint Sylvester's parochial school in Brooklyn. David McPherson had wasted a couple of years at Bucknell University before deciding that two years in the Marine Corps might be a more valuable way to help him focus on what he wanted to do with his life. Walter Sygman had immigrated with his family to the United States from Germany before the outbreak of World War II to avoid Nazi persecution. Earl Grabowski spent his early years at Boystown in Kearny, New Jersey. Edward Jones, Richard Lawless, and Lewis Leake were trying to escape from the gritty and decaying neighborhoods of Newark, New Jersey. Leroy Thompson, Donald O'Shea, and Norman Wood were just three faces among the rest.

Off they went—young, eager, nervous, feigning fearlessness—as young men from generations before them had done. Black and white youths joined in a common adventure as B&O train number 1 sped toward Washington and Richmond and into the darkness of a world unknown.

At approximately 8:30 A.M. on Wednesday, February 22, Atlantic Coast Railway train 77 pulled into Yemassee, South Carolina, a gloomy rail junction

15

some thirty miles inland from the South Carolina coast. From there, the same motley aggregation that had departed from Manhattan nearly twenty hours earlier was transported by Palmetto Bus Lines on a journey of more than an hour to Parris Island.

Meanwhile, other buses and trains conveyed small groups of young men from such scattered locales as Florida, Ohio, Kentucky, and Connecticut to the same final destination. These apprehensive youths, who by circumstance of fate happened to converge at Parris Island at the same time, were amalgamated into a single training unit to be designated as Platoon 71. At that time platoons were numbered consecutively as they were formed in each calendar year. Thus, Platoon 71 was the seventy-first organized in 1956. After a day of initial processing, responsibility for this newly formed band of human rabble was turned over to its three drill instructors, and eleven weeks of basic training began.

As described by Col. William B. McKean, who was the officer in charge of the Weapons Training Battalion in February 1956,

> Platoon 71 seemed much the same as any other. Good American names on its roster might have been drawn from a jury panel or college football squad: Baneshefski, Daszo, Grabowski, Hartman, Kochis, Martinez, McGuire, Mihalcsik, Nehrenz, Vaughn, Whitmore, Zeigler. There was but one Brown and Jones, no Smith or Miller. No two Boots had the same surname. New England Yankees with hazy knowledge of the War Between the States met unreconstructed Rebels who would talk of nothing else. There was a strong leavening from Great Lakes states and Appalachian foothills. There were country boys, city boys, boys from industrial towns—who would term themselves neither.

The first week at Parris Island was devoted to such preliminary matters as hygienic processing, uniform issue, medical and dental examinations, psychological testing, and initial indoctrination. Each boot was shorn of his civilian hairdo, whether crew cut or ducktail, in favor of the distinctive Parris Island style—shaved sides and a half inch on top.

By February 29, the preliminaries had been completed and the bewildered ragtag herd was ready to begin serious training. Pvt. Jerry Thomas, who had missed some training because of illness, was held back from Platoon 67 to join Platoon 71. Privates Acker, Blair, Brower, Hardeman, Hendrix, and Reilly had just completed four weeks of preliminary instruction in the "slow learners" platoon. They also joined the platoon on February 29. S.Sgt. Edward A. Huff, S.Sgt. Matthew C. McKeon, and Sgt. Richard J. King were the three DIs assigned to lead Platoon 71. At least one of the three men would be with the recruits twenty-four hours a day for the next eleven weeks.

Staff Sergeant Huff was the senior of the three DIs, having completed approximately twelve and a half years of military service. He had been a drill instructor for more than a year and a half and had trained four previous platoons as a junior or senior drill instructor. Neither McKeon nor King had prior experience. Both had graduated from DI school on February 5, 1956.

Huff was a salty thirty-eight-year-old veteran of both World War II and the Korean War. As senior DI he could and did exercise his prerogatives to assign most evening and weekend duties to the junior DIs, McKeon and King. Of the three, Huff was held in the lowest esteem by the recruits in Platoon 71, who described him variously as "tough," "gruff," "most feared," "by the book," "no teacher," and "hard-boiled." It seemed to one recruit that "he just wanted to get it over with."

Sergeant King was in many ways Huff's opposite. Less than four years earlier he had been a recruit himself. He was only a few years older than most of the youths he was training. Handsome and fastidiously neat, King was in the eyes of some of the boots a "Hollywood marine." Others characterized him as a "good guy," "easygoing," "friendly," and "sharp," but also lax about discipline and "less strict" than Huff or McKeon. One man recalled forty years after boot camp that after Huff ordered the men to forgo cigarettes for two weeks for a disciplinary infraction, King countermanded his superior's order during a break from drill and surreptitiously allowed the men a smoke.

S.Sgt. Matthew McKeon was born and raised in central Massachusetts, one of eight children in an Irish Catholic working-class family, He left high school in 1942 before graduation to serve in the navy and was assigned to the carrier *Essex*, which saw extensive service in the South Pacific until the battle of Okinawa was won. After toiling in a factory for two years on his return home, he decided that he preferred the military life. In 1948 McKeon enlisted in the Marine Corps. He was subjected to the rigors of boot camp, which, according to him, included crawling through pig manure, apparently as a perverse form of hazing or punishment. He was also led into the marshes behind the rifle range into water up to his knees and ordered to drop into the mud when his drill instructor simulated an air raid alert. Four months after his enlistment expired in 1952, McKeon reenlisted and saw combat as the platoon sergeant of a machine-gun platoon in Korea. Following his third honorable discharge in 1955, he promptly reenlisted and volunteered for DI school.

On February 4, 1956, McKeon completed the intensive five-week drill instructor's training program, finishing fourteenth in a class of fifty-five graduates (the class had begun with ninety students). A report of January 3, 1956, from the Psychiatric Observation Unit found him to be a "mature, stable appearing career Marine." By all accounts, Matthew McKeon had the maturity, experience, motivation, and ability to be an excellent drill instructor. Only later, after the events of April 1956, did a psychiatric examination by the depot psychiatrist reveal that McKeon, while not psychotic or emotionally disturbed, tended toward impulsive judgments. The psychiatrist concluded that McKeon tended to act hastily and think about it later.

Once the forming-up week was complete, Platoon 71 began training in earnest. For the next three weeks, from 5:00 A.M. until after evening chow, the new recruits drilled together and learned the fundamentals of Marine Corps history, discipline, rifle care, and other basic skills. They marched wherever they went. They shined their boots, cleaned their rifles, wrote letters during off-hours, and enjoyed no liberty on or off the base. The only semblances of pleasure were chow, sleep, receiving mail, and Sunday church call.

On Saturday, March 24, the initial phase of training was complete, and the men packed their seabags for truck transport. The platoon was then marched a mile down Wake Boulevard to the rifle range, where the men were quartered in one of the four squad bays in Building 761. This large building represented an upgrade from the World War II–vintage Nissen huts that were still in use in the Third Battalion's training area.

The next three weeks were to be devoted to marksmanship training primarily with M-1 rifles. Unlike the preceding month, when all their activities had been conducted in unison under the intense supervision of one of their three drill instructors, the men now shifted their focus to learning new skills under the guidance of range instructors.

By Saturday, April 7, the platoon had been at the rifle range for two weeks, twisting and stretching long unused muscles. They learned the intricacies of sighting and adjusting the sights on their rifles depending on the prevailing winds, and they practiced firing from standing, sitting, kneeling, and prone positions. The week of April 9 was to be the last and most significant; the long hours of practice and dry firing called "snapping in" were to culminate in firing for record. The marksmanship skills of the platoon as measured on record day would be a significant factor in the evaluation of the platoon's overall performance as well as in the evaluation of its drill instructors. Consequently, the recruits had been subjected to repeated intimations of the dire personal indignities they would suffer if they failed to attain the qualifying score of 190 out of a possible 250. Unlike today, each recruit had only one opportunity to qualify on record day.

It was not the men's performance on the firing line that most worried Sergeant McKeon and his two colleagues, however. Their real concern was that the cohesiveness and discipline they had endeavored to instill during the first month of training seemed to be deteriorating. McKeon thought that "the spirit and eagerness to learn seemed to leave them. . . . [T]he first couple of weeks they were [at Parris Island] they were very eager to learn, and they could learn, and they picked up quite quickly, but now it seemed like instead of picking up something of value they were picking up these goof-offs. . . . They were picking up bad habits." When McKeon was later asked whether or not the platoon had spirit, his response was, "No sir, it wasn't there."

How to restore the spirit and discipline with only five weeks of training left before graduation—that was the predicament that confronted Matt McKeon as he assumed the weekend duty on Saturday, April 7, 1956.

# FOUR

# Final Straws

lthough he was not scheduled to assume responsibility as the duty drill instructor for the weekend until noon on Saturday, April 7, Sergeant McKeon came "aboard" the base at about 5:00 A.M. Sergeant King was then on duty. McKeon chatted with King that morning while the men were occupied on the rifle range. When the platoon returned from the firing range at about 11:30 A.M., McKeon relieved King. The recruits were instructed to clean their weapons and launder their shooting jackets and cartridge belts on the large concrete wash racks behind the barracks. Later in the afternoon, the Catholics were allowed to attend confession. The platoon was then marched to the mess hall for evening chow. As no training activities were scheduled for the remainder of the weekend, McKeon was faced with the need to keep his recruits sufficiently active to avoid further slackness. Saturday evening was no problem. Sergeant Huff had authorized the platoon to attend the evening movie at the Lyceum only about a hundred yards south of the barracks on Wake Boulevard.

Sunday was typically the slowest and therefore the longest day of the week. Sunday, April 8, was no exception. McKeon had spent the night in the drill instructor's room adjacent to the squad bay. He arose between 5:00 and 5:30 A.M. After attending to personal hygiene and morning chow, he gave orders to police the squad bay. The Catholics and Protestants were released in separate details to attend church services. (The record is silent as to the religious arrangements made for Walter Sygman, the only Jew in the platoon.) After church, men with dirty laundry were again dispatched to the wash racks to finish cleaning their gear. Others wrote letters or shined shoes.

20

Seeing that everything was normal and under control, McKeon returned to his room to lie down. For the preceding three weeks he had been experiencing pain that radiated from his hip to his foot. Despite twice visiting the dispensary, his discomfort seemed to increase daily. He felt better when he was off his feet.

After briefly dozing, McKeon was awakened by the familiar voice of T.Sgt. Elwyn Scarborough, the range instructor assigned to Platoon 71. Scarborough was a ruddy veteran who had had a checkered military career. On this occasion his stated purpose was to express his grievance with the performance of the platoon. Although he spoke with a touch of humor, Scarborough's message confirmed McKeon's greatest concerns about his boots. Later, at his trial, McKeon described their conversation:

Q. [By defense counsel] What was the general conversation?
A. Well, the general conversation was regarding the platoon on the range, regarding their marksmanship and the big topic was the discipline of the platoon. Sergeant Scarborough was kind of pee'd off at them.
Q. We say tee'd off around here.
A. Yes, sir, I'm sorry.

But Sergeant Scarborough's unannounced visit was motivated by more than just a desire to discuss Platoon 71's performance. Not long into the conversation Scarborough said that he was feeling pretty rough and asked McKeon if he had anything to drink. Scarborough related that he had been partying until the late hours the night before and needed a drink to clear his head. Since he had nothing to drink on hand, McKeon drove Scarborough a few hundred yards down the road to the range instructor's car to retrieve a partially consumed fifth of vodka. When they returned to the drill instructor's room shortly after 11:00 A.M. Scarborough was carrying the bottle.

Soon after that, Sergeant Muckler, the drill instructor for the platoon housed in the squad bay above, entered the room. He, too, was the bearer of bad tidings, only now in a clearly demonstrable form.

Q. And what . . . did he say?
A. Well, Sergeant Muckler came in and he said, ". . . Whose platoon is that back there crapped out on the lawn, crapped out in the back of the barracks?" I said, "It can't be mine, impossible," and he had a little grin on his face, and he said, "I believe it is yours." So I went out . . . and Sergeant

Scarborough was behind me. I opened the door and there they were, laying on the grass out there, some on their elbows. . . . Some were crapped
out on their backs; others were lying face down with their arms under-
neath their head.

Q. Was there anything wrong with that?

A. Well, that's a cardinal sin; they should never do it. I can't explain, but they
should never.

McKeon was embarrassed and irate. He immediately ordered the troops
to scrub down the squad bay—in military terms, to "hold a field day." Gerald
Langone, the recruit section leader, was summoned to McKeon's quarters
and told in no uncertain terms "that [McKeon] wanted to see those people
turning to it . . . and didn't want to see any of them goofing off."

After the brief exchange with Sergeant Muckler and the commencement
of the field day, Scarborough set the bottle on the table. He poured himself a
drink in a paper cup and offered one to McKeon. Normally a beer drinker,
but not wanting to offend his guest, McKeon bought a Coke from a nearby
machine in the barracks to mix with the alcohol. Shortly afterward Sergeant
King joined them. King was a bachelor who lived on base and had little to do
on off-duty weekends. During the next hour, King took at least one swig
from the bottle when offered, Scarborough had at least two drinks, and
McKeon had two or three drinks.

After socializing in McKeon's room for about an hour, Scarborough asked
McKeon to take him to the Staff Non-Commissioned Officers' Club. McKeon
was willing to accommodate him, particularly as he was intending to drive
to Mainside to pick up the platoon's mail. King readily agreed to take the
men to noon chow and cover for McKeon until his return.

Before they left, McKeon looked at Scarborough and said, "Here's your
bottle, Gunny. Take it with you."

"Leave it here. I'll pick it up later," was the response.

McKeon and Scarborough left for Mainside in McKeon's car. After picking up the mail they drove to the Staff NCO Club and went inside. When
someone called to Scarborough from across the room, McKeon went up to
the bar alone. He ordered a can of Schlitz beer. After taking a few sips, he left
his beer to go and chat with an acquaintance he recognized across the bar. A
moment later his companion offered to buy McKeon a drink for every stripe
he had made since they were last together. Apparently there had been quite
an interval. McKeon found himself looking at a triple shot of whiskey. As he

later recalled it, he "reached over and took the glass, and just out of gratitude, appreciation, . . . took a sip of it and put it down."

The two men stepped briefly outside to admire the friend's new sports car. When they returned, the beer and whiskey had been taken away. At the same time, McKeon noticed that the clock in the club indicated that it was 1:40 P.M. He immediately left and drove back to Building 761 to relieve King. Scarborough remained behind at the club.

After chatting awhile with King, McKeon dozed off. He slept intermittently for two to three hours. At about 5:00 P.M., King and Langone awakened him. He washed up, got himself squared away, and marched his men the short distance down Wake Boulevard to evening chow.

While the platoon was sitting in the mess hall another incident occurred that further aggravated the already exasperated McKeon.

> I was sitting there talking to other drill instructors and drinking coffee, and Private Langone come by, and I asked him where he was going and he said he was going for seconds, and I said, "Langone, what did you do today to deserve seconds?" and he gave me some kind of a sarcastic remark. I won't say what he did say. . . . I told him, "I want to see you when I get back to the barracks. I want to see you in my room."
>
> Q. Did other members of platoon 71 go for seconds at that chow?
> A. Yes, sir, they did.
> Q. . . . Had Sergeant Huff issued any kind of an order about that subject?
> A. Yes, sir. He didn't want them to eat seconds while on the ranges for the simple reason he said it would be hard [for] them to get into positions.

By the time the platoon returned to the barracks, McKeon's frustration was becoming more and more evident. He immediately ordered a second field day. While it was in progress, a number of the Catholic boys were allowed to leave to attend a novena. Shortly thereafter a detail of Protestants was released to attend evening hymn singing at the chapel. Before each group left and after they returned they were to continue scrubbing down the squad bay.

After ordering the second field day, McKeon summoned Langone to the drill instructor's room. McKeon later recalled the ensuing events.

> I told [Private Langone] I wanted to see him in my room when I got back, and Private Langone knocked, and I told him, "Langone, when you step across that threshold, you had better start swinging." And Langone came in and he said he didn't want to start swinging, he didn't want to hit me

or words to that effect, and I think that what I said to him then was, "Did you ever hit your father or your mother?"

Q. What did he say?

A. He said, "No, sir, I never did." I said, "Why haven't you?" and he said, for the simple reason he respected them, and I asked him, "Don't you respect your superiors?" and Private Langone said he did, and I said, "Was that any respect in the mess hall this evening?" and just before then that is when I [slapped] him, sir. I slapped him. . . . Sir, I wasn't out to hurt him, sir. I slapped my own [five-year-old] kid, to be frank with you, harder than I slapped him. . . . [Langone] said he was sorry the way he had sounded off in the mess hall.

Q. What then happened?

A. I told Langone to sit down, and told him to have a cigarette. . . . I said, "Langone, do you realize the responsibility you have in that platoon? . . ." I said, "Here you are as a section leader and you are goofing off as much as those other kids." I said, "When those kids see you goofing off, naturally, they are going to follow you." I also spoke as regarding discipline. The discipline in the Marines, that the main thing of the Marines is discipline.

Q. Is that what you told him?

A. Yes, sir. I said, "Without discipline you have nothing." I told him that the purpose of a recruit training, the purpose of training here is not to go out of here with being an honor student more or less, but to go out of here with good discipline, that some day they may call upon you to defend this country of ours and if you don't have discipline you will have nothing."

Langone was instructed to send in Privates Maloof and Wood. McKeon recalled,

Maloof came in in a sloppy way. . . . I asked him, "Is that the position of attention?" is when I slapped him. . . . It was my way, sir, of showing him that I didn't approve of the things that he did. That was the only reason I did it when I ever slapped a kid.

McKeon told Wood and Maloof to fight with each other. When they declined, he did not press the point and claimed that he would not have let them do so even if they had been willing. He later explained why he had sent for them.

Well, the purpose of calling Wood and Maloof in, I told them to sit down and I spoke to Wood first, which was a colored boy, and I said to Wood,

"Just because you are colored, Wood"—and we have quite a few colored boys in that platoon—"there's no difference between you and the other people in your platoon." I said, "You people are equal until you prove yourselves different," and Wood—I noticed a tear or so came in his eyes when I was speaking to him that way. Maloof and Wood, they were two big men, I said, "Your people are goofing off as much as those little guys in there and when you people goof off these little guys are going to goof off. . . . I told Private Wood to square those other colored boys away . . . and Maloof and Wood agreed to it.

After finishing with Wood and Maloof, McKeon ordered Pvt. David McPherson to enter. McPherson was a tall man who had dropped out of college before joining the Marine Corps. His General Classification Test score of 139 was the highest of the platoon. McKeon described his encounter with McPherson as follows:

McPherson came in . . . he was a pretty good boy, had good common sense. . . . I spoke to McPherson regarding the discipline of the platoon and McPherson had the attitude that, "I'm just a recruit myself and I don't care what those other people are doing," says, "I'll take care of myself," and that's when I slapped McPherson. . . . I told McPherson to sit down, and I sat down on the rack right next to him and that's when I noticed the bottle. . . . I picked up the bottle and asked McPherson . . . , "Would you like a drink?" McPherson said, "It's up to you, sir." At that time I said to him, "When you prove to me that you are a man, then you can take a drink," and that's when I put the bottle up to my lips.

Q. When you put the bottle up to your lips was the cap on or off?
A. The cap was on it, sir.
Q. Did any of the liquid get into your lips, on your lips or in your throat whatsoever?
A. No, sir.

When David McPherson testified at the court of inquiry a few days later, his testimony did not quite agree with that of Sergeant McKeon:

Q. . . .[D]id you see any evidence that Sergeant McKeon might have been drinking?
A. Yes, sir.
Q. What did you see?
A. Sir, I saw Sergeant McKeon take one drink, sir.

McPherson was more equivocal at the court-martial some three and a half months later.

Q. What did you actually see there, McPherson?
A. Actually, I saw him raise the bottle to his mouth and bring it back down.
Q. Was the cork on or off?
A. I don't know, sir.

Inexplicably, at the court-martial the prosecution never sought to impeach McPherson with his earlier statement.

McKeon put the bottle down. He and McPherson talked a bit about the problems with the platoon. McPherson volunteered that the trouble with the platoon was that the men had it too easy. He considered them to be poorly disciplined. McKeon said to McPherson:

> "We tried everything on you people regarding teaching you people discipline." We spoke on discipline for a while, and I said, "Tonight we are going to try something different." I said, "I'm going to take you people to the boondocks, take you people to the swamps."

McPherson left the room shortly after 8:00 P.M., having confirmed McKeon's own observations and conclusions about the slackness of the platoon. The decision had been made. All else seemed to have failed, and the platoon was more than halfway through its training cycle. The time had come for a wake-up call. At approximately 8:15 P.M. the order was issued to fall out for a night march.

# F I V E

# "The Whole Marine Corps Has Had It, Too"

T.Sgt. John B. Taylor was the commander of the guard at the rifle range on Sunday, April 8. At approximately 8:45 P.M., a sentry at one of the ammunition sheds on Dog range called the corporal of the guard to report hollering and commotion behind the butts. The corporal of the guard relayed the message to Taylor, who immediately drove his automobile to the rear of the range. Seeing nothing but hearing noises a hundred yards or so farther on, he drove behind the Charlie range butts and faced his car out across the marsh toward Ribbon Creek with the headlights on. He heard someone shout, "Turn the lights off, they're blinding us."

Taylor dimmed his lights to the lowest level and began walking toward the source of the strange clamor. He was astonished to see a bedraggled procession approaching him.

> There was two little white boys carrying a colored boy. They were partly dressed, and I tried to talk to them, asked them what was going on and they wouldn't talk. . . . I was trying to talk to about a dozen of them there, but there was no answer at all. They were carrying one another and a few of the boys were naked and half dressed and I imagine they were just too cold to talk then. . . . In a few minutes Sergeant McKeon came up to me and I asked him, "What the hell is going on?" and he just made this statement: "Sergeant, I'm responsible for this."

Taylor told McKeon to take his men back to the barracks and get a head count. He then put the first three recruits he had spotted into his car to drive them to sick bay. Anxiously he drove past the other stragglers to the sentry post near the five hundred yard line on Charlie range. The three young men whom Sergeant Taylor transported have never been identified on the record. The available evidence indicates that they were Mims Brower, Lewis Leake, and Carl Whitmore. Using his cigarette lighter for the little illumination it would generate, Taylor dialed the corporal of the guard and instructed him to get Captain Patrick, the officer of the day, and bring him to the Charlie range butts on the double. Taylor then tried to call Col. William McKean, the officer in charge of the Weapons Training Battalion. In his anxiety he forgot the colonel's number. At the same time his lighter fluid gave out, leaving him in darkness.

At that moment, Captain Patrick drove up. Taylor told Patrick as much as he knew and then drove the three shivering recruits to sick bay. He successfully dialed Colonel McKean's number from sick bay just as Captain Patrick entered. Taylor handed the receiver to Patrick and left to meet Sergeant McKeon back at Building 761.

Meanwhile, the remnants of Platoon 71 straggled back to their barracks like a routed detachment, cold, wet, and in various stages of shock. One of the New York boys sat on his bunk, eyes glazed, babbling and praying with his rosary beads. A head count revealed eleven men missing. That number was reduced to seven when the three men Sergeant Taylor had delivered to sick bay were accounted for and it was realized that another man was already in sick bay and had missed the march.

Behind the butts, temporary lights were already being set up. The lights soon revealed Pvt. Clarence E. Cox, a country boy from the Carolina hills, perched on the opposite bank of Ribbon Creek. Someone with a bullhorn asked Cox if he was all right. He yelled back that he was just cold. Initially (and unbelievably, after what had just occurred) his offer to swim back across Ribbon Creek was accepted. Fortunately, a small boat arrived and delivered Cox to shore. As he was helped onto firm ground he walked past a Catholic priest ominously delivering prayers over the now still waters.

Cox, in a state of temporary shock, was transported by ambulance to sick bay to join his four platoon mates. The news of Cox's rescue reduced to six the number of men missing. Norman Wood, Leroy Thompson, Donald O'Shea, Jerry Thomas, Thomas Hardeman, and Charles Reilly remained unaccounted for.

At this point Elwin Scarborough, whom McKeon had left at the Staff NCO Club just after 1:00 P.M., reemerged as a figure in the events of the evening. At about 8:40 P.M., Sergeant Huff was dozing in front of his television at home when he was awakened by a call from Scarborough, who was still at the club and was seeking a ride back to his automobile at the Weapons Training Battalion. Huff went and picked up Scarborough, who, as Huff politely described it, "had been drinking," and drove him to the rifle range. Scarborough asked Huff to stop at Building 761 to visit Sergeant McKeon (but in all likelihood to enable him to retrieve his bottle). When they arrived at about 9:00 P.M. the squad bay was dark and empty. Huff thought little of it, as he assumed the platoon was down the road watching the movie at the Lyceum.

Huff had barely had time to return home and take off his clothes when Captain Patrick called at approximately 9:40 P.M. and told him to return to Building 761. Huff, a gruff and hard-nosed man by nature, was extremely upset at being called out for a second time on his night off. Rather than taking the time to determine what had happened, he immediately confronted the bedraggled assemblage he found in the squad bay, screaming that they were a bunch of pussies and candy asses. His tone changed when he realized that a number of the men were missing. Thereafter, in a scene reminiscent of Stanley's discovery of Livingston, he encountered McKeon:

> I walked [into the drill instructor's room] and I seen Sergeant McKeon sitting down and as I walked in I just said, "Hi, Mac," and he just said, "Hi, Huff." I walked right straight into the washroom that we have there and got a cup of water. . . .

After McKeon returned to the squad bay with the remnants of his platoon, Colonel McKean ordered him to be placed under arrest. Pfc. Fred Magruder, an MP, was detailed to confine McKeon temporarily to the drill instructor's room. When Magruder saw McKeon nervously take a liquor bottle and place it behind the toilet, he ordered Corporal Lyons, the corporal of the guard, to fetch the bottle. Lyons gave the bottle to Magruder, who placed it in the hallway. Lyons testified that there was about an inch and a half of liquid in the bottle. At the court of inquiry on April 16, Magruder testified that the bottle had "about a fourth left in it." At the court-martial on July 25, he hedged his estimate to "about a fourth or less."

Shortly thereafter, Magruder gave the bottle to the sergeant of the guard, who in turn delivered it to Lt. Oral Newman, the depot officer of the day. Newman later confirmed Lyons's testimony that there was about "one and one-half to two inches of clear fluid in it." McKeon, now under arrest, was brought by the MPs to the dispensary on the island to be tested for sobriety by both visual and verbal means. In addition, a Bogens test was performed to determine his blood alcohol content. Lt. Robert J. Atcheson, a navy physician, was on duty at the dispensary. Atcheson performed a basic physical examination on McKeon and a number of tests of coordination. His report of April 8 stated that blood drawn at 11:30 P.M. revealed 1.5 milligrams of alcohol per unit of whole blood. The doctor also reported that McKeon's breath was suggestive of alcohol; however, his self-balancing test was normal, as were his gait, pupils, and speech. His reflexes were normal and he was able to walk a straight line. Curiously, Dr. Atcheson then indicated that there was clinical evidence of intoxication but commented that the sergeant was "possibly under the influence of alcohol but still in control of himself."

At the court-martial, Dr. Atcheson expanded on his report of April 8.

I had the patient stand with his feet close together and close his eyes, which probably is a little more severe than the actual test is supposed to be, but his equilibrium was completely normal. He had complete control of his equilibrium. His gait I said was normal. . . . I had the sergeant walk over approximately 20 feet, and he did so without any difficulty whatsoever in a straight line. . . . His speech was completely normal. The sergeant answered me accurately and explicitly and immediately upon questioning. There was no difficulty in speech.

Dr. Atcheson sought to explain his comment that there was clinical evidence of intoxication in the following manner:

When I answered [the question on the record form regarding] clinical evidence of intoxication "yes," it was not as a result of my findings that I said this. Rather, I had asked the Sergeant during the course of the examination, which is not recorded here, I asked the Sergeant if he had had anything to drink in the recent past and he said "Yes" he had a few shots of vodka that afternoon. Then, going along with the breath, which was suggestive to me of alcohol, I had to say that there was some evidence that the patient may have been under the influence of alcohol, although my physical examination, as far as I could determine, was that he was in complete control of himself.

When he was asked about McKeon's condition at the court of inquiry on Saturday, April 14, 1956, Dr. Atcheson concluded that Sergeant McKeon had full control of his physical and mental faculties. He also related that to his knowledge the Bogens test did not give an accurate picture of the percentage of alcohol and would not stand up legally in court.

* * *

For the preceding thirty-three months Col. William B. McKean had been the officer in charge of the Weapons Training Battalion. An outspoken veteran of twenty-six years of service in the Marine Corps following his graduation from the Naval Academy in 1930, McKean had served in the South Pacific during World War II and had done several tours of duty both at sea and on land before he came to Parris Island in 1953.

About twenty minutes after Ed Sullivan signed off the air on Sunday night, McKean was alone in his den when Captain Patrick called. As McKean remembered it, Captain Patrick opened the conversation as follows: "Colonel, this is Patrick. We're in trouble. There are a bunch of recruits coming back to Building 761 and it seems that the DI has been marching them through the swamps. I'm going down now to investigate it."

McKean's immediate response was, "Lock up the DI. Send to sick bay those that need it. Get the rest of them policed up and call me back as soon as you know the number of the platoon and the battalion."

At about 9:40 P.M., Patrick called McKean again. In all likelihood this was the call Sergeant Taylor originated from sick bay. He relayed the platoon number and the information he had been able to obtain and alerted the colonel that a search was being organized behind the butts on Charlie range. McKean responded that he would pass the message on to the chief of staff and advised Captain Patrick to call again if there was any further news.

In the nearly three years that McKean had been in charge of the Weapons Training Battalion there had been numerous searches. "In some cases it's a lost fisherman; in others a recruit decides he can take no more and heads off into the swamps." Usually the unfortunate soul was found within a matter of hours, often muddy and tormented by the ubiquitous sand fleas. The messages McKean received from his officer of the day seemed to suggest a similar event that called for routine handling.

Although he was not alarmed, McKean was sufficiently concerned by the calls from Patrick to drive out behind the butts and see for himself what was happening. When he arrived, Major McLeod, the provost marshal, and the fire chief were already there. Overhead searchlights were in place, and foot patrols had been sent out. McKean's expectation was that six wet, scared, and muddy recruits would soon be found floundering about in the nearby marshes.

Shortly after midnight, General Burger arrived, alerted by the chief of staff, and was briefed by McKean. The patrols were still out, and S.Sgt. George W. Sparks was exploring the adjacent waterways in a small boat. At 1:30 A.M. Sergeant McKeon was brought back behind the butts by the provost marshal to pinpoint where the events in the waters had occurred. Colonel McKean, continuing to believe that there was no likelihood of a loss of life, returned home a few hours before twilight and slept briefly.

During low tide at between 2:30 and 3:00 A.M., Sergeant Sparks discovered clothes, utilities, underclothes, tops and bottoms, socks, shoes, cigarette cases, a cigarette package, and a wallet at the edge of Ribbon Creek, about one hundred yards downstream from an old wooden pier behind the far end of Charlie range. He also discovered footprints "where it looked like a body of men had come through."

Colonel McKean returned to the scene as the sun was rising behind the assembled group of exhausted searchers. Captain Patrick was trying to get some rest in the back of a nearby vehicle. All patrols had reported no sign of the missing men. At about this time McKean began to realize, as he described it, "that we probably had a tragedy on our hands."

Beaufort County sheriff J. E. McTeer volunteered his services shortly after dawn on Monday, April 9. Experienced at pulling bodies from the tidal waters, he advised McKean that a body is invariably found near the spot of drowning, even in swiftly moving tidal waters. McTeer offered his grappling hooks and suggested that the best way to retrieve bodies would be with a trawler and a shrimp net. McKean gave his approval, and McTeer radioed a nearby shrimper friend, who readily volunteered to assist. The shrimper proved to be of no practical use, however, as his boat ran aground in the ebbing tide.

While the trawler waited for the tide to turn, a number of smaller boats with grappling hooks combed the area where the panic had occurred the preceding night. A few minutes after twelve noon, the first body was found. Colonel McKean later described the scene:

> As we turned to look at the boats in the creek, there is a low whistle. Gooch, Whitlow, and Hughes have hooked one. They have him in the boat. Well, this is it. The whole Marine Corps has had it, too! Cautioning the idlers to stand well clear, I go over to the dilapidated little pier beyond the other end of the C butts to meet them. . . .
>
> . . . His face has been covered with a field jacket. It is the Section Leader, a tall husky Negro boy. He is in grotesque *rigor mortis*. . . . His arms and legs are in positions similar to a boxer's stance: there had obviously been a struggle; he went down fighting.

Twenty minutes later the second body was recovered. Within half an hour two more bodies were pulled from the murky waters just before low tide. At about 4:00 P.M. the fifth body suddenly appeared and was brought in for a prayer, identification, and photographing before the ambulance retraced the route to the morgue at the Beaufort Naval Hospital. All five of the young men had been found within forty yards of each other in a depression in the creek bottom known to local fishermen as the "trout hole."

The positioning of the bodies at the trout hole confirmed the accounts of several of the survivors that the stream bottom suddenly dropped off. In all likelihood, Sergeant McKeon, David McPherson, and the other boots who remained at the head of the column had stayed close enough to the creek's edge to avoid the sudden depression. Those nearer the rear who had fanned out after they turned downstream had probably walked into this unforeseen hollow on the creek bed.

The remains of Norman Wood, Leroy Thompson, Donald O'Shea, Jerry Thomas, and Charles Reilly were now accounted for. Only Thomas Hardeman, the lone swimmer of the six, had not been located.

Dragging operations continued into Tuesday but were finally suspended at about 1:00 P.M. to allow a different approach. A marine frogman named Gerald Seybold had offered to don his wet suit and comb the creek bed. After waiting a short interval to allow the mud to resettle, Seybold began methodically crisscrossing the stream from side to side while the tide was out. For more than two hours he probed every square inch of the watercourse, gradually moving upstream to where the other bodies had been found.

As the tedious effort continued, Thomas Hardeman's brother and stepfather appeared at the scene to observe the search. Colonel McKean discouraged them from remaining.

> I tell the brother I won't prevent his viewing the body—if we recover it—but I recommended against it. I describe how the other looked after some nibbling by crabs—in this case the crabs have had another twenty-four hours for nibble. . . . The two eventually leave, with the older man making the only kind remark I hear: "May the good Lord be with you and help you. Colonel, I know you're doing everything you can."

At 3:17 P.M. on Tuesday, April 10, with General Burger present and most of the rest of the weary search crew making idle chatter, Seybold discovered the body of Thomas Hardeman. A photographer from *Life* magazine who had ventured into the marshes captured the dramatic shot of the small skiff tilting sharply as Hardeman's body was pulled aboard. Moments later the ambulance departed with the remains of the last victim of Ribbon Creek while the exhausted frogman caught his breath and gulped a cup of coffee.

Most of the search party had been at the site for more than thirty-six hours. Emotionally and physically fatigued, they secured their remaining gear and shuffled off to face the unknown consequences that would flow from the events of the last two days.

# S I X

# The Reaction

As the night wore on and the elevated searchlights and scattered patrols failed to flush any survivors from the shoulder-high grass and marshes along the west side of the island, Colonel McKean's optimism that the missing men would be found gradually waned. Near dawn, General Burger and his chief of staff, Col. William Buse, arrived to survey the rescue operations. Their thoughts turned to the public relations aspect of the situation and the dilemma they faced. If the missing men were found alive, the matter could be handled internally without the inevitable damage to the reputation of the Marine Corps that would result from publicizing the events of the preceding evening. Certainly in the eyes of the top brass, there were already enough critics of the military in general and the Marine Corps in particular. No need to feed those sharks. On the other hand, if any of the recruits had actually drowned, the longer the story was withheld, the greater the anticipated repercussions. As Buse left McKean he related that Burger had made a decision: if the missing men were not found by 7:45 A.M., General Pate, the Marine Corps commandant, would be notified in Washington, D.C.

At approximately 7:45 A.M. Burger placed a call to Washington. As it turned out, General Pate was away at his alma mater, Virginia Military Institute, at the time. When his staff reached him later on Monday morning he decided to make a personal visit to Parris Island. Arrangements were hastily made for Pate and the inspector-general, Brigadier General Roberts, to fly to South Carolina that day to investigate the situation firsthand.

While Pate was en route to Parris Island, Headquarters Marine Corps in Washington began implementing immediate measures to handle the public relations aspect of the impending crisis. Col. James Hittle, who had developed close contacts with influential congressmen, was dispatched to Capitol Hill to alert allies of the Marine Corps of the situation.

According to historian Keith Fleming,

> Colonel Hittle left the chief of staff's office and immediately jumped into a car and went directly to Capitol Hill. Within the next hour, he saw and alerted Representatives Carl Vinson and Davey Short, plus Senators Leverett Saltonstall and Richard B. Russell, all of whom were very strong supporters of the Marine Corps and who held key leadership positions in the House and Senate Armed Forces Committees. Their support was especially vital to the Marine Corps that April because both Armed Services committees were in the midst of their annual hearings on the defense budget. The Marine Corps was counting on its friends in Congress to ensure that the Corps received its fair share of the austere defense appropriations requested by the Eisenhower administration.

Meanwhile, a news release was prepared in Washington for dissemination by Capt. Ralph Wood, the public affairs officer at Parris Island. Wisely, the release was held in abeyance for a short time until Colonel Hittle could brief the most important congressmen. At approximately 1:00 P.M. on Monday, April 9, some sixteen hours after the incident, the wire services received a terse announcement:

> Six Marines are missing from the Marine Recruit Depot at Parris Island, South Carolina, following a night training exercise conducted last evening.

The absence of details, including the names of the missing marines or the unit to which they were attached, raised more questions than were answered. There were more than five thousand recruits then in training at Parris Island, and incoming telephone calls from concerned families flooded the depot switchboard. The brevity of the press release also gave many inherently suspicious reporters the impression that the Marine Corps was being less than forthright about what had happened.

When the commandant arrived later in the day, he met with General Burger and briefly visited the scene where the search was under way. Five of the six bodies had been found. General Pate then met Colonel McKean, who was by that time emotionally and physically weary from his lengthy vigil. An embittered McKean would later recount his version of the ensuing exchange at the scene.

"Hello, Bill. Bill, what orders do you have or what Depot Order do you recall which specifically forbids a thing like this?"

"General, to the best of my knowledge there isn't any. This sort of thing just isn't done—but I can't recall any order that would apply."

"There has to be something to cover this."

"There may be—I hope so—But I haven't had much time since last night to read orders. . . . To the best of my recollection we have no order which covers a deal like this."

McKean claims that after watching the shrimp trawler make a few passes in search of the last body, "chauffeurs, aides, and generals mount up. I salute all the brass as their cars pull off. That is the last I see of our visitors."

General Pate had been advised by headquarters in Washington that the press had been alerted and would be present on his arrival at Parris Island. Once he had familiarized himself with the details, the commandant would address a press conference and inform the media of what had been and would be occurring. Headquarters had suggested to Pate through one of his aides that he advise the reporters that he would personally investigate the matter and keep them apprised. Maj. Duane Faw, the depot's legal officer, was present when General Burger briefed the commandant on the events at Ribbon Creek. Major Faw urged Pate to address the factual issues but to express no opinion as to McKeon's guilt or innocence. He was simply to tell the press that the matter was under investigation.

The commandant delivered his prepared statement as planned on the steps of the headquarters building at Parris Island, then offered to answer reporters' questions. When asked if Sergeant McKeon was guilty of breaking regulations, Pate responded, "It would appear so." He also related that Sergeant McKeon had no authority for disciplinary action or for scheduling such a march. Major Faw recalls a reporter asking the commandant if, in effect, the Marine Corps was going to let the drill instructor get away with murder. General Pate responded that McKeon would be punished to the fullest extent of the law.

Major Faw and Colonel Buse were shocked. The commandant had done exactly what they had tried to guard against. He had for all intents and purposes condemned McKeon well before the court of inquiry could begin to weigh the facts and assess responsibility. Furthermore, having peremptorily declared McKeon's guilt, General Pate was automatically disqualified thereafter from convening a court-martial. In an effort to eliminate command influence in criminal proceedings, the Uniform Code of Military Justice precludes a commanding officer and all officers in the command of lesser rank from ordering a court-martial if the superior officer has expressed an opinion of guilt. The Marine Corps now faced a dilemma. In expressing his opinion of McKeon's guilt, the commandant of the Corps had disqualified not only himself from convening a court-martial, but every other marine officer under his command as well.

Despite the major blunder at the press conference, the immediate steps taken to manage the crisis at the political level were paying off. As anticipated, there was an outcry from some congressmen for a congressional investigation. Within days of the drownings, Congressman Lester Holtzman of New York, a member of the House Armed Services Committee, called for a full-scale congressional probe of the incident. Holtzman's request was endorsed by Rep. L. Mendel Rivers of South Carolina. An Associated Press news report carried by the *New York Times* on April 12 reported that "growing concern over the Corps's basic training methods was expressed in Congressional quarters. Demands were heard for an Armed Services Committee investigation if the Marines' own inquiry did not reassure the nation."

At best, a congressional investigation would generate widespread negative publicity for the Marine Corps as well as risk further budgetary constraints. Election year politics would undoubtedly shift much of the focus of any investigation from dreary fact finding to events more appealing to the public appetite.

What the general public did not know about, but the top Marine brass did, was the wealth of raw material that a publicity-seeking congressman could find and use to stir up public passion against the Corps. For years, recruits and their families had been complaining about training abuses to their representatives and senators. The Marine Corps had taken no significant steps either to rectify the underlying problems or to assure the families and their congressmen that the complaints were taken seriously. Exposure of that foreknowledge in the wake of the Ribbon Creek deaths would only compound the adverse reaction to recruit training in particular, and the Marine Corps in general. In a worst-case scenario, the Marine Corps itself could be in jeopardy.

A strategy was formulated at headquarters to avert a congressional investigation: the Marine Corps would conduct its own full-scale inquiry, publicize the results, and make a number of substantive and visible changes in the training regimen. Rep. Carl Vinson, chairman of the House Armed Services Committee and a longtime supporter of the Marine Corps, agreed to forestall an investigation by his committee provided the Corps took immediate steps to implement its promised inquiry and changes.

Vinson's aim was not to conceal the truth. Rather, his objective was to work with the Marine Corps to enable it to satisfy Congress that the Corps had made a full inquiry into the Ribbon Creek tragedy and taken constructive steps to reduce the potential for future maltreatment of marine recruits. The events of Ribbon Creek were too devastating and too public to be wished away. If the Marine Corps was to survive as a unique institution and the essential features of boot camp were to continue, there had to be an acknowledgment of error as well as a plan for structural improvement. Congress clearly would settle for nothing less.

General Pate and his advisers recognized the threat to the Corps immediately and set about addressing the situation in a manner that would be most effective in mitigating the damage. As will be seen, the strategy they developed proved to be largely effective, but there was a cost. If General Pate's comments at the press conference on April 9 foreshadowed the official position of the Marine Corps, the future did not bode well for Matthew McKeon. As the strategy of damage control began to become more apparent in the days that followed, it became clear that McKeon's fate was caught up in circumstances far more complex than he could ever have imagined when he decided to instill a dose of discipline in the old-fashioned way.

# SEVEN

# Inquiry

While the commandant was still en route to Parris Island, the top-level staff at the depot was hastily preparing plans to begin a formal inquiry. On the morning of Monday, April 9, less than twenty-four hours after the ill-fated march, General Burger appointed Col. John B. Heles, the depot inspector, to preside over a court of inquiry. Burger ordered the court to convene at 1:00 P.M. on Monday, April 9, "or as soon thereafter as practicable." Joining Heles were Maj. Gerald B. McIntyre of the G-3 (training) department and Lt. William J. Spann, a navy physician in the depot's medical department. Maj. Donald J. Holben, who was both an infantry and a legal officer, was named counsel for the court. His task was to orchestrate the proceedings, examine the witnesses, and introduce the documents that were to be placed in evidence. Holben was not supposed to be a prosecutor; he was to assist the court in seeking to determine the truth within the scope of the convening order. All three members of the court as well as Holben held staff positions at Parris Island at the time.

In some respects the court of inquiry was similar to an inquest or grand jury proceeding. The court was empowered to issue subpoenas, to take testimony under oath, and to follow the formalities of basic due process of law. Sergeant McKeon was made a "party" to the proceeding. Although a party was not technically a defendant, as the inquiries were essentially investigative in nature, the conduct of a party could be the subject of criminal charges. As such, McKeon was entitled to be represented by a lawyer, to be present at all proceedings, and to decide whether or not to testify.

The scope of the court's responsibilities was spelled out in precise detail in General Burger's convening order.

> The court shall make a thorough investigation into all of the circumstances connected with the marching of Platoon 71 into the swamp and the disappearance of subject named men. The court shall report its findings of fact, opinions and recommendations with respect to the circumstances surrounding the marching of Platoon 71 into the swamps, and the deaths, injuries or disappearance of naval personnel and their line of duty and misconduct status, and responsibility for the incident, including recommended disciplinary action.

As the order reveals, the inquiry was called so soon after the incident that it was not then known whether the six recruits unaccounted for were dead, injured, or simply missing.

When Major Faw arrived at his office in the headquarters building on Monday, April 9, he was immediately briefed about the events of the preceding evening by Major Holben, who had been on duty on Sunday. At this time no bodies had been found, but it was suspected that some recruits had drowned. Holben told Faw that the drill instructor who had instigated the march was in the brig.

Faw had considerable experience as military defense counsel. He knew the importance of protecting a defendant's rights by offering the immediate assistance of a lawyer. After hurriedly—and unsuccessfully—scouting about for an available staff lawyer to assign to McKeon, Faw walked over to the brig and spoke directly to the sergeant through his cell bars. After introducing himself, Faw advised McKeon that he had no knowledge of any drownings at that point because the dragging operation was just getting under way. He also told McKeon that he was entitled to a lawyer. McKeon responded that he didn't want a lawyer and that he knew there was at least one body in the stream. Faw tried his best to stop the disconsolate drill instructor from continuing, but to no avail. McKeon said that he felt he deserved whatever punishment he got because it was all his fault.

Faw now faced a dilemma himself. He had a confession, but it would be inadmissible in any court-martial because no Miranda-type warning had been given. He returned to his office after the brief exchange and assigned 2d Lt. Jeremiah Collins to defend McKeon. Collins was selected because he had previously represented drill instructors charged with various offenses. Faw decided that the fairest way to deal with McKeon's unsolicited comments was to just keep them to himself, which is exactly what he did for the next forty-one years.

At 8:31 A.M. on Tuesday, April 10, the court of inquiry was called to order in the administration building at Mainside. By that time, five of the six bodies had been recovered; only Thomas Hardeman was still unaccounted for. The rapidity with which the court was assembled and called to order left virtually no time for any preliminary investigation, interrogation of potential witnesses, assembly of needed documents, or general planning as to how this rather unusual proceeding was to be conducted. The recruits, who must still have been in a state of shock, had prepared sketchy handwritten statements only hours before legions of reporters arrived to interrogate them. Lieutenant Collins had had only hours to meet with McKeon and begin preparations to represent him. Yet once the drownings became public knowledge, there was little the Marine Corps could do but try to get to the bottom of what had occurred with as much dispatch as possible.

After preliminary introductions, the court members and counsel immediately reconvened behind the Charlie range butts to view the scene. McKeon and Collins chose not to attend. Sergeant Sparks was present. He pointed out to the court some of the salient features of the terrain, described where he had found the tracks leading into the water, and pointed out the location of the trout hole, which he testified was about one and one-half feet deeper than the rest of the creek bed. After standing on the bank of Ribbon Creek and observing the surroundings for half an hour or so, the court members returned to the hearing room to begin listening to descriptions of the events of April 8 from the mouths of the men who made the march. All witnesses were sequestered so that no man's testimony would be affected by what he had heard from another witness.

Joseph A. Moran was the first recruit to testify. One of the New York boys, Moran was the son of actress Thelma Ritter. He had become something of a celebrity himself when his mother prevailed on one of her colleagues to write to Moran in the early days of boot camp. Moran achieved an elevated status in the eyes of his companions when he showed them a letter from none other than the goddess of sex herself, Marilyn Monroe.

Moran gave a rather coherent description of the march across Baker range and into the water and the subsequent panic. He described his heroic efforts with Donald Porter to try to save Leroy Thompson and others. He had continued his efforts with Private Truitt on his back, he said, and "a lot of people . . . trying to drag me under."

Private Porter was called after Moran. For the three summers before enlisting, Porter had worked as a lifeguard at Riis Park and Coney Island in New York, where he had been credited with saving four lives. He confirmed the essential features of Moran's description of the effort to save Leroy Thompson. Both told of helping Thompson to a point where he could stand in shoulder-deep water and leaving him there, thinking he was safe. Porter had then assisted Leonard Myers to firm ground and organized a human chain to pull the other recruits to safety. Porter's efforts were confirmed by a number of other boots. He was certainly one of the heroes of the evening.

In all, twenty-three of the sixty-nine survivors testified. Understandably, none claimed that he had panicked or jumped on the back of another man. Yet by piecing together the sketchy and often conflicting testimonies, one can draw a composite of the minutes preceding and following the outbreak of pandemonium: the moonless night; the disintegration of the platoon's formation in the water; the nervous and frightened young men, many quelling their apprehension by joking and fooling around; the ever deeper water; the force of the outgoing tide; and the precipitous drop-off of the creek bed leading to the sudden eruption of panic and chaos followed by a number of valiant and sometimes futile rescue efforts. Donald Porter, Edwin Leonard, William Rambo, John Martinez, Richard Acker, Earl Grabowski, and David McPherson all told of McKeon's efforts to save his men.

Presumably the members of the court and Major Holben knew that Sergeant McKeon had tried to conceal the nearly empty bottle of vodka behind his toilet just before his arrest. One would expect, therefore, that one of the critical areas of inquiry would have been the extent to which each of the recruits was aware of McKeon's drinking—any noticeable effects of alcohol on his breath, in his speech, or on any aspect of his behavior before or during the march. Yet no concerted line of questions was put to the men who would have had the most direct knowledge of McKeon's condition. The absence of such an inquiry is particularly odd since much of the inquiry focused on that very subject.

Of the twenty-three recruits who were called to testify, only eight were asked questions in any way related to McKeon's alcohol consumption or the possible effects of it. Of those eight, five testified that there was no evidence that McKeon was drunk or impaired by drinking.

Donald Porter, when asked if McKeon appeared drunk, replied:

No, sir, not to me he didn't. I wasn't that close to him to smell alcohol. I found the man from what I saw to be in a normal condition, not to be under the influence of drinking.

William Rambo, when asked bluntly, "Do you think he was drunk?" replied that he couldn't say, as he had never seen McKeon drunk and wouldn't know how he would act if he were. However, Rambo testified that he saw nothing unusual about McKeon's conduct.

Stephen McGuire, Eugene Ervin, and Gerald Langone also reported to the court that they saw nothing unusual about their drill instructor's behavior. When asked directly, McGuire responded that McKeon seemed to be his normal self.

Lew Ray Brewer, the only married man in the platoon, was more equivocal. When asked if he noticed anything unusual about Sergeant McKeon's condition, he responded,

Sir, it seemed to me that he was unsteady on his feet and I don't know . . . I know he drinks, and it seemed like he was tired, sir. He seemed like he was real tired, sir.

Richard Drown also noticed that McKeon seemed tired or fatigued, "kind of unsteady on his feet." He also said, however, that in the preceding weeks McKeon had walked with "kind of a slight hitch."

Incredible as it seems, fifteen of the twenty-three witnesses were never asked about McKeon's drinking. Each man was offered an opportunity to make a voluntary statement about any matter he thought significant for the court. Many statements were offered, but none hinted at McKeon being under the influence of alcohol.

The most damaging evidence on the subject of alcohol was offered by David McPherson, one of the men who had been called into the drill instructor's room shortly before the march began. McPherson had seen McKeon lift the bottle to his lips and take one drink. McPherson also related that McKeon had acted normally and seriously. When asked if in his opinion McKeon was drunk, McPherson replied, "No, sir." When interviewed forty years after the incident, McPherson was still of the opinion that McKeon did not appear to be under the influence. What was not asked at the time, and what never came out in any of the testimony, was that McKeon was not the only one to take a swig of vodka; McPherson had one too.

The questioning of the recruits tended to be quite superficial, with little follow-up. On the first day, after the court returned from viewing the site, eight witnesses were called, examined, cross-examined, and excused between 10:00 A.M. and 4:16 P.M. All twenty-three had completed their testimony by midday on Wednesday, April 11, the second day of the hearing. It must be kept in mind, however, that the court had been convened in haste and was under considerable pressure to ascertain the essential facts and make its report and recommendations without delay. Under those circumstances, and perhaps because many of the recruits were still suffering from the aftereffects of their ordeal, the court's objective seems to have been to inquire briefly and directly about only those matters that seemed central to the investigation. Full details could be fleshed in if and when a court-martial was ordered.

Understandably, none of the surviving witnesses was asked by the court or by Major Holben for an evaluation of Sergeant McKeon as a drill instructor; that topic was well beyond the scope of the inquiry. However, when each recruit was offered the opportunity to make a voluntary statement at the conclusion of his testimony, several chose to speak about the sergeant. McKeon had had no opportunity to coach or intimidate any of the witnesses. What follows are some of the men's assessments of their drill instructor—the man who only days earlier had led these same young men into what was undoubtedly the most traumatic and frightening experience of their lives—that the court must have found remarkable.

If everybody had stayed in ranks and followed Sergeant McKeon, nothing would have happened. [Joseph A. Moran]

I would like to say that Sergeant McKeon to my knowledge really did work in that water to get those boys out. I mean he really worked hard, and he was really exhausted when he got out of the water. And there was no two ways about it he was really downhearted for what happened to those men. [Donald J. Porter]

I think that Sergeant McKeon did—he was only trying to help us and teach us further training that we should know if we ever go into combat. I don't think that he ever intended for any of the boys to be hurt. I think that it was an unfortunate accident, sir. [Edwin Leonard]

I'd like to say that Staff Sergeant McKeon has been a great help to me and I'm pretty sure he has been for the rest of the boys. And he's always been good to us. He's been patient with us and he's trying to teach us certain things we should know in boot camp. A lot of things that he has helped us on. I knew he has me, and I am grateful to him for that. [William Rambo]

Yes, sir, I know Sergeant McKeon didn't mean any wrong by what he did. [Stephen McGuire]

Sergeant McKeon was trying to help as many men as he could, sir, that were drowning. [Richard Acker]

I noticed Sergeant McKeon was in the water and he was helping most of the boys and he was trying his best to get the other boys out. . . . I know Sergeant McKeon was the last one out because that's when I saw him coming by. [Earl Grabowski]

Sergeant McKeon did his best to get everyone out of the water that was in distress. I also saw Sergeant McKeon, sir, that he felt hurt and sorry at what had happened. [David McPherson]

Although several of the witnesses made no voluntary statements, not one of those who did had anything negative or critical to say about Sergeant McKeon. Whether it was a form of survivor's guilt, residual intimidation, or genuine respect for their former instructor, no man seemed to blame him for the gruesome deaths of six of their companions.

Having disposed of the recruit witnesses by April 11, the court now turned its attention to the surrounding details. T.Sgt. Samuel Cummings authenticated a two-page statement he had obtained from Sergeant McKeon at 8:30 A.M. on the morning after the march. In his statement McKeon described his anger at finding the men "crapped out" on Sunday morning. He attempted to cover for Scarborough and King, relating that "someone" had brought a bottle of vodka into his room and "all during the afternoon I had some drinks from the bottle. I believe at the most I had three or four drinks." He claimed that he thought of taking the men into the swamps shortly after noon, described the route of the march, and recounted his efforts to save the men after some of the recruits "out toward the center of the stream" began yelling for help.

Sergeant King was called. He described joining Scarborough and McKeon in the drill instructor's room between 11:00 A.M. and noon on Sunday. The vodka bottle was half full when he entered. He took one drink, he said, while Scarborough and McKeon each had two or three drinks. King had noted nothing unusual about McKeon's condition before he left or after he returned with the mail. He was of the opinion that McKeon was not drunk.

Elwin Scarborough's testimony added little to what was already known. He acknowledged that the fifth of vodka was his, that it was "a little over half" full when he retrieved it from his car, that he and McKeon "had a couple of drinks," and that he did not see McKeon again after they parted at the Staff NCO Club shortly after 1:00 P.M.

Lt. Charles B. Herlihy, the depot psychiatrist, was called initially to authenticate the records of the psychiatric screening examination done when McKeon was entering DI school. The psychiatric evaluation performed at that time rated McKeon in the highest category in motivation, emotional stability, and control of hostility.

Herlihy's duties as the depot's record keeper were incidental to his primary reason for being called, however, for it was he who had examined Sergeant McKeon on the afternoon following the drownings. He described McKeon as appearing "quite dejected, remorseful, . . . stunned . . . and . . . depressed," but with a clear memory of what had occurred. The responses to the psychiatrist's many questions revealed a man who "was clear and coherent and logical in his thinking." It was at this point in his narration that Dr. Herlihy commented that his examination revealed that McKeon's judgment had "shown itself at times in the past to be based upon impulsive thinking. He tends to act hastily and think about it later." What were the events in the past that had shown impulsive judgment? Was Herlihy alluding simply to the events of the preceding evening, or was there something in McKeon's past that reflected impetuous behavior? The witness was never asked, nor did he volunteer. Major Holben quickly moved on to establish that McKeon knew right from wrong and had the ability to cooperate with counsel in his own defense.

After Dr. Herlihy stepped down, Lieutenant Collins reported to the court that Sergeant McKeon had decided to ask his brother-in-law, Thomas C. Costello, a young civil lawyer in New York City, to join Collins in representing him. Collins requested a brief recess until Mr. Costello could be asked if he was willing and able to rush down to assist in the proceedings. Colonel Heles accepted the request for a brief delay and adjourned court for the day on Thursday, April 12, at 11:25 A.M.. In all likelihood, all present were relieved to have an afternoon to gather their wits and a momentary break from the pressures of the proceedings.

The afternoon break turned into a day-and-a-half recess because of a second development. Col. William McKean, the officer in charge of the Weapons Training Battalion, who was about to testify, outranked Colonel Heles. Under military protocol, the president of the court should outrank the major witnesses. Consequently, Heles had to be replaced by an officer senior to Colonel McKean. Brig. Gen. Wallace M. Greene Jr., a future commandant of the Marine Corps, was dispatched by General Pate to preside over the balance of the inquiry.

Greene, of Vermont Yankee stock, was a graduate of Annapolis. Although he was somewhat diminutive in size, his military demeanor and habits were those of a professional soldier. He was regarded by his colleagues as a firm and capable officer. He showed that he meant business by reconvening the court of inquiry on Saturday, April 14, at 8:10 in the morning. Greene was sworn in, offered a prayer, requested the "guidance of Almighty God," and announced that he had read the transcripts of the prior proceedings and had viewed the scene. By this time Thomas Costello and an associate, attorney James McGarry, had also arrived from New York and had reviewed the record of the testimony to date.

Dr. Robert Atcheson, a navy lieutenant assigned to the medical corps at Parris Island, was the first and most significant witness of the day. Atcheson had conducted a series of sobriety tests on McKeon immediately after he was brought in between 9:50 and 10:00 P.M. on Sunday night. None of the five separate tests Atcheson conducted revealed that McKeon was intoxicated or under the influence of alcohol. However, when Atcheson stood close to the sergeant he detected a suggestive odor of alcohol on McKeon's breath that prompted him to ask McKeon if he had had anything to drink. McKeon volunteered quite candidly that he had had "a few shots of vodka that afternoon." Atcheson then prepared his report indicating that there was clinical evidence of intoxication. When he was on the witness stand a week later, Dr. Atcheson sought to wriggle free from the apparent contradiction by suggesting that while the objective tests were all negative, McKeon may have "subjectively" been under the influence of alcohol. Either Costello or McGarry (the record does not indicate which) emphasized this contradiction on cross-examination. Not until the court-martial nearly four months later would Dr. Atcheson admit that there was no clinical evidence of intoxication. By that time, however, much of the damage was long since done.

Dr. Atcheson was followed by Sgt. Algin Nolan, a clerk in the depot sergeant major's office. Nolan's duties were to prepare the tide tables for the surrounding waters. He testified that high tide on the evening of April 8 was at 6:34 P.M. and that the sun set at 6:48 P.M.. The exchange between the witness and the court was somewhat confusing with regard to when the tide would have crested on Ribbon Creek behind the rifle range. The witness's opinion seems to have been that high tide would have occurred no more than ten minutes earlier or later than 6:34 P.M., but that point was never clarified.

Lt. Col. David Silvey, who supervised the recruit training program, next testified that no night marches had been authorized. Silvey responded to a line of irrelevant questions that depot regulations prohibited swimming in the waters around Parris Island because of pollution. Major Holben adroitly avoided asking if there were any regulations prohibiting recruits from entering the waters of Ribbon Creek or the surrounding marshes; he knew there were none. Silvey's primary mission, it appears, was to enter into the record exhibits of detailed plans for swimming instruction and other forms of recruit training.

By this time the two civilian counselors and Lieutenant Collins were better prepared, mutually supportive, and more acclimated to the proceedings. Their growing confidence was reflected in the team's increasingly vigorous cross-examination. Their examination of Silvey illustrated the remarkable gulf between training as set forth in the "book" and the reality of recruit training at that time at Parris Island.

Silvey, who had been in charge of recruit training for two and a half years, had never heard of the marsh areas being used for recruit training. He never heard that drill instructors were expressly taught that recruits went through a "shock and fear" stage of training at the outset (although the officer in charge of the DI school would testify to the contrary). Discipline, according to Silvey, was "orderly conduct," which was taught in one hour in the classroom during the ten-week training period. He refused to concede that drill instructors were allowed some latitude in teaching discipline. A drill instructor who, for example, ordered recruits to do fifty push-ups for disciplinary purposes after they breached a regulation would be "out of bounds." Any drill instructor seeking to impose any form of discipline as punishment would have to go first to the battalion commander for permission. According to Silvey, no drill instructor was authorized to deviate from the detailed lesson plan without the approval of his battalion commander or had any independent authority to exercise disciplinary action. A drill instructor who kept his men standing at attention because they marched sloppily or who held them on the drill field longer than usual because they did not respond promptly enough to his orders during close-order drill would himself be subject to disciplinary action from his superiors.

The DI described by Lieutenant Colonel Silvey was a benign automaton carefully nudging his platoon through ten weeks of orderly and constructive instruction. He would run to his battalion commander if there were any deviation from his lesson plan. The battalion commander would then spend his days granting audiences to concerned drill instructors before authorizing a round of push-ups or extra time on the drill field. All this was coming from the mouth of the man who for nearly three years had been responsible for a training program in which officer oversight was almost nonexistent. A mere month later General Greene would find ten of these carefully nurtured recruits hospitalized with fractured noses.

When Colonel McKean was called as a witness, he recognized that his conduct the night of the drownings might lead to one or more charges against him. He openly waived his privilege to remain silent and announced that he was ready to testify. Unlike Lieutenant Colonel Silvey, whose programmed and sometime evasive responses sounded like high-level bureaucratic double-speak, the voluble McKean was anxious to tell all. Questions calling for "yes" or "no" responses often produced lengthy explanations. McKean was clearly anxious to set the record straight. Unlike Silvey, McKean was not evasive. He described in considerable detail the vigil at Ribbon Creek from Sunday night until Tuesday afternoon when Thomas Hardeman's body was finally located. And also unlike Silvey, he acknowledged that drill instructors had considerable discretion in teaching discipline without seeking dispensation from their superiors.

Major Holben next called T.Sgt. John Perdeas, the liaison NCO at the Weapons Training Battalion; Capt. Charles Patrick, the officer of the day on Sunday, April 8; Lt. Col. Robert Thompson, commanding officer of the Third Recruit Training Battalion; and Capt. Richard Grey, commanding officer of Able Company in the Third Battalion. Ostensibly, each man testified to establish that there was adequate officer supervision of the drill instructors both at the rifle range and back at Mainside. McKeon's attorneys were not concerned with that issue. Rather, they labored to establish the obvious: that the drill instructor in practice had considerable latitude to teach and discipline his troops beyond the black-letter training schedule.

Meanwhile, General Greene allowed no let-up in the proceedings. He kept the court in session for the entire day on Saturday, April 14, and reconvened shortly after 1:00 P.M. on Sunday, April 15. First Sgt. Hershel Baker, the field sergeant major for the Third Battalion, was called. In his three years in that position he had never heard of a platoon going into the swamp for training purposes. M.Sgt. Hans Manthey, the chief drill instructor for Able Company, offered nothing of significance except to verify that McKeon was a good DI.

The final battery of witnesses was on and off the stand in a matter of minutes. Private First Class Magruder testified that he saw McKeon pick up the vodka bottle and place it behind the toilet, and that he had Corporal Lyons retrieve the bottle and place it in the hallway. S.Sgt. Malcolm Overpeck told of Magruder giving him the bottle, which he then turned over to Oral Newman, the depot officer of the day. Newman gave the bottle to Sgt. Loren Raddatz, the investigator on the case. Raddatz completed the chain by producing the bottle. The fifth of vodka that Elwin Scarborough had needed to calm his nerves eight days earlier had become a potentially incriminating piece of evidence against the man who was unwise enough to accommodate Scarborough's need.

Holben wrapped up his presentation with Dr. Lowell Smythe, the pathologist at the Beaufort Naval Hospital. Dr. Smythe had examined and conducted the autopsies on the six bodies delivered to him. His findings were virtually identical for each victim: all had died from asphyxiation from drowning in salt water.

After the roster of Platoon 71 was admitted as an exhibit, Major Holben announced that he had no further witnesses to call. General Greene turned to Costello and his colleagues to offer them the opportunity to call any witnesses they wanted the court to hear. McKeon's lawyers, having anticipated this eventuality, reported that the witnesses they wished to call to "throw some light" on the issues before the court and "aid in bringing to the court the true facts" were afraid to come forward. According to counsel (the record does not indicate which of McKeon's three attorneys was speaking) these potential witnesses (McKeon's fellow DIs) "felt if they came forward and testified and their testimony was in any way critical of the methods used here at Parris Island, that their careers as Marines would be finished."

Although Major Faw had offered limited immunity, McKeon's lawyers indicated that the men still refused to come forward, and for that reason they would present no further evidence. At approximately 9:00 P.M. on Monday, April 16, General Greene stated that all evidence had been presented by Major Holben and Sergeant McKeon. He reserved for the court the right to call additional witnesses or present additional evidence after reviewing the transcript. Inasmuch as both Costello and McGarry were returning to New York the following morning, however, the court agreed to hear closing arguments from Holben and Costello before adjourning for the evening.

As Major Holben began his closing argument, his comments removed any doubt that he was treating his designated role of counsel to the court as essentially prosecutorial. Admittedly, Holben had been in a difficult position in that Sergeant McKeon, while officially designated as a party, was in all respects the focus of the inquiry into potential violations of the Uniform Code of Military Justice. McKeon had three lawyers representing him through most of the proceedings, all of whom assumed the role of defense counsel, cross-examining each of the witnesses (except the recruits, whose testimony was generally favorable to their former DI). Major Holben had no need to be concerned about developing exculpatory evidence or other testimony that would mitigate any wrongdoing on McKeon's part because the sergeant's defense counsel made vigorous efforts to bring out the facts in his favor.

In his closing remarks Holben pointed out to the court that General Burger's order of April 9 was to recommend how to assign the responsibility for the Ribbon Creek incident. He noted that while a drill instructor had some discretion as to training and no regulation explicitly prohibited a march into the marshes and surrounding waters, that discretion had to be tempered with common sense. Adroitly turning the cumulative evidence that McKeon was *not* drunk against him, Holben argued that drunkenness was, therefore, not an excuse for the march.

Holben then professed to have examined the other side of the responsibility issue, asking rhetorically, "What was the command's responsibility?" He went to some lengths to exonerate the command from any responsibility. He pointed out that McKeon had been thoroughly screened before being assigned as a drill instructor, that the command had set high standards for all drill instructors and had alerted each of them as to what constituted maltreatment. Holben asked the court to recognize the problems involved with supervising a large command and asked for sympathy for "Colonel McKean's problems and also . . . [to] realize that he took steps to see that his command was properly supervised." Noting that the officer of the day could not supervise all the platoons that were on the rifle range, and that Colonel McKean himself had made personal inspections, Holben concluded,

> I feel that I have shown the court through competent evidence that the man who has a definite responsibility for the acts of persons in that command has taken adequate steps to supervise and see that the personnel in that command carry out the regulations. I feel that the command is exonerated entirely for anything that happened on Sunday, 8th of April.

Major Holben's position on the staff at Parris Island placed him in a very difficult situation. Any finding that General Burger or Holben's other superior officers were in some way responsible for the Ribbon Creek incident could adversely affect his career. Although Duane Faw would later vouch that Major Holben was a man of the highest integrity, his staff position at Parris Island created at least the appearance of a conflict of interest.

Costello's summation revealed the importance of having counsel independent of command authority. As a civilian, his career could not be affected by Colonel McKean, General Burger, or the Marine Corps. He could devote his full energy to his client—Matthew McKeon. He immediately set out to do just that.

Pricking what must have been a sore spot, Costello noted that the repetitive evidence that McKeon had been cautioned about maltreating his recruits suggested there "must be an awful lot of it, else why the necessity of so much warning." After that quick shot across the bow, he challenged General Burger to disqualify himself as the officer reviewing the evidence and the recommendations of the court because he had openly expressed judgment as to McKeon's guilt. Moreover, Burger, as the officer ultimately responsible for the depot, would in effect be sitting in judgment on himself.

Costello then sought to portray the events of April 8 as an unfortunate accident. He noted that the survivors had spoken not of maltreatment, but rather "almost to a man have sung [McKeon's] praises." He reminded the court that no one knew that the waters were dangerous or the current so severe. The men who drowned were those who wandered out too far.

Costello noted that Depot Order 348 expressly authorized each drill instructor to conduct extra activities to bring out the best in his platoon. Conversely, there was no specific regulation in effect prohibiting the use of the Ribbon Creek area for night training exercises.

Staff Sergeant Huff's testimony that he had threatened to take the platoon into the swamps authorized McKeon by implication to do the same (although there was no evidence that McKeon was aware of that threat). Costello concluded that the knowledge that his senior drill instructor had threatened to lead a swamp march "and many other reasons" (presumably potential testimony of other drill instructors who never testified because of lack of immunity) led McKeon to believe that a night march into the swamps "was customary procedure . . . on Parris Island." The argument was an excellent one, but utterly without foundation in the evidence before the court.

Costello then took the command to task. Noting that Colonel McKean had testified that individual recruits had entered the swamps at night seeking to escape (which Costello cleverly characterized as a rash of training accidents in the swamps) together with the fact that swamp training was explicitly prohibited at nearby Elliott's Beach, McKeon's lawyer suggested that the absence of a specific prohibition against entering Ribbon Creek implied that the area was not out-of-bounds and that perhaps the Marine Corps was responsible for not ordering all drill instructors to stay out of the waters if that was what was intended.

Costello appealed to the court to recognize Sergeant McKeon as one of their own. He had been trained by the Marine Corps and had fought under the Marines' banner during the Korean War. Costello implored the members of the court to exercise courage in the face of public opinion and congressional scrutiny, advancing the blunt observation that

> this Court and this Corps that has proved itself in battle not to be afraid of foreign enemies such as Japs, Krauts, or Chinese certainly should not be afraid of any segment of public opinion.

The argument advanced by McKeon's brother-in-law was a masterful and clever interweaving of the facts that pointed toward an unforeseen accident, tried to shift at least some of the responsibility for what occurred to the Parris Island leadership, and finally appealed to the special loyalty that binds one marine to another.

Protocol allowed Major Holben an opportunity for rebuttal. Having previously argued for exoneration of the command, he turned his focus to the most damning evidence against McKeon. Acknowledging that the sergeant had been the first one in the water because he knew he could swim, Holben pointed out that McKeon also knew that there were men in his platoon who could not swim. It was the taking of men into water up to their necks knowing that they were unable to swim that made this case more than just an unfortunate accident. Holben characterized it as a "gross and willful disregard of probable consequence . . . [that] . . . someone would drown."

The inquiry was all but over as Major Holben concluded his remarks and General Greene adjourned the court at 9:40 P.M. on Monday, April 16. All that remained on the following day was for Holben to introduce evidence that the moon set at 4:38 P.M. on April 8, some four hours before the fatal march. With that last bit of information, Holben rested his case.

General Greene turned to Sergeant McKeon and his remaining counsel, Lieutenant Collins, and offered them a final opportunity to present evidence. Collins declined, probably for two reasons. First, both he and McKeon must have known—from the comments of the commandant and congressmen as well as from the fact that six innocent young men had died—that there would be a court-martial. That being the case, the best strategy was to use the inquiry to discover the specifics of the prosecution's evidence without revealing any information that might strengthen the prosecution's case. Second, at that juncture, only nine days after the drownings, there was little exculpatory evidence to be presented. McKeon's best defense was his claim that night swamp marches were a well-recognized and unofficially condoned means of disciplining a laggard platoon. However, the only people who could confirm the existence and extent of the practice were other drill instructors. That there were other drill instructors with that knowledge was alluded to by Thomas Costello but never established. If such men did exist, they were not about to step forward and risk prosecution or jeopardize their careers by taking the witness stand.

At 2:36 P.M. on Tuesday, April 17, the court of inquiry was recessed. During the eight days it had been in session it had heard from fifty witnesses and had received twenty-one exhibits. Thirteen- and fourteen-hour days had been the norm because of the tremendous pressure brought to bear on the Marine Corps to explain what had occurred and what would be done about it. Major Holben had marshaled a considerable amount of evidence and presented it in a comprehensive fashion in a short time span. His counterparts, Thomas Costello and Lieutenant Collins, had done the same. Costello's closing argument, while somewhat free and loose with the evidence, was quite persuasive considering the time constraints under which all parties had labored.

At 7:36 P.M. on Wednesday, April 18, General Greene called the court into session and declared,

> With my hand on the Holy Scripture and in the presence of Staff Sergeant McKeon and these witnesses, I swear before God that this court has arrived at what it considers to be the truth, the whole truth and nothing but the truth in this case, and it makes its recommendations seeking only justice for all parties concerned.

As Greene prepared to announce the court's decision, the courtroom was cleared. The findings were not to be made public until they had been reviewed and approved by General Burger and the Corps commandant. Only Sergeant McKeon, Lieutenant Collins, Major Holben, the court reporter, and the members of the court remained. The president then spelled out the facts and opinions as found by the court.

Greene traced the undisputed events of McKeon's background and train-ing as well as the basic activities of the fateful Sunday. McKeon's heart must have sunk as he listened to the litany:

> That Staff Sergeant McKeon drank an unknown quantity of vodka during the morning, afternoon, and early evening of 8 April 1956 while on duty as the drill instructor in charge of Platoon 71.
>
> That Staff Sergeant McKeon knew that certain members of his platoon could not swim.
>
> That prior to entering the water of Ribbon Creek, Staff Sergeant McKeon took no measures to insure that the water area into which he was about to lead his platoon was safe to enter.
>
> That the recruit platoons while stationed at the Rifle Range are adequately supervised by personnel of the Weapons Training Battalion.
>
> That Staff Sergeant McKeon did not have written or verbal authority to conduct a night march of recruits into Ribbon Creek.
>
> That Staff Sergeant McKeon at the time he marched his platoon into Rib-bon Creek was under the influence of alcohol to an unknown degree.
>
> That the deaths . . . were the result of [the] recruits being led into the deep water of Ribbon Creek by Staff Sergeant McKeon, who was engaged in the execution of a punitive act against the members of Platoon 71 on the night of 8 April 1956.

The coup de grace was delivered with the concluding declaration:

> That Staff Sergeant Matthew C. McKeon, 668581, U.S. Marine Corps, by his actions in drinking intoxicating liquor while on duty in a position of great responsibility, and in conducting an unauthorized and unnecessary march by night into an area of hazard which he had failed to first reconnoiter and which resulted in the deaths of six brother Marines, not only broke estab-lished regulations but violated the fine traditions of the noncommissioned officers of the United States Marine Corps and betrayed the trust reposed in him by his Country, his Corps, his lost comrades and the families of the dead.

The court had been charged by General Burger to determine the facts and assess responsibility for the Ribbon Creek march. It had done that and had recommended a general court-martial, a procedure reserved for the most serious offenses under the Uniform Code of Military Justice. Specifically, the members of the court of inquiry recommended that Sergeant McKeon face the following charges before a court-martial:

CHARGE I: Possession and/or use of alcoholic beverages in barracks (Building 761) housing enlisted personnel;

CHARGE II: Oppression of seventy-four recruits by leading them into the mud and water of Ribbon Creek, and by leading them around in said water thus subjecting them to depths of water up to and over their heads, for a period of about twenty minutes for purposes of punishment knowing that some members of said platoon were unable to swim.

CHARGE III, Specification 1: Culpable negligence in that he did unlawfully kill six recruits "by leading them into the waters of Ribbon Creek in the dark without proper precautions for their safety and without first familiarizing himself with the hazardous conditions of the creek."

CHARGE III, Specification 2: Oppression in that he did unlawfully kill six recruits by leading them into Ribbon Creek.

CHARGE IV: Unlawfully drinking intoxicating liquor in the presence of recruit David H. McPherson.

Ordinarily the commandant would have been the proper authority to convene a court-martial. Because of General Pate's prejudicial remarks to the news media during his visit to Parris Island, however, Major Faw, at Colonel Buse's urging, immediately set out to determine whether there might be civilian jurisdiction if a trial were warranted. Ultimately, it was determined that the secretary of the navy was the only available person superior in status to the commandant who could order a court-martial. With the commandant's disqualification, Secretary of the Navy Charles S. Thomas, an Eisenhower appointee, was left to weigh the findings of the court of inquiry and convene a general court-martial. In all likelihood, this was the first time that a secretary of the navy has ever been called on to convene a court-martial because of the disqualification of the entire command. Not unexpectedly, Thomas accepted the recommendations of the court of inquiry and ordered McKeon to face the five charges recommended before a general court-martial.

The announcement that Sergeant McKeon would face a court-martial for his responsibility in the deaths of the six recruits probably was no surprise to the general public. However, the finding that McKeon was under the influence of alcohol during the march was—and it was not supported by the evidence. Such a prejudicial finding was sure to provide a feast for the tabloids and irresponsible press starving for details after more than a week of secret proceedings.

Perhaps more damaging was the character attack contained in the court's concluding opinion. McKeon was declared to be a traitor to his men and the Marine Corps. Having completed its thorough assessment of responsibility, the court had made its final and ultimate pronouncement. Not only had Matthew McKeon violated the military law, he was now declared to be a moral reprobate as well.

# E I G H T

# Media Feast

Although the court of inquiry had concluded its investigation and made its findings by April 18, no public announcement would be forthcoming until the results were reviewed and approved by General Burger, the commandant, the judge advocate's office, and ultimately Secretary of the Navy Thomas. Remarkably, by today's standards at least, confidentiality was maintained during the entire course of the review process.

General Burger wasted little time in digesting and passing on to General Pate a copy of the record of the court of inquiry together with his own sixteen-page report. In his report Burger briefly described the geography of Parris Island and outlined the format of the training programs for drill instructors and recruits. He devoted considerable detail to the various layers of supervision of drill instructors and recruits, followed by a detailed narration of the highlights of the march and the events leading up to it. The remainder of Burger's report was aimed at justifying the status quo and exonerating himself and the persons in his command from responsibility for the incident. Burger cleverly parried the anticipated criticism that there were no orders prohibiting swamp marches by suggesting that the prohibition was unnecessary because such conduct was considered prohibited "as evidenced by McKeon's prompt arrest"—surely something of a non sequitur. He argued that there was no reason to anticipate that any platoons would be led into the swamps, and hence no need to issue a special order addressing the nonexistent problem.

Burger's report went to some lengths to conclude that there was adequate supervision on April 8, that this command, including subordinate units, has taken all reasonable precautions from the standpoint of regulations, training, supervision and security to prevent foreseeable conduct injurious to the person or property of the recruits; . . . [and] that Staff Sergeant McKeon willfully and deliberately violated the known policies of this command with respect to methods of recruit training in order to substitute unauthorized methods of his own.

Burger concurred with General Greene in recommending a general court-martial for McKeon. In Burger's view, he and his subordinates were in no way responsible for the events of April 8, and no substantial changes were needed in the training program. He did, however, suggest that one further order would be prudent. Henceforth, "all marshes, tidal streams, beaches and water [should be] out-of-bounds for recruit training."

From General Burger's perspective, the deaths in Ribbon Creek were the result of an isolated and willful act of disobedience by an inexperienced drill instructor. General Pate, whatever his personal inclination may have been, could not afford to view the situation as narrowly as Burger. The commandant knew that Congress was poised to act unless the Marine Corps addressed in a constructive way the mounting complaints of maltreatment and abuse, which had culminated in the Ribbon Creek march. Hanging McKeon out to dry and proceeding with business as usual, as Burger was in essence proposing to do, would not be sufficient. The commandant recognized that either the Marines had to get their own house in order or the politicians would do it for them.

On April 30, the commandant delivered his report to the secretary of the navy via the judge advocate general. General Pate summarily endorsed the recommendation that Sergeant McKeon face a general court-martial. Having disposed of that issue, he promptly disowned the well-drafted and cleverly worded defense of recruit training that General Burger (actually, it was probably Major Faw) had drafted. General Pate had a much broader agenda:

The case of Sergeant McKeon is a matter for disposition in accordance with the Uniform Code of Military Justice, but there are other matters which must be considered. The Marine Corps system of recruit training has been drawn into question. In a very real sense the Marine Corps is on trial for the tragedy of Ribbon Creek just as surely as is Sergeant McKeon. I will not blind myself to this fact, nor will I seek to disown the responsibility which is mine as Commandant of the Marine Corps. Since World

War II some practices have crept into the handling of recruits which are not only unnecessary but do not comport with the dignity of the individual or his self-respect. Such practices were extremely rare in the past. While they are still relatively rare, I attribute their increasing appearance in recent years to the lack of mature judgment on the part of certain few drill instructors.

General Pate noted that despite efforts to eradicate maltreatment of recruits, the steps taken were never fully effective, and certain forms of hazing, mass punishment, and abuse continued. The time had come, he declared, to address such long-standing problems with systemic changes. Recruits were still to be trained by drill instructors, but with greater oversight by officers. The recruit depots at San Diego and Parris Island would be under the control of separate recruit training commands supervised by an inspector general reporting directly to the commandant. Selected officers were to be assigned to each recruit training command "to supervise and monitor but not to supplant the drill instructors in the conduct of recruit training."

Thus, not only would Sergeant McKeon be facing a court-martial for his conduct, but the commandant now declared that the Marine Corps itself was on trial. A very skilled lawyer named Emile Zola Berman would later recognize that the trial of the Marine Corps could have considerable bearing on the trial of Sergeant McKeon as the commandant had framed the issues. But at the end of April 1956, that strategy was still unforeseen. Whatever changes might be in store for the Marine Corps, Matthew McKeon was facing a general court-martial, and his future looked bleak.

On May 1, 1956, one day after sending his report to the secretary of the navy, General Pate appeared before the House Armed Services Committee as promised. The findings of the court of inquiry were announced publicly, as was Pate's report to Secretary Thomas outlining the proposed changes in recruit training. The commandant also announced that General Burger was being transferred to Camp Lejeune, North Carolina, and that Colonel McKean would be transferred as well. General Greene had been selected to command the newly created Recruit Training Command at Parris Island. While neither McKean nor Burger was found to be at fault or in any way responsible for the Ribbon Creek march, the commandant undoubtedly viewed a change in the top command at Parris Island as both a necessary component of the revised training program and a means to give General Greene a fresh new command with which to implement the envisioned changes.

The Armed Forces Committee and particularly its chairman, Carl Vinson, received Pate's report favorably. Vinson, in particular, praised General Pate for recognizing the perceived deficiencies in the recruit training program and addressing the situation with "courage and forthrightness."

Pate's prompt and straightforward acceptance of responsibility was successful in defusing the call for a congressional investigation. In sharp contrast, the release of the findings of the court of inquiry to the public was like tossing red meat before starving dogs. The headlines in the tabloid *New York Daily News* on May 1 proclaimed: "Marine Drunk, Call Death of 6 Manslaughter." The *New York Post* in an opening paragraph purportedly reporting the commandant's congressional appearance erroneously reported that "the Marine Corps said today Sgt. Matthew McKeon was drunk after an all day vodka drinking bout when he led his 78 man recruit platoon into the Parris Island, S.C., swamplands on a death march that killed six." The *Daily News* followed up its May 1 story by reporting on May 2 some of the changes in Marine Corps training anticipated "because a vodka-swigging sergeant who faces manslaughter charges, led a 'death march' at Parris Island, S.C."

Perhaps the most reckless commentary on the events surrounding the march were contained in a six-article purported exposé by correspondent Stan Opotowsky, a former marine, that ran in the *New York Post* in early May. Opotowsky "reported" that McKeon ordered a Sunday-morning drill "for no apparent reason." When some weary boots slumped to the grass for needed rest, he "bull-voiced them back to attention." McKeon then retreated to his room "and his vodka," where he was joined by King and Scarborough. "King had a bottle too." McKeon fumed and brooded after marching the platoon to lunch. At about 3:00 P.M., after returning from the NCO Club where he had been drinking for a while, he called a couple of boots into his room. With vodka still in hand, he told them they were going to the swamps. Nothing seemed to please [Sgt. Matt McKeon] except the bottle of vodka he nursed along in his little cubbyhole adjoining the barracks room.

Every "material fact" related by Opotowsky was either false or misleading. Yet the story with its sensationalist slant was disseminated as a factual account in the country's largest media market. Anyone who relied on such reports would have difficulty considering McKeon, and perhaps drill instructors in general, to be anything but a drunken, sadistic brute.

On July 24, while the court-martial was in progress, the *Post* continued on the same theme, falsely claiming that survivors of the march testified that McKeon drank vodka as he lined up his recruits for the fatal march.

The only testimony regarding McKeon's drinking was, of course, David McPherson's statement at the court of inquiry that he had seen McKeon apparently take one swallow from the vodka bottle while alone with him in the drill instructor's room.

The *New York Times,* as might be expected, was more restrained. It reported the story in a factual manner, balancing the opinion of the court of inquiry that McKeon was to some extent under the influence of alcohol on the night of the drownings with details about the charges and the proposed changes at Parris Island. The wire services, too, seem to have taken a more subdued posture than the New York tabloids. Nevertheless the term "death march" became almost a cliché in describing the march to Ribbon Creek.

The extent to which some elements of the press stirred up public hostility cannot be measured accurately. Maj. John DeBarr, an attorney appointed to McKeon's defense team, recalls receiving large quantities of mail, about 65 percent of which was negative; in some cases the letters were simply addressed to "Murderers" or "Butchers." It is hard to believe that the inflammatory and often inaccurate reporting of the tabloids was not instrumental in generating the volume of messages as well as the outrage and hostility many of them expressed.

What the court of inquiry had found, and what the commandant had made public, was that Sergeant McKeon "drank an unknown quantity of vodka during the morning, afternoon and early evening of 8 April 1956." General Pate also reported that the court of inquiry was of the opinion that at the time he marched his men into Ribbon Creek, McKeon "was under the influence of alcohol to an unknown degree." Neither the findings and opinion of the court of inquiry nor General Pate's report to Congress and the public indicated that Sergeant McKeon was drunk, that he had been drinking all day, or that he had been "swigging" vodka. Certainly such sensationalism was highly irresponsible, but with millions of people reading such hyperbole, both McKeon and the Marine Corps were taking a public relations beating.

By early May, the Marine Corps was desperately, and successfully, moving to minimize the institutional damage of Ribbon Creek and rectify some of the apparent shortcomings in its training program. But Matthew McKeon had no such resources to control his future. He was facing a general court-martial, charged with manslaughter, while major elements of the popular press were characterizing him as a drunkard who callously led six young men under his command to their deaths.

As the Marine Corps was seeking to recover from the Ribbon Creek incident and reestablish its image with the public—both as a matter of self-
preservation and to attract the necessary supply of new recruits—a fortuitous
event was unfolding that bears mentioning, even though its effects were of
no immediate benefit to McKeon or the Marine Corps. Shortly after the
Ribbon Creek incident, one of the major film studios wanted to produce a
film about brutality in the Marine Corps, perhaps using the Ribbon Creek
incident as a centerpiece. Needless to say, the Marine Corps wanted no part
of it and refused to cooperate. Meanwhile, however, Jack Webb, who had
already attained considerable notoriety as *Dragnet*'s Sergeant Friday, was
intent on producing a movie based on a Kraft Television Theatre production
entitled "The Murder of a Sandflea." The story, written by James Lee Barrett,
a former Parris Island recruit, centered on the burial ritual ordered by a drill
instructor for one of the ubiquitous Parris Island sand fleas executed by a
boot contrary to all protocols of recruit behavior.

Webb, a very patriotic American who had served in the Army Air Corps
during World War II, wanted to create a movie realistically depicting the life
of a Parris Island drill instructor, weaving the sand flea incident into the plot.
By all accounts, Webb was a stickler for detail. He sent a production crew to
Parris Island in late 1956 to examine and record the details of recruit training
As the script outline made no reference to Ribbon Creek, the Marine Corps
was more than willing to assist Webb. Barrett, who was to write the movie
script, spent several weeks at Parris Island with the crew observing First Battalion DIs applying all the well-honed physical and verbal techniques for
recruit motivation. The sarcasm, profanity, and jargon were all captured on
tape. The barracks were filmed in minute detail for precise re-creation on a
Hollywood set.

Lt. Col. Wyatt Carneal, the First Battalion's commanding officer, and Maj.
Richard Mample, the senior marine officer in the Armed Forces Information
Office in Los Angeles, were recruited by Webb as technical advisers. Webb was
so impressed on hearing the melodious cadence of Cpl. John R. Brown, a
junior drill instructor of nearby Platoon 351, that he brought Brown to
Hollywood as a technical adviser and gave him the role of Sergeant O'Neil in
the film. Actual recruits from the San Diego Recruit Depot were selected to
play similar roles in the production.

The movie, entitled *The D.I.,* premiered at Parris Island in May 1957.
Despite a rather conventional plot, the sand flea story is a classic, and Webb's
"T.Sgt. Jim Moore" is a vividly realistic portrayal of a dedicated, hard-nosed

drill instructor molding a pathetic malingerer and raw recruits into basic marines. *The D.I.* portrayed the Marine Corps and its drill instructors in a positive light at a time when the wounds of Ribbon Creek were still fresh. After the painful events of 1956, DI Jim Moore must have been a morale booster for real drill instructors, for the fictional hero presented to the public not the sadist or the abuser but a composite of the fine qualities of so many of their number.

Unfortunately for McKeon and the Marine Corps, there was no T.Sgt. Jim Moore to lift their spirits in the summer of 1956.

# N I N E

# The Tide Turns

J ames B. M. McNally was a powerful and savvy senior judge on the New York Supreme Court in 1956. Raised in one of the toughest Irish neighborhoods in Manhattan, McNally had completed law school and ultimately attained his lofty position as chief administrative judge through sheer brains and perseverance. McNally possessed a commanding de-meanor to complement the power of his position. At the same time, he never forgot his roots and his struggle for survival as a youth on the streets of New York.

After the conclusion of the preliminary hearing by the court of inquiry, Thomas Costello returned to the law firm of James E. Whalen, where he was a young attorney defending insurance cases. Whalen had been a student of McNally's in law school and had tried many cases in his court. While Costello was still participating in the court of inquiry at Parris Island, McNally called Whalen and told him to have Costello come over to his courtroom for a meeting as soon as he was available. When Costello returned to New York and received the summons, he promptly responded. The meeting was held in the robing room off the courtroom where McNally presided. Costello was apprehensive, not knowing the purpose of the invitation. McNally got right to the point. He told Costello that he had been following the McKeon affair. It was his view that the Marine Corps was setting out to make a scapegoat of McKeon for the events that had led to the drownings. McNally bluntly said that he was going to do everything in his power not to let that happen, including making sure that McKeon had the best possible defense. Costello, he said, was too young and inexperienced to handle a case of this complexity. Further, being a member of the family would rob him of the objectivity that would be needed to plan and implement a successful trial strategy.

Instead, McNally told Costello, Emile Zola Berman, a fifty-three-year-old personal injury lawyer with an active civil trial practice, should handle the case. In his many years on the bench, McNally had seen most of the good trial lawyers in New York City. He thought Berman was the best, primarily because his trial skills were complemented by a unique ability to adapt to the unforeseen circumstances that inevitably arose during a trial. When faced with sudden adversity, Berman had the ability to shift his tactics and often turn misfortune to his advantage.

At this juncture Berman was unaware of what McNally had in mind for him. Costello was told to consult with the McKeon family. McNally assured Costello that if the family approved, Berman would take the case and ask no fee other than, perhaps, his actual expenses.

Costello had already had the benefit of watching Berman in action. Having seen Berman's skills firsthand, and with the imprimatur of Judge McNally, Costello met with the McKeon family and urged them to accept the judge's proposal. McNally had also promised that if the family accepted Berman as defense counsel, he would form a committee of respected New York Supreme Court judges who would see to it that Matthew McKeon received a fair trial. A committee comprised of men of such stature would send a clear message to the Marine Corps that McKeon was not to be railroaded in order to protect his superiors or to cover up the circumstances at Parris Island that surrounded the fatal swamp march.

In the meantime, then Senator John F. Kennedy had been in touch with the McKeon family, undoubtedly in part because they were his constituents. Kennedy had called or written several times, even offering to recommend a lawyer. Needless to say, the members of this humble family were honored by the interest of a man of Senator Kennedy's stature. After some deliberation, and despite being flattered by Senator Kennedy's interest, the family decided to accept Tom Costello's recommendation and ask Berman to handle Matthew's defense. The decision was immediately communicated to Judge McNally, who contacted Emile Berman. Berman readily agreed to take the case without fee, his only condition being that the court-martial be postponed until later in the summer when the New York courts would be out of session and he would be free to devote his full time and energy to the defense.

Such a delay was easily arranged, as all parties needed at least two months to prepare for a trial that could last for several weeks.

With Berman in place, McNally could remain a shadowy figure in the background. As promised, he and Walter A. Lynch, a fellow judge on the New York Supreme Court, enlisted other judges to form an informal committee to oversee the trial. Once Berman had accepted the challenge, however, there was little need for the committee. Berman immediately took command of the situation.

Emile Zola Berman, known to friends and colleagues as "Zuke," was born in lower Manhattan shortly after his parents immigrated to the United States from Russia. His mother and father were both revolutionary socialists. Deeply moved by the unjust conviction of the French officer Captain Alfred Dreyfus, they named their firstborn son after the great French novelist, Emile Zola, who had publicly proclaimed Dreyfus innocent and exposed the virulent anti-Semitism in the French Army.

Berman was raised in the Bronx with his younger brother, Alfred (named after Dreyfus), and a sister, Miriam. Mr. Berman supported the family with his work as an expert woodcarver and designer of fine interior paneling. Emile graduated from New York University in 1923 and earned a law degree from the same school a year later. By 1956, at the peak of his career after more than thirty years of practice, he was considered by many colleagues and judges to be the top trial lawyer in New York City.

Thin, bald, and bespectacled, with large ears and a long, sharp nose on a small head, Berman seemed to be the antithesis of a military figure. But his odd appearance and strange name masked inner qualities that ultimately would induce respect and admiration from both his colleagues and his opponents at Parris Island. Ironically, this odd-looking son of Russian Jewish revolutionaries, raised in a city far removed in distance and mores from the southern low country, would soon be perceived as the staunchest of all the defenders of the Marine Corps and its traditional training practices.

Actually, Berman was no stranger to the military. In 1942, at forty years of age, he had left his thriving law practice to join the Army Air Corps. He was assigned to the China-Burma-India theater as an intelligence officer. Although classified as a non-flying officer, he flew on numerous dangerous missions in the Far East. On one occasion he wound up fighting in the jungle with Merrill's Marauders. By the end of the war he had been promoted to lieutenant colonel and had won the Distinguished Flying Cross as well as numerous lesser medals for his valor and performance.

After the war, Berman returned to his law practice in New York City with his second wife, Alice Rose Gaines, a South Carolina fashion model whom he had married in 1944 when he returned from Asia. Although he had very little experience in trying criminal cases, Berman's civil practice flourished, earning him a comfortable living and a spacious home in Roslyn Heights, one of the city's better suburbs. By 1956, most of the personal injury cases he handled had become routine for a man of Berman's skills and dynamism. He gained the most satisfaction from lecturing and teaching at New York University, Columbia, and the Practicing Law Institute.

With the McKeon case making national headlines, Berman was perfectly positioned to step into the picture. In fact, in some respects the impending court-martial appeared similar to the circumstances of the Dreyfus affair. McKeon was the unassuming enlisted man who was facing manslaughter charges for conduct that had long been condoned by the marine culture and by the officer corps at Parris Island. The top brass was running for cover, leaving a defenseless drill instructor exposed to take the rap for what was arguably no more than an unfortunate accident. Berman, modestly wealthy, bored with the routine of his law practice, and weaned on the belief that fighting for justice for the powerless was a great virtue, answered the call of Judge McNally without hesitation. With obvious understatement, he told writer Joe McCarthy of *Life* magazine, "I must have been seeking some kind of satisfaction I don't find in my regular work when I got into the McKeon case."

The emergence of Berman as lead defense counsel suddenly changed the whole complexion of the case. A master strategist as well as a superior advocate, he immediately set out to accomplish two objectives: to begin the detailed preparation necessary for a difficult trial and, equally important, to "humanize" his client. Although most marines and former marines supported McKeon, the news media's vicious portrayal of his role in the events of April 8 had convinced many civilians that six young innocents had been led to their deaths by a drunken sadist. No effort had been made to portray McKeon as a responsible family man with an honorable record of service to his country, or to point out how tenuous were the earlier findings that he was under the influence of alcohol on the evening of the march. If McKeon were to receive a fair trial, that image would have to be challenged immediately and vigorously.

Further, Berman must have realized from the outset that it was unlikely that McKeon would be acquitted of all the charges against him. Therefore it was necessary to plan a strategy to mitigate the damage and ensure that any punishment meted out fit the crime for which McKeon might be convicted. The ultimate arbiter of the punishment would be Secretary of the Navy Charles Thomas. As a political appointee, Thomas's decision would to some extent be governed by public opinion. If McKeon were perceived to be a rogue, there would be strong support for throwing the book at him. On the other hand, if McKeon were viewed as a decent and dedicated human being who had made a tragic mistake, Thomas would naturally incline toward leniency.

With his energies revived and a cause in which he could believe, Berman plunged into McKeon's case. Suddenly the momentum of the case began to shift. Although Matthew McKeon remained nominally the defendant, his counsel took the offensive. The commandant's declaration that in a very real sense the Marine Corps itself was on trial became Berman's trump card. He seized on those ominous words to shift the focus from the lonely defendant sitting in the brig to the very essence of long-established Marine Corps training practices. From that point on, the Marine Corps brass knew that their own future and perhaps that of the Corps was on the line if they chose to hang Matthew McKeon out to dry. At the same time, Berman made it clear that he had no desire to cause any further damage to the Corps. Adroitly turning the tables, he set himself up as the defender of traditional Marine Corps practices. If McKeon were to be condemned, the very system of which he was a part was equally at fault. Be fair with McKeon, Berman let it be known, and the defense was only too willing to be fair with the Marine Corps.

On May 4, 1956, just four days after the official record of the court of inquiry and the conflicting endorsements of General Burger and General Pate were sent to him, Secretary Thomas ordered a general court-martial to convene at Parris Island. Trial was to commence on May 14 "or as soon thereafter as practicable." Even in an era before extensive pretrial maneuvering and delays were common to felony criminal proceedings, the hiatus of only ten days was unrealistic. As it turned out, the court did not actually convene until Monday, July 16, 1956.

Secretary Thomas appointed Col. Edward L. Hutchinson to serve as president of the seven-member court. The other six members were Lt. Col. Nicholas A. Sisak, Lt. Col. Robert D. Shaffer, Lt. Col. Walter Gall, Maj. Edwin T. Carlton, Maj. John Demas, and Lt. Cdr. Hampton Hubbard of the U.S. Navy Medical Corps.

On July 9, Shaffer, Gall, and Hubbard were relieved and replaced by Lt. Col. Duane Fultz, Lt. Col. Daniel J. Regan, and Lt. Bentley A. Nelson, the latter attached to the U.S. Navy Medical Corps. No explanation was given for the substitution of the three members, which still left the court with six marine officers and one navy physician.

Colonel Hutchinson commanded the Sixth Marine Regiment at Camp Lejeune at the time of his appointment. He was no stranger to Parris Island, having completed boot camp there in 1931, three years before receiving his commission. Major Carlton had been a Parris Island recruit in 1932 before rising through the ranks to warrant officer in 1942 and receiving a commission in 1943. Major Demas enlisted in 1942. After boot camp at Parris Island, he participated in the V-12 program, ultimately receiving his commission in 1945. Although Lieutenant Colonel Sisak had entered the Marine Corps as a second lieutenant, he was probably more familiar with the Ribbon Creek area than any other member of the court. He had helped construct Charlie range in 1940 and 1941, an activity that had actually taken him into the waters of Ribbon Creek fifteen years before the events that were at the center of the impending trial.

Secretary Thomas designated Maj. Charles B. Sevier as trial counsel. Capt. Frederick M. Haden and Capt. William L. Otten Jr. were appointed as Sevier's assistants. Lt. Col. Alaric Valentin, Maj. John DeBarr, and 2d Lt. Jeremiah Collins were appointed as defense counsel to assist Berman and his associate, Howard Lester.

Although the military lawyers for the prosecution and defense were equal in number, Berman's trial experience far outweighed that of the opposing counsel. At the time they were appointed, Major Sevier was an executive officer in the tank battalion and Captain Haden was assigned to an artillery unit. Both were stationed at Camp Lejeune in 1956, although they had never met before being selected to prosecute McKeon. Sevier and Haden were capable lawyers, but neither had the extensive trial experience of Emile Zola Berman. In fact, Sevier had not been in a military courtroom for two years. As Haden later related, "They went and got Charlie and I, who were really neophytes at this point. . . . I really hadn't worked this area."

Navy captain Irving N. Klein, a 1927 graduate of Brooklyn Law School, was appointed to serve as the law officer, a position created under the Uniform Code of Military Justice when it was adopted in 1950. At the time of his appointment, Klein was the district legal officer for the Third Naval District in New York City.

How Klein came to be selected as the law officer remains a mystery. According to Frederick Haden, Klein had minimal experience in presiding over criminal cases. Colonel McKean, in his embittered analysis of the events surrounding the swamp march and subsequent proceedings, had little regard for Captain Klein. In fact, McKean devoted an entire chapter of his book *Ribbon Creek* to a critical and unflattering examination of Klein's rulings. Duane Faw, the depot legal officer, who was integrally involved in the trial arrangements, claims that Klein volunteered for the position. This despite the fact that he had limited understanding of the rules of evidence and the Uniform Code of Military Justice that had been adopted six years earlier. Faw relates that Klein had never tried a case under the Uniform Code of Military Justice.

To a considerable extent, Klein was to be the equivalent of a judge in a civilian trial, ruling on points of law and evidence and to some extent orchestrating the orderly process of the trial. The seven members of the court were in many respects analogous to a civilian jury, although Colonel Hutchinson, as president, had broader authority than would a jury foreman. As titular supervisor of the courtroom, Hutchinson was responsible for scheduling, decorum, and oversight of the proceedings.

Ordinarily a general court-martial would have been held in the courtroom located in the administration building at Mainside. However, the commandant had whetted the interest of an already aroused public when he declared that the Marine Corps had nothing to hide and that "in a very real sense the Marine Corps is on trial for the tragedy of Ribbon Creek just as surely as is Sergeant McKeon." The press had descended on Parris Island in droves right after the drownings, and were no less intent now on covering one of the most sensational courts-martial of the twentieth century. That being the case, a decision had to be made whether to hold the proceedings in the courtroom, which could accommodate only a handful of reporters, or move the trial to more spacious facilities.

As late as May 10, 1956, the *Beaufort Gazette* confirmed that no final decision had been made on the courtroom location, noting that "inasmuch as the Parris Island court room will comfortably seat no more than a dozen, ... the trial, which will be public, would have to be held in the post lyceum or some other large building."

Soon thereafter, a decision was reached, at the behest of the defense and with the acquiescence of the Public Information Office, to convert the auditorium of the depot school at Mainside into a makeshift courtroom. The *Parris Island Boot* reported on July 20, 1956, that a room adjacent to the auditorium had been set aside and "equipped with teletypewriters and telephones to accommodate more than 45 news correspondents from major cities throughout the United States." Although the acoustics were poor and the building lacked air-conditioning to ward off the South Carolina heat and humidity, the facility was spacious enough to accommodate the large number of anticipated spectators. According to Duane Faw, Captain Klein was one of the proponents of the change to a larger facility, even suggesting revisions to the law officer's platform to double the elevation of his position within the courtroom. Although the installation of air-conditioning was not feasible, large fans were installed and jury-rigged to blow some of the hot air out the windows around the top of the auditorium, thereby keeping the temperature at a more bearable level.

The initial trial commencement date of May 14 was unrealistic from the outset. As soon as Berman agreed to serve as chief defense counsel he requested a postponement, ostensibly to clear his existing schedule of cases. Undoubtedly the reason he advanced was legitimate. Berman was a busy trial lawyer and could look forward to fewer demands on his time in the summer months when court business slowed down. But there was an even more pressing reason for delay. Berman and his assistants had an enormous amount of work to do in planning strategy, interviewing witnesses, and familiarizing themselves with military law and procedure. The Navy Department readily granted the request for postponement and scheduled the first day of trial for July 14. Ultimately, a pretrial conference was held on Friday, July 13, with the trial set to begin on Monday morning, July 16, 1956. As any trial lawyer knows, the amount of time spent in the courtroom is only a small fraction of the time needed to attend to the unending details of preparation. The delay of almost two and a half months gave both sides adequate time to do their homework before the formalities were to begin.

Beginning with the time of their appointment in May, Sevier and Haden left their homes at Camp Lejeune at the beginning of each week and drove approximately three hundred miles down the North and South Carolina coasts to Parris Island. At the end of the week they returned home to their families. Eventually, as demands on the men's time increased, their families found temporary housing in the Port Royal area.

Aside from their work demands, the months preceding the trial were not happy ones for the prosecution team. Enlisted men, particularly drill instructors, were protective of McKeon and fearful that further changes might emanate from the trial and its attendant publicity. Many officers recognized that the impending trial could expose them to some responsibility for things they had done or failed to do. Sevier and Haden were, in a sense, two outsiders brought in to prosecute one of their own, and to some extent to prosecute the Parris Island culture itself. With the exception of the depot legal personnel and General Greene, who extended them full courtesy, the two prosecutors were treated as pariahs during the weeks leading up to the trial. Haden remembers that period as one of the loneliest times he ever spent in the Marine Corps—away from his home base and with few people wanting to have anything to do with him.

The prosecution team's strategy was simple and straightforward. As they viewed the situation, essentially there was nothing wrong with Marine Corps training. The system that was in place had worked well for many years and was not on trial. Both Sevier and Haden had firsthand knowledge of the rigors of boot camp because both had been Parris Island recruits during World War II. From their perspective, McKeon was a "bad apple" who deserved to be convicted for taking people whom he knew couldn't swim into unknown waters at night. Neither Sevier nor Haden agreed with or was influenced by the broader issues raised by the commandant. Matthew McKeon was on trial, and the prosecution would simply focus on proving beyond a reasonable doubt that he and he alone committed the offenses he was charged with.

Berman immediately recognized that he must approach the defense of Matthew McKeon with a more elaborate strategy than simply seeking acquittal by showing reasonable doubt as to each charge. The lesser charge of possession of alcoholic beverage in the barracks, for example, would not be difficult for the prosecution to prove. Further, the fact that McKeon took a number of nonswimmers into unknown waters, leading to six deaths, could not simply be written off as an unforeseen occurrence. Knowing that his client was going to be punished in some form, Berman's basic objective was to gain acquittal on the more serious manslaughter charges in hopes that his client would receive a reduction in rank and perhaps minimal brig time rather than the maximum of ten years in prison and a dishonorable discharge that he was facing. His strategy was to ignore the alcohol issues as being trivial and establish that although McKeon may not have exercised good judgment, he was simply following a well-established boot camp procedure for instilling discipline. The deaths, he would claim, resulted from recruit panic rather than from any circumstances that McKeon could reasonably have expected to occur.

Within days of his appointment, Berman made his first move, appearing on the nationally televised *Today Show* to announce that he was taking on McKeon's defense without fee and suggesting that the case presented broader issues than those covered by the charges against this client. Here he was adroitly tapping into Americans' well-known support for the underdog, framing McKeon's role as less than the only plot in the upcoming drama, and subtly putting the Corps on notice that if McKeon went down, others might fall with him, all without openly challenging the Marine Corps to a confrontation.

The *New York Journal-American* and associated Hearst papers had assigned popular author and journalist Jim Bishop to cover the trial. In Bishop, Berman saw the opportunity to generate favorable publicity for McKeon and soften the image of the heartless sergeant who had callously led his young charges to their deaths. Berman was wise enough, and both he and Bishop were professional enough, not to try to misrepresent the facts. Rather, Bishop was given unlimited access to and cooperation from Matthew McKeon and his family. During the week before the trial Bishop wrote an eight-part series describing McKeon's humble background, his close-knit Irish Catholic family, his long working hours and devotion to the difficult task of making basic marines out of recalcitrant recruits. He described the large McKeon family as patriotic, good-hearted, hardworking Americans. He told of the affection and loyalty each felt for Matt. Old neighbors of the McKeons were quoted in folksy terms telling how Matty McKeon "loved kids, going fishing and having a good time." The nun who taught him in grade school volunteered that while Matt was not the most diligent student, he was a "youngster who was always devoted to God and his country." Bishop portrayed McKeon as a man who embodied the honor and pride that had always been the hallmark of the Marine Corps: "he fights hard for the pride and honor of his wife, his two babies, his mother and the Corps."

Unlike McKeon, who displayed the manly virtue of acknowledging that he had done wrong and deserved punishment, the marine brass, Bishop said, were "standing on something the size of a pinhead called righteousness and they were trying to shove the sarge off." Bishop suggested that the commandant's declaration that he wanted to see McKeon, Scarborough, and King "punished to the fullest extent of the law" was in fact a bold hint to his subordinate officers who were assigned to their courts-martial to "hit them with the book."

After reading the Bishop articles, only the most hard-hearted reader could have thought of McKeon as less than a well-meaning, hard-working marine and family man who made a terrible mistake. Bishop himself became so attached to the cause that he posed for a group photograph with McKeon, Berman, and the defense team at the conclusion of the trial.

Bishop was not alone in gaining access to the defendant and his lawyer. In fact, Berman, who enjoyed Dewars Scotch, often in more than modest quantities, spent many an evening entertaining the press at the Golden Eagle Hotel in Beaufort, where, as Jim Bishop described it, "the spittoon is still a challenge to a marksman." During the trial, Berman would invite members of the press to join him for a drink in his air-conditioned room, where he could discuss the day's events and give the reporters good copy with just the spin he wanted on it.

As part of his public relations effort, Berman made sure that Sergeant McKeon and his attractive and pregnant wife, Betty, were accessible to reporters. *Life* magazine ran an article during the trial that showed McKeon frolicking with his year-old son. *Life*'s journalist, Joe McCarthy, had arrived at Parris Island with the impression that "McKeon was a first class son-of-a-bitch," but after meeting him declared that "you couldn't ask for a nicer guy."

As Sevier and Haden were diligently interviewing the prosecution witnesses and preparing themselves to present the evidence, their counterparts on the defense team were assiduously preparing the defense. Berman had brought with him to Parris Island a young associate named Howard Lester. Lester and Berman, as civilian counsel, were treated as though they were majors and offered housing at the depot bachelor officer's quarters. In these temporary quarters, Lester, Colonel Valentin, and Major DeBarr, assisted by Lieutenant Collins and Thomas Costello, prepared their case. The defense interviewed all available members of Platoon 71 in preparation for potential cross-examination. How fresh the recollections of the former recruits were is a matter of speculation, as all had been subjected to repeated interrogation by the press as well as during the preparations for and proceedings of the court of inquiry.

Sevier, Haden, and later Otten knew firsthand what the witnesses they were planning to call would say because they had personally interviewed them. Berman was busy planning defense strategy, preparing Sergeant McKeon for his anticipated lengthy testimony, and attending to the many details of trial preparation. Lester and the remainder of the defense team interviewed all the potential witnesses and recommended which ones to call as well as briefing Berman on the anticipated testimony.

As July 16 approached, the defense team was still working aggressively to generate public support while keeping the prosecution and the Marine Corps on the defensive. On Sunday, July 15, Berman held a full-scale press conference to announce that he had asked Secretary Thomas to release the results of approximately twenty-seven thousand questionnaires about training methods that had been sent at the commandant's behest to former marines. Berman had also requested the names and addresses of all marines discharged or separated from Parris Island since January 1, 1956. The secretary had denied both requests, claiming that the questionnaire was for the commandant's personal use in evaluating training methods and that both requests appeared to seek information not relevant or material to the trial. Thomas did agree to cooperate if the law officer at trial ruled that the information sought was, in fact, relevant.

Thomas's reasons for denying the request were reasonable. In fact, Berman later received the results of the questionnaire pursuant to an order by Captain Klein. He never used any of the information contained in the survey results. However, in the game of legal chess he was playing, Berman had set the stage for his next moves. First, he was able to announce publicly that his request for information had been turned down, thereby suggesting that the Marine Corps had something to hide. Second, he was able to use the refusal as the basis for a nationally televised press conference in which he asked marines to contact him by collect call or telegram to confirm that night swamp marches were standard Parris Island procedure.

Within hours of the dramatic appeal letters, telegrams, and telephone calls poured into Parris Island. Betty McKeon and other comely marine wives were shown on television responding to the overwhelmingly positive response to Berman's appeal. The move was both a public relations masterpiece and a source of vital information to buttress the defense's claim that night swamp marches were a long-accepted means of instilling discipline into recalcitrant platoons.

Captain Klein had suggested at a pretrial conference that the commandant might have to be called as a witness if the defense was intent on pursuing the release of the information contained in the responses to the questionnaire. Berman dangled that possibility before the press. When asked if he intended to call General Pate as a witness, he shrewdly toyed with that interesting possibility by responding, "Do you think he would come?"

By the morning of July 16, as the trial was about to begin, the canny Berman and his support team had engineered a remarkable turnaround in public opinion. They, and not the prosecution, were holding themselves and Matthew McKeon out as the defenders of the Marine Corps. The commandant's sweeping declaration in April that in a very real sense the Marine Corps was on trial, however necessary such a confession may have been in the face of a hostile Congress, was now the shield McKeon was raising to defend himself against the institution that was bringing him to trial.

The strategy formulated by the defense had worked remarkably well during the two months since Berman entered the picture. He was the choreographer of the dance on the stage of public relations. But the facts were the facts, and no degree of showmanship could change them. On the eve of the trial, Parris Island and much of the nation was anxious to see whether Berman's legal skills could match his public relations performance.

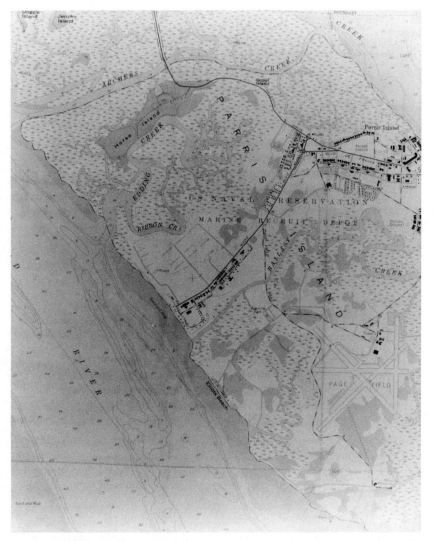

Overhead view of Parris Island. *Courtesy of Parris Island Museum*

Recruits arriving at Yemassee, South Carolina (ca. 1940s). Yemassee was the rail junction at which most recruits arriving from the north were met for bus transportation to Parris Island. *Courtesy of Parris Island Museum*

The author in front of Building 761 showing where Platoon 71 fell out on the evening of April 8, 1956, to begin the march. The platoon was housed in the lower left-hand squad bay.

Rear of Building 761 showing the wash racks where Staff Sergeant McKeon found a number of his recruits "crapped out" at midday on April 8.

Ribbon Creek as it appeared in 1996 at the approximate spot where the platoon entered.

Ribbon Creek near low tide as it appeared in 1996. The view is toward the ocean in the direction the platoon was heading when the panic broke out.

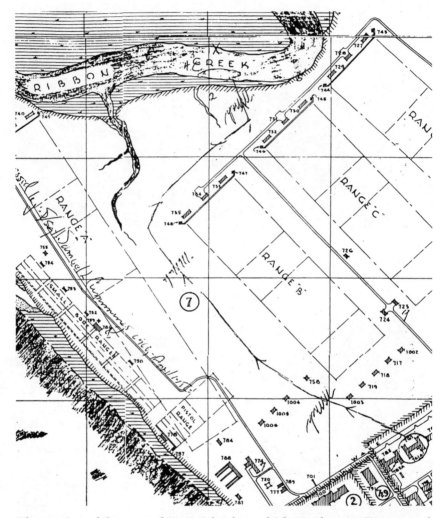

The portion of the map of Parris Island on which Matthew McKeon traced the approximate route of the fatal march from Building 761 into Ribbon Creek. The initials on the line from the barracks to the water are McKeon's, witnessed by Staff Sergeant Cummings, who noted the time as 0900, 9 April 1956. The map was introduced in evidence at McKeon's trial and became part of the official record.

The members of the court. *From left to right:* Major John G. Demas, Lt. Col. Daniel J. Regan, Lt. Col. Nicholas A. Sisak, Col. Edward L. Hutchinson (president of the court), Lt. Col. Duane Fultz, Maj. Edwin T. Carlton, Lt. Bentley Nelson. All were marines except Lieutenant Nelson, a navy physician. *Courtesy of Bentley Nelson, M.D.*

The former depot schoolhouse. The auditorium was converted to a makeshift courtroom to accommodate the media throng covering the trial. *Courtesy of Parris Island Museum*

Staff Sergeant McKeon and his brother-in-law, Thomas Costello, enter the courtroom as the trial begins. *Courtesy of Thomas Costello*

The McKeon support team, including chief defense counsel, Emile Zola Berman, at front center. Celebrated author Jim Bishop is on Berman's left. *Courtesy of Thomas Costello*

Matthew McKeon with Thomas Costello and two of his military lawyers, Maj. John DeBarr and Lt. Col. Alaric Valentin. *Courtesy of Thomas Costello*

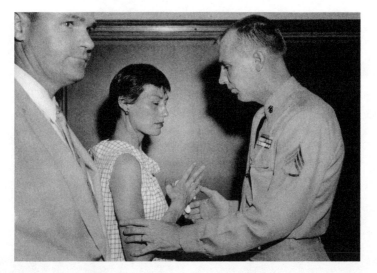

The anguish of the verdict and all the strain of the events since April 8 are reflected in the faces of Betty and Matthew McKeon. *Courtesy of Thomas Costello*

Maj. Richard Mample, Jack Webb, and Jackie Loughery, a former Miss USA, during the filming of *The D.I.* I recall my recruiting sergeant assembling me and about twenty other would-be recruits in front of City Hall in Worcester, Massachusetts, and marching us to a nearby theater to view *The D.I.* in June 1957. It must have been a good investment, because I believe that all of us followed through and enlisted. *Courtesy of Richard Mample*

TOP LEFT
David H. McPherson in 1996. Mc-
Pherson, a retired United Airlines
pilot, was the recruit before whom
McKeon allegedly took a swig of
vodka just before the march.

TOP RIGHT
Fred Haden outside his law office in
1996. Haden, Maj. Charles Sevier,
and Capt. William Otten Jr. were
appointed to prosecute McKeon.

BOTTOM
Matthew McKeon outside his home
in central Massachusetts in 1996.

# T E N

# Trial Begins

On Tuesday, July 17, 1956, at 11:01 A.M. the court-martial of Matthew C. McKeon was convened. The makeshift courtroom in the auditorium of the depot elementary school was packed with newsmen, spectators, and the defendant's family as well as the principals in the drama. Emile Zola Berman, fastidiously neat despite the wilting heat and humidity of midsummer South Carolina, sat next to the erect sergeant whose fate was to be determined. Also at the defense table were Thomas Costello and Howard Lester as well as the three military lawyers, all of whom had been laboring for the preceding two months in preparation for the events that were about to begin.

Facing the defendant and his battery of counsel were the three members of the prosecution team. Without fanfare or publicity, they too had devoted every workday since May to interviewing witnesses, researching legal precedents, and preparing to introduce the evidence, block by block, that would build the case for conviction.

Before the presentation of evidence, protocol required the prosecution to read the pending charges to the seven members of the court. The formal reading of the charges was followed by a voir dire, or preliminary examination of each of the seven court members by counsel for each side to determine if any of them was biased or otherwise unsuitable to sit in judgment.

Major Sevier briefly asked each of the seven court members whether he had any prejudicial information concerning the case, whether he had formed an opinion of guilt or innocence, and whether the defendant was personally known to him. Satisfied with the negative responses, Sevier sat down and gave Berman his turn.

Berman's questions were subtler than Sevier's. Recognizing that the commandant of the Marine Corps, the ultimate superior of all members of the court except navy lieutenant Nelson, had initially condemned McKeon and testified before Congress, Berman asked each member of the court if such statements would influence his decision. Accepting the negative response of each, he then moved on to address the issue of intoxication. Each man was asked if he equated taking a few drinks with intoxication or drunkenness. The question was cleverly phrased, for McKeon had never been found (except by the press) to be drunk or intoxicated. As expected, none of the court members equated a few drinks with intoxication; however, the very question elicited an advance commitment that no one would assume intoxication unless the evidence was there to prove it.

Finally, Berman had to contend with the fact that one member of the court, Major Carlton, had served as an officer at Parris Island from 1953 to 1955. His personal knowledge of recruit training practices, as well, perhaps, as his personal acquaintance with some of the personnel still serving, might interfere with Carlton's impartial judgment. Instead of challenging him, Berman politely but firmly confronted Major Carlton with his concern. Carlton responded that he had given thought to that issue and concluded that he could make his judgment based on the evidence he heard rather than his personal knowledge.

The voir dire provided the first hint of what Berman's approach would be. Rather than confront a potentially adversarial witness, he candidly laid out his concerns and, receiving favorable responses, demonstrated his trust in the fairness of the court by not exercising his opportunity to challenge. He was suggesting that he trusted each member of the court to be fair and impartial rather than risk alienating the group by removing one of their colleagues. Implied in his approach was a tacit expectation that his trust in them would be reciprocated.

Before the formal presentation of the evidence, a lawyer representing each side had an opportunity to outline the facts of his case that he expected to establish through witnesses and documents. This initial summary, called the "opening," while not evidence, gave each lawyer the chance to try to focus the jury on what he considered to be the essential points of his case.

Major Sevier, as the prosecutor, or "trial counsel," made only the briefest of openings, telling the court that it was

the intention of trial counsel . . . to reconstruct in as much detail as the rules of evidence will permit, the events and occurrences which are the subject

matter of the charges and specifications now before this court. . . . The prosecution is ready to produce direct testimony bearing on the facts and issues
of this case. Thank you, gentlemen.

Sevier was on his feet for perhaps three minutes. When he concluded, the
seven members of the court who would judge the case knew no more about
the facts of the case or the man who would present it than they had known
when he first arose. Sevier apparently saw his job as presenting the evidence
and letting the facts speak for themselves.

Then it was Berman's turn. His opening foreshadowed the dramatic contrast
in styles that would mark the entire proceedings. As an experienced litigator he
knew the importance of establishing rapport with the jury as well as outlining
what he hoped they would believe to be the truth of the matter before them.

Beginning humbly by asking the indulgence of the court for his ignorance
of the idiom and technical language of the Marine Corps, he immediately
addressed one of the issues that he feared could cloud the court's judgment
on the most serious charges of oppression and manslaughter. He again reminded the court that

> nowhere in the charges and specifications thereunder which have been sub-
> mitted to you and which form the foundation upon which this trial is to
> proceed, is there one word, one claim, one charge, even one suggestion that
> the accused Staff Sergeant Matthew McKeon . . . was either drunk, intoxicated
> or under the influence of liquor in the slightest, affecting the performance
> of his duty in the slightest.

Berman then set out to do with the court what he had been doing with
the media for the preceding two months—to personalize the man who had
been demonized in much of the popular press. He narrated McKeon's exemplary service record, his earlier honorable discharges, and his leadership in
combat during the Korean War. As Berman described him, McKeon was "in
truth . . . a fine Marine . . . dedicated to the U.S. Marine Corps and to the mission of that Corps."

Having linked his client to the long and honorable tradition of the Corps,
Berman then shifted his narrative to contrast the quality of the recruits
McKeon was charged with molding into marines.

> This platoon . . . was . . . a little lower than perhaps the usual amalgamation of
> young lads. . . . It became obvious to the accused as a junior drill instructor, as

it did to others, that in the terms of Marine Corps training this platoon was not sharp—it was undisciplined, it had some of the characteristics of that technical term, which is indigenous to Parris Island called a herd.

Berman pointed out that McKeon had been the first man into the water on the evening of April 8, and that he at all times led his men for the sole purpose of instilling discipline. The drownings occurred when panic set in—"sheer, stark unreasoning terror." The mission of the command was to produce marines, and the methods employed by McKeon during the ten-week training period were "indeed part and parcel, the very warp and woof by which this Corps has its wondrous traditions and its well-deserved history." Although the loss of six lives was a tragic accident for which "no man could have been more remorseful," McKeon's goal was at all times "dedicated to the purpose of making Marines of those entrusted to him."

Berman concluding by noting,

I like to think of myself as a responsible lawyer, Mr. President and officers of the court, I believe that when the time comes for evidence [you can] say to yourself, 'Mr. Berman told us several days ago that this will be his proof, we have a right to measure him by accepting that proof.' I accept that responsibility.

In contrast with Sevier's cryptic remarks, Berman's speech, which must have lasted for at least half an hour, was designed to create a sense of mutual trust and respect with the court members and to lay before them some of the basic themes on which he hoped to focus their attention as they heard the evidence.

It is interesting to note that at no time did Berman suggest that McKeon was not guilty; nor did he frame his comments in legal terms except to point out that the term *oppression* implied a form of tyranny, and certainly his client was no tyrant. Rather, Berman sought to establish a "man-to-man" relationship with each of the seven men on the military jury. He avoided legal jargon and addressed them directly, outlining what he felt was most important and asking that they trust him and hold him accountable to his word. Rather than blame the Marine Corps, he praised it lavishly, all the time bonding McKeon to its long and proud tradition.

Although he never said so, the opening also reflected Berman's knowledge that he was not going to get a full acquittal. In describing the drownings as arising from a tragic accident for which "no man could have been more remorseful or is to this day more remorseful," he was suggesting that while

McKeon may have been negligent, there was no intent to do harm, nor was malice involved. Whatever responsibility McKeon bore, he was not guilty of the two most serious charges: manslaughter and oppression resulting in death. Having no hope of an acquittal on the relatively minor charge of drinking in the barracks, Berman simply ignored it as being too trivial for consideration.

On the morning of July 18, the second day of the proceedings, the prosecution called Capt. Charles Weddel as its first witness. Weddel, as depot adjutant, was the custodian of the official records. He authenticated Depot Order 5000.1, which prohibited the possession or use of alcoholic beverages in barracks housing single enlisted personnel.

Sevier also sought to introduce another section of the same general order, which provided: "Because of the contamination of the water adjacent to Parris Island, all personnel of this Command are prohibited from bathing or swimming therein." Captain Klein was intending to admit the second section routinely when Berman rose to object on ground of relevancy, for "nobody has suggested that anyone has gone out swimming or bathing." Klein, caught off guard, sought cover.

KLEIN: Certainly it is a prohibition against entering the water adjacent to Parris Island.
BERMAN: Oh, no, it is not, it is a prohibition against swimming and bathing because of pollution.
KLEIN: I believe it is self-evident.
BERMAN: I present my objection on the grounds that there had been no showing of materiality whatsoever.
KLEIN: I will admit it on the basis that the reason, because of contamination, implicitly carries with it the question of entering.

Berman was right. Certainly an order relating to swimming and bathing was not relevant to the charges against the defendant. Although the law officer had the last word, he must have known that the brief exchange was a wake-up call for what would follow.

The cross-examination of Captain Weddel marked the beginning of another skirmish with the law officer over proper procedure. Under the protocol applicable to courts-martial, questions on cross-examination are limited in scope to subject matters raised in the direct examination. The purpose of the rule is to allow the prosecution to put on its case cleanly without the development of extraneous material on cross-examination. The defense has the right to recall the witness when it presents its case and may seek to introduce favorable testimony at that time. The benefit of the procedure is that it allows each side the opportunity to present its case with a minimum of confusion. The downside is that it is burdensome and often inefficient to have the same witness testify on two occasions, often days apart.

After Sevier finished with Weddel, Berman sought to introduce another depot order through his cross-examination of the witness. The prosecution objected on the ground that the topic was beyond the scope of the direct examination. Berman argued that recalling the witness would unnecessarily prolong the case. Klein agreed but sustained the prosecution objection "inasmuch as trial counsel insists on orderly procedure."

As the routine questioning was about to resume, a fortuitous event occurred. Berman suddenly halted his cross-examination to announce, "I have been advised that General Pate's secretary, Colonel Simpson, is on the telephone. It has been reported to me that it is an emergency call. Do I have your permission, Mr. President, to respond to that call?" Permission was, of course, granted, setting everyone present to speculating about why the commandant was so anxious to speak with the lawyer for the man he had promised would be punished to the fullest extent of the law. The mysterious summons while court was in session did nothing to diminish the aura of control that Berman seemed to be establishing over the proceedings.

When Berman returned, M.Sgt. Hans Manthey, the chief drill instructor for McKeon's former company in the Third Battalion, testified that the regulation prohibiting alcoholic beverages in enlisted quarters was posted in an area where drill instructors who entered company headquarters would see it. Berman again sought to use a witness to introduce evidence unrelated to the limited purpose for which he had been called. Captain Klein again vacillated on how to handle this fundamental procedural issue.

SEVIER: I object. This is outside of the scope of the document of which the man entered to testify.

KLEIN: Objection sustained.

BERMAN: Nothing is going to be served here by a parade off and on the stand, as they will have to be recalled to get the full scope of their testimony.

KLEIN: I agree with the observation and with that purpose I will permit you to go ahead.

SEVIER: Sir, I object. Is the defense allowed to place their case before the court by cross-examination?

KLEIN: Hold it. In view of your objection, your objection will be sustained.

As soon as that colloquy was completed another procedural issue arose. President Hutchinson asked the law officer if questions by the court were appropriate. Klein advised him that the members of the court could ask only clarifying questions; they could not inject any new matter or new evidence in the trial. After the luncheon recess, however, Klein announced, "I should like to change and amend and eat humble pie in connection with such instructions." Klein sheepishly acknowledged that under the recently adopted Uniform Code of Military Justice any member of the court may ask a witness any question that either side might properly ask of the witness.

The defense then recalled Captain Weddel. Under questioning he acknowledged the fact that had so concerned General Pate on his visit to the scene of the drownings on April 9. There were no explicit orders in effect on April 8 that put Ribbon Creek out-of-bounds except for swimming or bathing.

Lt. Col. Robert A. Thompson, the commanding officer of the Third Battalion, was the prosecution's third witness. Thompson related that in February 1956 McKeon had been among the new drill instructors who had assembled for an orientation lecture. Among other topics, each new DI was warned that incidents of maltreatment or hazing would be investigated, and appropriate action taken.

Here Berman made his first major blunder. In trying to persuade the witness to differentiate between the defendant's activities and the term *maltreatment*, he posed a lengthy hypothetical question. Assuming that a drill instructor took his platoon "into the marshes of a creek for the avowed purpose of teaching them discipline and improving their morale," he said, "would you consider that . . . maltreatment . . . ?"

Thompson's blunt response was, "I would." Berman immediately cut his losses and sat down. Here Sevier could have walked away with a clean victory. Instead, he chose to try to frost his cake with a few more questions, giving Berman time to gather his wits and undercut some of the earlier damage by gaining an admission from the witness that he had never issued any instructions about training or drills being conducted in the marshes or swamps around Parris Island.

When Berman asked Thompson if he knew of any night exercises in the swamps and boondocks behind the Third Battalion's huts, Sevier again raised the objection that the question was beyond the scope of direct examination. Berman replied:

BERMAN: I'm just asking him.
KLEIN: He's just asking about it.
SEVIER: Well, I object; it is way beyond the line of the direct . . .
KLEIN: I'll permit the question.

At this point the prosecution faced a dilemma. Continued objections to Berman's expansive cross-examination were getting nowhere except possibly to create a record of error for appeal. On the other hand, the law officer had now begun ruling consistently that Berman could work in part of his own case through his questions to the prosecution witnesses. Exasperating the law officer would certainly not help the prosecution's case.

Sevier, having laid a foundation of the depot orders and McKeon's knowledge of them, was now prepared to call witnesses who would describe the events of April 8. Maj. Stanley McLeod, the depot provost marshal, told of organizing the search behind Charlie range, dispatching boats and foot patrols, setting up portable lights, ferrying Clarence Cox back to safety, and continuing the search until the last body was found. He remembered the night being "rather cold" and "extremely dark." On cross-examination he clarified his testimony to mean that it was cold at about 2:00 A.M. and he didn't recall if the moon was out.

Berman used Major McLeod to introduce a photograph of the area, asking only if it portrayed the area in a general way. Sevier objected, but Klein let it in. Berman then had the witness mark on it the C butts, the pier, and a drainage ditch. What began as a general representation of the area was gradually becoming one of the central exhibits of the case. Berman would later use it to try to establish specific distances and water depths. At this point, Sevier's patience was exhausted. He had never been extended the courtesy of seeing the photograph, nor was there any foundation testimony as to how accurate a representation of the area it was.

On redirect examination Sevier established that McLeod had ordered each of the bodies to be photographed. Sevier had eight-by-ten-inch photographs of each corpse on a stretcher in a state of rigor mortis. He proposed introducing the photographs as exhibits for the court. Berman vehemently objected.

I object to them on the grounds that it is inflammatory and of no purpose in this trial. I . . . state in your court that there is no issue in this case as far as defense is concerned and it is conceded in the record that the persons named in the charges and specifications thereunder lost their lives as a result of drowning in Ribbon Creek while on a march of April 8, 1956, while members of Platoon 71. That . . . there is no issue in this case at all, no need for proof of this kind except to encumber the record with inflammatory and gruesome material.

Major Otten responded,

The prosecution feels that we should not be restricted as to how we present our case. We feel that the best way to establish the identification of the deceased persons in this case is by the use of photographs which we intend to try to enter into evidence.

Berman continued to protest the admission of the photographs. He conceded in open court the identity of the deceased, making the photographic evidence superfluous.

Berman was correct in objecting. The evidence was cumulative and proved nothing that was in dispute. Judge Klein, who earlier had expressed an interest in expediting the trial, overruled the objection and allowed the photographs of each of the six corpses into evidence. Why he did so remains a mystery; the photographs were indeed inflammatory and established nothing that the defense had not already conceded in open court.

M.Sgt. John E. Clement, attached to the Weapons Training Battalion, followed the provost marshal to the stand. Clement had spent a total of seven or eight years at Parris Island since he first arrived there in 1945. He had been assigned to water transportation and was familiar with Ribbon Creek. Clement testified that the water at an average high tide was about six feet above the level of low tide. He pointed out on one of the photographs previously introduced by defense counsel the area of the creek where the search was conducted on April 9. According to Clement, at low tide the water was neck deep on the searchers at the deepest point, which was about three-fourths of the way across the creek. At high tide the water at that point would be about six feet higher, or approximately five feet over the top of a man's head. Clement estimated the water in the marsh and the grassy area between the creek and the filled land behind Charlie range to be two and a half to three feet deep at high tide.

On cross-examination Clement acknowledged that certain portions of the creek bed were actually out of the water at low tide. This line of questioning by the defense was probably designed to lay a foundation for further testimony that if the platoon had been in the shallower areas, the water would not have been more than chest deep even near high tide.

Suddenly Berman popped the explosive question that went to the heart of his defense:

BERMAN: Tell me this: In all the years you have been on this base, have you ever seen platoons marching in the swamps, marshes and creeks in the area of the Weapons Training Battalion or the Third Battalion or any other area, Sergeant Clements?

PROSECUTION [Sevier or Haden]: May it please the court, we would like to object to that question. It's beyond the scope of direct examination. All this witness has testified to today is the area—

BERMAN: He has been speaking about the area, and that's what I want to ask him about.

KLEIN: I don't think he testified he ever saw anybody marching in the area.

PROSECUTION: Further, we think it's irrelevant and immaterial.

KLEIN: I will admit the question of the witness, who has expressed a familiarity with the area, and it hasn't been limited to the present time by the prosecution or the defense.

PROSECUTION: May it please the court, the only purpose we can see that the defense has got in asking this question and attempting to elicit his answer—and it also applies to witnesses whose names have been submitted to us to bring down here and testify—is to show some custom or usage in going into these—

BERMAN: Custom, usage or practice.

KLEIN: Of marching into water—is that what you are offering—marching into water or swamp areas?

BERMAN: I offer the proof to show that it was the practice on Parris Island, in connection with the matter of training, discipline and morale, to march the troops into swamps and marshes and waters, as an exercise.

PROSECUTION: May it please the Court, I still have some further matters—

KLEIN: I would like to hear you. I think that is going to be a decided question and I would like to hear you on that question.

PROSECUTION: If it's going to be an extended discussion, I don't think the witness should remain.

KLEIN: I suggest we take a recess at this point. If the offer is to get a ruling on questions of that nature, I would expect to have extensive authorities and discussions from both sides. I think, Mr. Berman, it is an avenue you intend to pursue.

BERMAN: I do. I think it is the only issue in the case.

KLEIN: I think, on the other hand, you intend to object specifically to that?

PROSECUTION: That is true.

KLEIN: The question is being raised here definitely out of order, except as the discretion of the Law Officer would permit cross-examination to be extended beyond the direct scope; and I have that discretion. If both sides are fully prepared at this time . . . to present their arguments and their authorities, then we can proceed . . . with consideration of that question. As far as I am concerned, it's as good a time as any.

After some discussion, it was agreed to defer argument on this critical question until the following morning to allow each counsel to prepare and submit briefs. Berman then resumed his efforts to try to persuade Clement that the water depth at the deepest point in the creek bed at high tide was about eight feet. Clement refused to budge, estimating the depth to be about ten and one-half feet. Berman, not getting the response he hoped for, quickly shifted gears and established that Clement's estimate was based on observation, not on a formal survey or measurements.

During the course of the redirect examination of Sergeant Clement, a telling bit of information was disclosed, but its significance seems not to have been realized by the prosecution because no further mention was made of it. Clement was asked by the prosecutor what happened when the skin diver discovered Thomas Hardeman's body. The witness responded, "He pulled it out of the mud and it came up like a cork." Much would be made of the depth of Ribbon Creek where the march occurred. However, one of the primary reasons the creek was so perilous, regardless of the depth of the water, was the mud on the creek bottom. Clement's testimony that when Hardeman's body was released from the mud it came up like a cork suggests in vivid terms the suction of the mud on an object as large as a body. Had Clement or the frogman, Sergeant Seybold, been asked, either of them could have expanded on the danger posed by the heavy mud filling the boots of the recruits struggling to safety. Berman was certainly not going to touch the subject, but why the prosecution ignored it as well is difficult to understand.

Sgt. Algin Nolan was the first prosecution witness when court resumed on July 19 after the luncheon recess. Through Nolan, a former administrative clerk in the depot sergeant major's office, Sevier was able to establish that on

April 8 the tide crested at Ribbon Creek at 6:34 P.M. approximately seven feet, three inches above low tide, and that the sun set that evening at 6:48 P.M. That information established that it would have been fully dark or very nearly so when McKeon assembled his men outside Building 761 shortly after 8:00 P.M. They entered the water on an outgoing tide no more than two hours after it had reached its peak level.

The first six witnesses called by the prosecution had laid the groundwork necessary to prove all the preliminary elements of the charges. Having established the existing legal regulations, conditions of the weather, lighting, tides, topographical features of the Ribbon Creek area, and identity of the six victims, Sevier, Haden, and Otten could now turn to the events of April 8. Their first witness was Richard King, the other junior DI of Platoon 71. At the time of the incident King was a sergeant. By the time of trial he was a corporal, having already lost one stripe for drinking in Building 761 on the morning of April 8.

King was unmarried and living in the same barracks with his platoon while they were at the rifle range. He was present in the squad bay when McKeon ordered the first field day. He then joined Elwin Scarborough and McKeon in the drill instructor's room. He saw a bottle of vodka that was about half full on the table. The three men made small talk. King saw McKeon have "a drink, maybe two, I'm not positive of the exact amount." King was offered a drink and, having no glass, took a swig from the bottle. When McKeon offered to drive Scarborough to Mainside shortly after noon, King volunteered to take the platoon to noon chow. McKeon returned around 1:30 P.M. McKeon told King he was going to sleep for a while. King left but returned to wake McKeon before evening chow.

Berman's objective on cross-examination was to mitigate the damage done by King's testimony. He had King verify that McKeon had been on duty since Saturday morning, that he walked with a limp, that he had a legitimate purpose in driving to Mainside with Scarborough (to get the platoon's mail), and that King had assumed supervision of the platoon during the time McKeon was sleeping.

King had identified the six bodies at the Beaufort Naval Hospital. Sevier wanted to have him confirm the identity of each of the six corpses shown in the photographs previously admitted. Berman again pleaded with the court to allow him to stipulate to the identity and death of each of the victims. Having already admitted the photographs for no useful purpose, Captain Klein must have had second thoughts. A brief exchange between counsel and the law officer not only shows Klein now attempting to save face while backpedaling but also offers a brief vignette into the personalities of the participants.

KLEIN: Before the witness leaves, it might be desirable for Mr. Berman to indicate the extent of his concession. . . . It might expedite considerably proof of death and such other things if we had for the record that concession at this time, assuming Mr. Berman is of a mind to do precisely what he indicated he wanted to do a little while ago.

BERMAN: I am of that mind.

KLEIN: In other words, I don't want to appear to be eliciting from you something you don't want to do.

BERMAN: Not at all. At the pre-trial conference I offered to concede that the persons named in the specifications thereunder were members of Platoon 71, who participated in a night exercise on April 9 [*sic*], 1956, and that they lost their lives by drowning in Ribbon Creek.

KLEIN: You say who participated in the exercise. You meant were led in it?

BERMAN: Were led by platoon into the area of Ribbon Creek and lost their lives by drowning.

KLEIN: And that they are dead, of course?

BERMAN [who obviously had about had his fill of Captain Klein]: The legal presumption, Mr. Legal Officer, is that when one loses his life there is a certain degree of permanency about it.

SEVIER: I can't accept any stipulation that includes any [authorized] exercise.

BERMAN: We concede that the members of Platoon 71 designated in the specification and now identified in and depicted by the exhibits lost their lives by drowning in Ribbon Creek while members of Platoon 71. I concede identification and death.

SEVIER: And the time?

BERMAN: Yes, of course; the 8th of April 1956.

KLEIN: All right, that will facilitate our hearing proof.

Sevier next called Sergeant Huff to identify and enter into the record the platoon roster and training schedule for Sunday, April 8. Presumably the purpose of Huff's appearance was to authenticate a document showing that no evening training marches were scheduled.

When court reconvened on Friday, July 20, Berman had another dramatic announcement:

A matter has come up very, very recently which requires my personal attention at some distance from Parris Island. It is a matter of serious purport [import?] and I have no way of delegating this to anyone else. It will require my leaving Charleston by the first available plane on Saturday, which is one o'clock, and my experience with transportation across from this place and vice versa is that if I allow two and a half hours, especially on a Saturday, I would be operating on a very thin line indeed.

Berman asked that the planned court session on Saturday be waived and that he be excused at the end of the day's session until Monday morning. No reasonable objection could be made to such a request. Berman was again the center of attention. The obscure references to a matter of great import prompted considerable speculation among the reporters present and reinforced the notion that Berman was running the show.

The purpose of Berman's mysterious mission was never revealed. In all likelihood, General Pate had agreed to meet with Berman to discuss a possible appearance as a defense witness.

After thus setting the press gallery abuzz, Berman turned to Huff to begin his cross-examination as the trial entered its fourth day. Huff, who had been a drill instructor for nearly two years, viewed Platoon 71 as the most undisciplined of the five recruit platoons he had worked with. He was dissatisfied with their response to discipline and command as well as their morale. Asked to evaluate Sergeant McKeon's performance, Huff said that he considered it to be outstanding.

Sevier again rose to object as Berman asked Huff about his orders precluding seconds at chow. The question was beyond the scope of the direct examination, but Klein was inclined to give Berman considerable latitude. Sevier asked Klein if the prosecution would retain the right of cross-examination of new matters introduced by the defense. The reply:

You are not precluded from the right to cross examine. They will speak for themselves. Mr. Berman will not be called upon necessarily to say, this is my witness for this question, and when you ask a question which is in the nature of cross-examination concerning matters which Mr. Berman has initiated and objection is made at that time, each specific question will be answered and ruled on.

Any hope the prosecution had of presenting its case first was now dashed. The law officer was, in effect, declaring that the defense could present its case through the prosecution witnesses if it chose, leaving Sevier and Haden with the right to cross-examine their own witnesses on any new matters opened up by Berman. This was a tactical victory for the defense because it allowed Berman to further disrupt an orderly presentation by the prosecution. Any confusion that might result could only assist the defense by helping to create reasonable doubt in the minds of the court members.

The issue of prior swamp marches arose again when Huff was asked if he knew of such a practice. Both sides were now prepared to address and argue that critical issue, which had been deferred from the preceding day. The court members, as fact finders, were excused because the issue was strictly a legal one—whether evidence of prior custom and practice was admissible to shed some light on the standard of reasonable conduct that would be used in weighing whether or not McKeon had been negligent or guilty of oppression.

Ordinarily, evidence of prior custom and usage would be inadmissible in a criminal trial. Evidence that other people had committed rape, robbery, larceny, or murder in circumstances similar to those in which the defendant acted would have no bearing on the question of guilt. A crime is a crime regardless of how many other persons have committed similar misdeeds.

The confusion in the present case arose from the fact that the major crime McKeon was charged with was "culpable negligence," a crime under the military code but rarely the basis for a crime in civilian courts. Negligence is a concept that normally pertains to civil suits between private parties for money damages. A party may be found liable for damages incurred by another person as a result of negligence or carelessness. However, careless or negligent conduct does not normally constitute a crime. Ordinarily, one must have either intended the criminal act or at least behaved recklessly before such behavior can be deemed criminal. Consequently, there was little precedent in the criminal law that either the prosecution or the defense could cite to support their arguments. The lawyers for both sides had to turn to a number of civil decisions and treatises in search of precedents to buttress their claims.

The prosecution lawyers were anxious to exclude any evidence of prior swamp marches. Their view was that the focus should be exclusively on McKeon's conduct, which they asserted was clearly blameworthy and negligent regardless of whether or not other drill instructors had led their recruits into the waters surrounding Parris Island at other times. Furthermore, as the march was in violation of an existing order, evidence of other marches should have no bearing on guilt or innocence.

In support of their second point, Sevier, Haden, and Otten cited a civil case in which an automobile was involved in an accident while making a left turn at an intersection where there was a sign that stated No Left Turn. In that case the court refused to allow the defendant to introduce evidence that drivers customarily turned left despite the prohibition, on the basis that a defendant cannot seek to excuse his conduct by custom and usage if it is in violation of a clearly established law or ordinance.

Berman and Lester argued that negligence means unreasonable conduct under the circumstances. However, customary conduct in such circumstances would have a bearing on just what would be considered reasonable. Consequently, evidence of similar swamp marches should be admitted to determine the appropriate standard of reasonableness. That standard, once determined, would enable the court to decide whether McKeon's actions so deviated from what was reasonable as to be considered culpably negligent.

The defense team responded to the prosecution's argument that McKeon was guilty of violating an existing order prohibiting entry into the surrounding waters of Parris Island by pointing out that there was, in fact, no such order. The order Sevier had introduced at the outset of the trial precluded entry into the waters surrounding Parris Island for swimming and bathing only. Berman and Lester correctly argued that that order was irrelevant to the circumstances of the present case.

The law officer sided with the defense and agreed to allow evidence of prior swamp marches to show an existing pattern of custom and usage. The only condition attached to the admissibility of such testimony was that the marches must have been under reasonably similar circumstances.

In reality, there may have been no need for this legal tussle, which consumed almost an hour of the morning, as it is likely that Captain Klein had already made up his mind before the debate began. Before either lawyer presented any argument or authority, the law officer announced,

> I want to say at the very outset that I am inclined to rule, on my own research thus far of the question prior to the hearing of argument, that evidence of custom or common practice with respect to night marches instituted or initiated by drill instructors, including evidence of the condition and place where such marches took place, is admissible, in connection with the allegation in specification 1 of charge 3 of death by culpable negligence.

Berman had won a major battle. Sevier's only hope at this point was to show that any other swamp marches were so dissimilar as to be inadmissible. But even if he were successful, before there could be such a determination, the law officer and all the court members would already have heard a parade of drill instructors say that they had been marching their troops into the mud and waters around the island for years, a practice that had apparently been met with a nod and a wink by those in command.

Sergeant Huff resumed the stand at mid-morning. When asked again if he knew of a practice, for the purpose of training discipline and boosting morale, of taking platoons on night marches into the boondocks, swamps, marshes, and waters around Parris Island, Huff replied, "As far as I know, yes, sir." He also acknowledged that he had earlier told the recruits of Platoon 71 that if their performance didn't improve, he would take them into the swamps.

Sevier went after Huff like a bulldog. Huff had to acknowledge that he had never seen a platoon marched into the marsh or swamps in the two years he had been a drill instructor. He knew of no specific platoon ever marched into the swamp. Huff never told McKeon to take the platoon into the swamp or that such a march was acceptable if the recruits were goofing off.

The prosecution did what it could to mitigate the damage done by Huff's testimony. Nevertheless, the question remains as to why he was called to the stand to begin with. The training schedule for Sunday, April 8, was of minimal significance and could have been introduced through Captain Weddel or another neutral witness. Huff's testimony had been more helpful to the defense than to the prosecution. Huff had testified at the court of inquiry that he knew of prior swamp marches and had threatened to take the platoon into the swamps. Certainly it was foreseeable that Berman would get that information into the record. Not only was it damaging to the prosecution's case, but it was also just the type of publicity the Marine Corps hoped to avoid.

Friday afternoon's session opened with Capt. Charles Patrick on the witness stand. Patrick had been the officer of the day at the Weapons Training Battalion on April 8. Following a call from the commander of the guard at about 9:00 P.M., Patrick had driven to the road that divides Baker and Charlie ranges to discover

> bunches of recruits coming up the road. They weren't in any particular formation, some of them were half undressed, . . . some were barefooted. They were wet, muddy, bedraggled. . . . Two or three of them were being carried.

Patrick established that Platoon 71 was not scheduled for fieldwork that evening, nor had the drill instructor requested permission to engage in any activity that night. He did acknowledge on cross-examination that the only time the area behind the Charlie butts was out-of-bounds was when there was firing on the range.

T.Sgt. Johnny B. Taylor's testimony dovetailed with that of Captain Patrick. He told of learning from the corporal of the guard that one of the sentries had heard shouting and hollering behind the butts. He drove down behind the Charlie butts. When he got out of his vehicle to see what was happening, "two little white boys carrying a colored boy" came by, followed by a number of stragglers. All were apparently in some degree of shock, as none would respond to Taylor's questions about what was happening. While he was behind the butts, Taylor spotted McKeon, who told him that he was in charge and was responsible for the events. After his futile effort to call Colonel McKean from the ammunition shed, Taylor drove the three stragglers he had first encountered to sick bay.

Berman asked Taylor a number of inconsequential questions about the location of the sentries. His purpose may have been to try to show that the route of the march was not intended to avoid the sentries, as Sevier had earlier intimated. If so, his questioning led nowhere. Probably, the primary objective was psychological—to mark time with the witness, giving the appearance that Berman was in control and allowing the witness to finish his testimony with a number of innocuous responses rather than end with the vivid account of the traumatized recruits straggling to safety.

As the first week of trial drew to a close, Sevier, Haden, and Otten had presented the first three phases of the prosecution's case. Applicable orders and regulations were part of the record. The lighting, tides, and natural features of Ribbon Creek had been placed in evidence. Sergeant McKeon's activities and the relevant events leading up to the march and its immediate aftermath had been described by the people who had the most direct knowledge of them. The court had yet to hear firsthand accounts of the events in the dark and rushing waters just before and after the panic set in. The prosecution intended to conclude with testimony surrounding McKeon's alcohol consumption and sobriety. It was now time for the young men of Platoon 71 to tell what had happened in the fifteen minutes after they were led into the mud and waters of Ribbon Creek.

# E L E V E N

# Trial Continues—Week 2

B y the time the court-martial of Sergeant McKeon began, the surviving members of Platoon 71 had long since completed their basic training. Following a month of infantry training at Camp Lejeune, North Carolina, and a brief leave at home, each of them was ordered to return to Parris Island as a potential witness. Lawyers for both the prosecution and the defense were given the opportunity to interview each young man. The prosecutors decided to call nineteen of them as witnesses. Nine of the nineteen had previously testified in April before the court of inquiry.

Earl Grabowski was the first of the former recruits to be called as a witness. Major Sevier used him to give the court an overview of the events during the course of Sunday, April 8. Grabowski told the court that McKeon met him and the other recruits returning from the Catholic detail in the evening, and that he "smelled a little liquor on him." Grabowski also claimed to have smelled liquor on McKeon before. After they fell out shortly after 8:00 P.M., McKeon told the platoon that they were going swimming, prompting a laugh from several of Grabowski's companions. Once the men were in the water, he heard McKeon ask where the nonswimmers were. Grabowski was near the rear and walked into water over his head. When the panic erupted, he tried to help Donald O'Shea, who was trying to climb on top of him. He recalled the strong current and the formation of a "chain gang" to pull most of the recruits into shallow water. After he was out of the water, he fell in chest-deep mud before Private Ferkel pulled him back out onto the grass.

On cross-examination, Grabowski confirmed that McKeon was at all times in the lead as they went over the bank and into the water, which was then about knee deep. The column turned right and went about thirty feet, turned left and walked for about thirteen or fourteen feet toward the center of the stream, and then turned left again, parallel to the initial route. The water was about waist deep at that point. Some of the men were fooling around—joking, kidding, and slapping others with twigs while yelling "Snake!" or "Shark!" Suddenly there was a cry for help, and panic broke out to Grabowski's rear, nearer the center of the stream. McKeon tried to help the recruits. Although it was dark, there were patches of light on the water.

Berman then took a gamble.

BERMAN: Had you heard anything about other outfits being taken into the boondocks?

GRABOWSKI: At mainside I did, yes, sir.

BERMAN: At mainside you heard that?

GRABOWSKI: Yes, sir, by other platoons.

BERMAN: That recruits were taken into the boondocks?

GRABOWSKI: Yes, sir; that would be the usual routine, I heard.

BERMAN: That was the usual routine, you heard?

GRABOWSKI: That's what I figured.

Sevier was asleep at the switch. Each of the questions called for hearsay testimony, which would have been excluded had an objection been made. Berman, finding no opposition on the issue, just kept hammering away until no one could miss the point.

In an unusual move, Colonel Hutchinson then interjected a question into the cross-current of interrogation, asking the witness to mark the route of march on the aerial photograph that Berman had previously marked as an exhibit. Grabowski had not seen the area since that dark night of April 8. Sevier properly asked if Grabowski could make an accurate estimate, to which the witness twice replied that he could only guess at it. That response should have disposed of the request, as testimony that is no more than speculation is inadmissible as evidence. Instead, Grabowski was permitted to trace what he guessed to be the route of the march on the photograph. No real harm would have been done to the prosecution's case if the route designated on the map was understood to be nothing more than reasonable conjecture. Instead, Berman would later use Grabowski's markings as a foundation for expert testimony intended to show that the route followed was in shallower water than the prosecution claimed.

The second former recruit to take the stand was Melvin Barber. He was examined by Captain Haden. Through his testimony, Haden established not only that he was a nonswimmer, but, even more significantly, that McKeon had spoken to him and Private Wood in the pool and said, "Big as you two were you should be able to swim."

Haden asked Barber if he thought the two field days were a form of punishment. Berman properly objected because the question called for an inadmissible opinion from a lay witness. Inexplicably, Klein allowed Barber to give an affirmative response.

Barber's description of the evening's events and route of the march was not materially different from Grabowski's. He did add that when they first went off the bank the men were slipping about in ankle-deep mud. When the water came up to his chest, Barber stopped in his tracks. He also commented that McKeon had seemed "sort of tired" and that his "face was sort of flushed" earlier in the day.

Barber was to be cross-examined when court resumed on Monday, July 23. Before Barber returned to the stand, however, the record reveals that a seemingly innocuous event occurred at the outset of the morning's proceedings. Berman rose to announce to the court that Mr. Morton Janklow "has been excused from further attendance at this trial with the express consent of the accused." Janklow, an attorney, had accompanied Berman, Lester, and Costello to Parris Island ostensibly to assist with the defense. However, Mr. Janklow had an agenda of his own, which, through the fortuitous presence of Tom Costello (while Berman was away for the weekend on his secret mission), never came to fruition. More on Mr. Janklow later.

Berman skillfully led Barber to acknowledge that although classified as a nonswimmer because he could not swim a certain distance in the pool, he and the other nonswimmers had been taught how to float, tread water, and dog paddle. All recruits in the platoon had received ten hours of swimming instruction before April 8.

Barber, like Grabowski, thought the platoon lacked discipline. Backtracking on his earlier testimony, Barber agreed that the field days, rather than punishment, were meant to point out to the men that they were not obeying instructions. Actually, he may have considered them to be both; his responses were somewhat ambiguous. He also spoke of the high regard he had for McKeon as a drill instructor.

Pfc. John Maloof was the third recruit witness. Maloof was one of the more articulate young men in the platoon. He described being called into the drill instructor's room with Private Wood in the early evening. McKeon tried to induce Wood and Maloof, both large men, to fight. Moments earlier he had slapped Maloof lightly on the left side of his face for not standing properly at attention. He told the two recruits that he wanted them to get the platoon squared away. It was Maloof's opinion that "Sergeant McKeon was at the end of his rope . . . he had tried hard, very hard and he got no results." McKeon talked to both men about the lack of organization and discipline in the platoon. Wood was sitting on the locker box while Maloof stood. McKeon told them he had decided to take the platoon out into the boondocks. After a brief conversation, Wood and Maloof were shown the door with instructions to send in "the next biggest man."

The "next biggest man" happened to be David McPherson. While McPherson was closeted with McKeon, the word was spread that they were going to the boondocks. According to Maloof, "everybody was feeling pretty good and happy and thought it was a great idea."

In Maloof's view the march to the rear of the butts was disorganized, "a mass of bunches" rather than a marching column. There was laughing and joking even after the men entered the water. He testified that McKeon led them into the water. After walking upstream in the slimy mud, the column made a U-turn and headed downstream as the water rose higher and higher. The bottom seemed to drop off like a cliff, and Maloof began floundering. He tasted saltwater and felt the pull of the current. In the ensuing panic he was grabbed and dragged underwater. After freeing himself, he shed some of his clothes and tried to rescue some of his companions who were farther downstream.

Berman established through Maloof that the cries for help were nearer the center of the stream. As there was little to be gained for the defense by dwelling on the events in the water and earlier in the evening, Berman shifted the subject to McKeon's qualities as a drill instructor. According to Maloof, McKeon had always been there to help. He was not violent or abusive. There was no indication that McKeon was under the influence of liquor that evening, although he did seem depressed about the failures of the platoon. Maloof and the other recruits he spoke with after leaving the DI's room with Wood felt that "we were going to square away on the double, and we all thought we had let him down, because he did everything for us and he got a knife in the back."

Lewis Leake was the "little colored boy" that Johnny Taylor had described being carried by "two little white boys" when Taylor first arrived at the scene. Leake, known as "Pee Wee," was one of the smallest men in the platoon. He was well liked because he tried hard. He was a particularly valuable prosecution witness because he was a nonswimmer, and McKeon knew that to be so before April 8.

SEVIER: Of your own knowledge, do you know whether or not the accused knew whether you were a swimmer or a non-swimmer?
LEAKE: Yes, sir.
SEVIER: You do or you do not know?
LEAKE: He knew I was a non-swimmer, sir.
SEVIER: Would you explain to the court why you think he knew that?
LEAKE: Because one time he took us to the swimming pool and I was on the side where the non-swimmers were and he spoke to me.
SEVIER: What did he say to you?
LEAKE: He said he didn't know I was a non-swimmer.
SEVIER: Can you swim at all, Leake?
LEAKE: No, sir.

The only positive testimony Berman could extract from Leake was that he thought McKeon was a good DI and that the discipline of the platoon was bad.

Sevier used Lester Hendrix to reinforce the fact that McKeon knew in advance of the march that a number of men in his platoon could not swim. Hendrix, being only five feet tall, was assigned to the last squad. He remembered McKeon's words after they fell out and were about to depart for the boondocks.

SEVIER: Did Sergeant McKeon say anything to the platoon at that time?
HENDRIX: What do you mean? When we fell out he asked for the non-swimmers.
SEVIER: He asked where the non-swimmers were or asked for them, or what?
HENDRIX: He just asked if there were some non-swimmers.
SEVIER: What happened?
HENDRIX: Some of them raised their hands.
SEVIER: Anything else said?
HENDRIX: Yes, sir, he said that those who could swim would be drowned, and those who couldn't would be eaten by the sharks.

Although Hendrix probably had the last comment reversed, McKeon's prediction seems to have been taken lightly by many of the recruits, who were joking and fooling around as they headed for the water minutes later.

Eugene Ervin was, like Maloof, an intelligent and articulate witness. He had been the right guide marching at the front of the platoon on April 8. Ervin was a swimmer of limited ability who, on reaching Ribbon Creek, wisely dropped back onto land, ostensibly to help Private Langone herd the rest of the platoon into the water. His testimony established that the mud was approximately five to seven inches deep. He also recalled hearing McKeon say while they were in the water, "Let's go out with the tide," thus confirming that McKeon was aware that the tide was going out when he led the column into the deeper water.

Berman could not counter the case the prosecution was building except to elicit some favorable personal testimony. Ervin considered discipline to be poor and found McKeon to be an excellent teacher who was never physically violent.

Gerald Langone, the former section leader, did his best to defend his former DI, whom he thought "was the best on the Island, in my opinion, and I think most of the men agreed with me, sir. He was patient and interested in the men personally." Langone, who had had a private audience in the drill instructor's room just before the platoon fell out, found no suggestion "by odor or conduct or discussion" that McKeon had been drinking.

Despite his protective bias, Langone admitted on direct examination that McKeon had slapped him and tried to get him to swing at him when he entered the DI's quarters. He also characterized the current in the creek as "fairly strong" and testified that he knew there were a couple of nonswimmers in the platoon.

As court opened on Tuesday, July 24, Berman rose to make an announcement:

> Before you call your witness, Mr. President, with your permission Mr. Law Officer, I have here a list of 108 former Marines that I desire the government to issue subpoenas for; that is subpoenas for their production on this trial. The matter came in informally on a previous occasion and I should like to know whether you prefer for us to discuss it in the absence of the court or what procedure you desire to be adopted.

Although Captain Klein instructed him to raise the matter in the absence of the court members (it was a procedural issue that had nothing to do with the evidence the court members as jurors would consider), the clever Berman had, in effect, already made his dramatic announcement in open court while framing the question of how the procedure should be handled. The request for 108 subpoenas suggested that an overwhelming number of defense witnesses would be called. The timing was a perfect counterpoint to the cumulative litany of evidence Sevier, Haden, and Otten were presenting to bolster the case for conviction.

A conference ensued among the lawyers and Captain Klein, still in the presence of the court, in which Berman was advised that in order for Sevier to subpoena the witnesses, the defense would have to furnish not only the name and address of each witness but also a synopsis of the anticipated testimony, the reason for the witness's presence, and an explanation of why the anticipated testimony was necessary.

By 1:35 P.M., when court reconvened after the luncheon recess, Berman was rapidly backpedaling.

> I have reconstituted that list and I have cut that number down to 82. However, I would like for the record to show now that I am presently furnishing, together with that list, a list to trial counsel of just 18 names, 18 out of the list of 82, and that with respect to those 18 names, if those 18 persons are subpoenaed I will not request that any others be subpoenaed until those 18 have testified and then only upon reflection as to whether there is a necessity for additional proof.

Captain Klein had said that such discussions should be held out of the presence of the court; yet the colloquy about the subpoenaed witnesses continued back and forth in open court with Klein a participant. Once again Berman had taken center stage. He originally requested 108 witnesses, trimmed that list to 82, and finally acknowledged that he really needed only 18. He actually called only 2 of the subpoenaed witnesses before resting his case.

After the first round of the subpoena controversy was completed, the prosecution called David McPherson. McPherson had followed Wood and Maloof into the DI's room, where he was chastised for not doing more to help the platoon act in a disciplined manner. He, too, received a slap or two and then was told to sit on the locker box. McKeon, frustrated with the lack of discipline and spirit in the platoon, told McPherson he was thinking of taking them out into the swamps. He talked at some length about how platoons lacking in spirit and discipline would not come through in combat. McPherson concurred that the platoon had had it too easy right from the beginning and that a march to the boondocks would be a good idea.

At some point, McKeon picked up the bottle of vodka from the floor, raised it to his lips, and brought it back down. McPherson was ambivalent about whether or not the top was on the bottle and whether McKeon actually took a drink in his presence. He identified Scarborough's bottle as being the one he saw. The issue of drinking in the presence of a recruit would rise or fall largely on McPherson's testimony.

The defense salvaged what it could on cross-examination. The witness described the lack of discipline and agreed that McKeon was an excellent DI with great patience.

After McPherson left the stand, Sevier, Haden, and Otten called ten more recruits as witnesses. The stories were tending to become repetitive and the evidence cumulative. Privates Drown and Leonard confirmed that the mud was near or over their boot tops. Private Brennan recalled hearing McKeon ask in the water if everyone was all right and reply to a negative response that they should do the best they could. Privates Serantes and Geckle related that they were not qualified swimmers. Geckle knew that Wood, Poole, and Leake were also not qualified.

The defense could do little to discredit the damaging testimony from the recruits. The best that Berman could accomplish was to show that McKeon's intentions were good, that he exposed himself to the same risks by leading his platoon into the water, that he was trying to snap his recruits out of their dispirited ways, and that he was a well-liked, patient DI. Considering that the two most serious charges against McKeon were oppression and culpable negligence (manslaughter), the defense hoped that the unanimous praise and support of his platoon would persuade the court that at the most the defendant was guilty only of the lesser offenses of drinking in the presence of a recruit, drinking in the barracks, and simple negligence.

Thomas O. Truitt, the last of the nineteen recruits to testify, was excused from the courtroom at 10:10 A.M. on July 25. After a thirty-five-minute recess, the prosecution team was ready to present its last battery of witnesses.

Pfc. Fred Magruder was a military policeman on duty on April 8. After Magruder was dispatched to Building 761 by the sergeant of the guard, Captain Patrick had him place McKeon under arrest and confine him to the drill instructor's room. Meanwhile, Sergeant Huff had arrived, but his conduct was so unruly that he, too, had to be placed under arrest. As Magruder was trying to calm Huff and place him under arrest, he saw that McKeon "had picked up something and was started into the head." Magruder followed him and saw him place an object behind the toilet. Magruder asked Corporal Lyons, the other MP present, to retrieve the object. Lyons returned with "a fifth of Vodka, I believe, sir, that was almost empty. It had about a fourth or less in the bottle, sir." The witness identified the bottle that had already been marked as an exhibit.

Berman had nowhere to go with this witness except to have him confirm that the top was on the bottle when Lyons brought it from the head (lending some credence to McPherson's testimony, and what would later be McKeon's testimony, that the bottle was capped when the sergeant lifted it to his lips in McPherson's presence).

Sevier called Corporal Lyons to corroborate the essence of Magruder's testimony. Lyons recalled that the bottle had an inch and a half of liquid in it when he brought it from the bathroom where McKeon had placed it.

Wednesday, July 25, was an unusually sultry day. At midday, the ever-polite and immaculately groomed Berman finally made a minor concession to the sweltering conditions in the auditorium/courtroom by loosening his tie. He apologized to the court for doing so.

The prosecution continued its methodical presentation by introducing the autopsy records near the end of the morning. Berman objected on the ground that the men's death by drowning in Ribbon Creek had already been conceded. The autopsy records were unnecessary and prejudicial because they contained gruesome details regarding the medical examiner's findings when he opened up the corpses. Berman must have seen that the end was in sight and that the case would turn on larger issues than the detailed records, for he suddenly withdrew his objections without explanation.

The prosecution team had two witnesses whom they intended to call in hopes of showing that the accused was under the influence of alcohol during the evening of April 8. The first of the two was Billy Redmond, one of the navy corpsmen who was on duty at the depot infirmary on April 8. Redmond was called to authenticate the log in which the results of all blood alcohol tests taken at the infirmary were recorded. The record would show that Dr. Atcheson performed a Bogens test on Sergeant McKeon at about midnight, with the assistance of Corpsman Fox. The reading of 1.5 Atcheson obtained, if valid, would indicate that McKeon was on the borderline for being under the influence of alcohol when the test was performed.

One of the fundamental rules of evidence is that hearsay statements (what someone other than the accused said out of court or wrote) are generally not admissible. Such utterances are considered inadmissible because the witness cannot verify the truth of what someone else said or wrote, and the speaker or author is not on the stand to be examined as to the reliability of the statement. There are exceptions to the rule if the nature of the hearsay statement is likely to be inherently reliable. Two such exceptions are for records kept in the ordinary course of business and official records. Although the Bogens log was hearsay, Sevier sought to have it admitted as an official record.

Berman sprang to his feet, requesting and receiving a "preliminary inquiry" concerning the admissibility of the proposed exhibit. Berman's aggressive and crisp questioning established that Redmond had had nothing to do with the drawing of blood or the performance of the test. Berman sought to exclude the test results on the ground that its validity hinged on the scientific reliability of the test and on those administering the test following proper technical procedures. Redmond had no personal knowledge of either. Captain Klein was not persuaded and admitted the log as an exhibit under the "official record" exception to the hearsay rule.

Sevier, having scored a victory with the admission of the record, then sought to have Redmond explain in layman's terms what the 1.5 reading meant. Again Berman objected. In just a few minutes he skillfully showed that the witness was not an expert in blood chemistry and was not competent to interpret the results. This time he was successful. Captain Klein suggested to Sevier that he call the doctor who had administered the test.

Berman, assisted by Lieutenant Collins, requested and was granted a brief hearing out of the earshot of the court during which they tried to persuade Captain Klein that any evidence of intoxication was inadmissible because it was not directly related to any of the charges against the defendant. The law officer was adamant that evidence of intoxication, if proven, might corroborate charges I and IV, which alleged violations of regulations prohibiting drinking in the barracks and drinking in the presence of a recruit. The prosecution lawyers wisely kept quiet. Berman's final comments lent a personal touch to the professional struggle that was under way.

BERMAN: I should not be quite so intense in this hot weather. I find that I set down in a bath of perspiration.
KLEIN: Your intensity is commendable.

At about 7:00 A.M. on Monday, April 9, T.Sgt. Samuel Cummings, chief investigator for the depot, received a call at his home telling him to "come aboard to interview a fellow who had 6 recruits missing from his platoon." When Cummings arrived, he had McKeon brought over to his office from the brig. After being advised of his right against self-incrimination, McKeon described what occurred, and Cummings wrote it out in longhand. McKeon read it, or appeared to, and signed it. A copy of that statement, authenticated

by Cummings, was offered as an exhibit. As the eighth day of trial was about
to conclude, the court was finally going to hear McKeon's version of the
events of April 8. Below are excerpts from his statement.

At [approximately 11:00 A.M.] I told the platoon to turn to and wash clothes
on the washing racks to the rear of our quarters Barracks 761.

Shortly after the platoon had gone out to the wash racks I went out to
check them and when I did I found several of the men "crapped out." I
became quite angry with this display on their part and as a result ordered
them back into the barracks and further instructed them to turn to holding
field day. . . . At about 1300 I went to get the mail and while getting same I
got the idea to take them out into the swamps that night thinking that I
could teach them a little more discipline. . . . Sometime during the previous
night someone had brought a fifth of vodka into my room and all during the
afternoon I had some drinks from the bottle. I believe at the most I had three
or four drinks. . . .

Around 1830 I told the Section leaders and squad leaders that I was going
to take the men out into the swamps later on and teach them some discipline. About three fourths of the platoon was squared away but the remainder were foul balls.

At a little after 2000, 8 April 1956 I fell the platoon out to take them into
the swamps. . . . I marched the platoon in a column of two's down to the
Baker range butts and from there over to Charlie range butts. When the
head of the formation had got abreast of the target shed on Charlie range I
gave them a column left and marched them out into the swamps . . . and,
then beared right in water about waist deep along the bank. When the
entire platoon was in the water I, who was at the head of the platoon, swung
the column around into deeper water and reversed the line of march back
toward Baker range. When we had gotten past the point where we had initially entered the stream still in somewhat of a formation, I heard some
men to my right, out towards the center of the stream, yelling for help. I
would say there were about six or seven men out there. . . . I told the men to
keep cool and go onto the beach. . . . I swam out to the men in the middle
of the stream. I grabbed one man and took him to the beach to a point
where he could stand up. I asked him if he could touch ground and stand
up, when he gave me an affirmative reply I headed back into the stream to
help the others. The remainder of the platoon who had gone onto the beach
were helping others who had been on the rear end of the column, to get

ashore. I swam out and as I passed one of the men, a colored boy who I thought was O.K. grabbed me and we both went down under the surface of the water . . . and then came back up to the surface. We went down a second time and at this point he let go of me and I could not find him after that. After several attempts to locate the boy and had had no success I headed for the beach as I could see no one else in the area. The tide I believe was high and at the time was going out as there was quite a current. . . .

After taking down McKeon's statement, Cummings had produced a large map of Parris Island. He circled Building 761 and asked McKeon to draw a line on the map showing the general route followed from the barracks into the water. McKeon complied. That map was produced and offered as an exhibit.

Sevier turned the witness over to the defense at 3:55 P.M. Citing the lateness of the hour, Berman asked permission to adjourn for the day to allow him to prepare for cross-examination. Colonel Hutchinson was only too pleased to comply. The day had been unusually hot, and everyone was feeling wilted.

On Thursday morning, Berman, having freshened his mind and body with his customary cold morning shower, was ready to make what headway he could with Sergeant Cummings. McKeon's statement, although already in evidence, was not in and of itself particularly harmful. Most of the damaging information had already been introduced from other sources. Furthermore, Berman was planning to put his client on the stand to admit most of what he had acknowledged in his interview with Cummings.

Berman's strategy with this witness was twofold. First, he intended to establish that Cummings had no knowledge of the events of April 8 other than what McKeon had told him. McKeon could thus clarify and elaborate on some of the things he had told Cummings when it was his turn to testify. Cummings could also be used to develop the second prong of the defense strategy, which was that while the defendant had had a lapse of judgment, he was far from the beast the news media had been writing about for months.

Berman quickly established that Cummings had no personal knowledge of the events of April 8. Everything he knew about the incident he had learned from the defendant. Berman then drew from Cummings testimony designed to evoke sympathy for his client from the seven members of the court.

BERMAN: And in what way, in his talk with you or in the statements that he made did his nervousness and concern show itself?

CUMMINGS: Well, at that time of the morning neither he nor I knew what the condition of the men were. He was concerned over the—his main concern was about those boys, the men who had been out there. He didn't know what had occurred to them.

BERMAN: In what way did he manifest that concern; what did he say?

CUMMINGS: I recall him making statements to the effect, "poor devils," and "those poor boys," and that sort of thing.

BERMAN: Did you gather the impression that he was despondent and very despondent?

CUMMINGS: In that regard, yes, sir.

BERMAN: In other words, would it be fair to say that you gathered that his overwhelming attitude at the time was one of tremendous concern for his men and that anything else was an effort for him to address himself to?

CUMMINGS: Yes, sir, I would go so far as to say that.

BERMAN: You gained the impression that he was cooperative and not attempting to hide or conceal anything from you?

CUMMINGS: No, sir, nothing whatsoever.

Dr. Atcheson, the young navy physician whose one-page report indicating "clinical evidence of intoxication" had been the central piece of evidence that led the court of inquiry to find that McKeon was under the influence of alcohol to an unknown degree, was the next witness. The cross-examination of Dr. Atcheson by Emile Zola Berman exemplifies why Judge McNally held him in such high esteem.

Atcheson had been in the navy only eleven months on April 8, having been commissioned directly after completing his internship. On direct examination he related that he had drawn the blood for the Bogens test and corroborated the reading, but two corpsmen had performed the mechanics of the test. On the other hand, Atcheson had performed the clinical sobriety test entirely by himself. The doctor candidly acknowledged that he had little familiarity with the Bogens test and did not consider himself qualified to evaluate the test results. Despite his own disclaimer, and over the defense's objection, Atcheson was permitted to state that the test result meant that the subject had ingested alcohol to some degree.

On cross-examination, Atcheson admitted that sobriety or lack of it is a matter of reaction of the brain to alcohol. He agreed that a number of objective tests are routinely carried out to measure the effect of alcohol on the brain and central nervous system. He had personally carried out those tests on

Sergeant McKeon. Berman named each of the tests, and each time Atcheson confirmed that the test results did not indicate that McKeon was under the influence of alcohol.

After showing that all objective tests for sobriety were normal, Berman led the doctor through the intricacies of the Bogens test. Atcheson acknowledged that there was a subjective element to the final reading and that any number of unknown variables could have influenced the test results. By the time Berman finished with Atcheson, it was clear that he knew far more about the test than the witness did.

In his report, which was later admitted as an exhibit, Dr. Atcheson had answered the question as to whether there was clinical evidence of intoxication by circling "yes," and added by way of addendum: "Possibly under the influence of alcohol but still is in control of himself." As Berman began homing in on the accuracy of that opinion, Atcheson struggled for a way to explain away the seeming inconsistency between his conclusion of intoxication and his objective findings. The best he could do was to state,

> As I recall, to the best of my recollection he answered "I had a few drinks or a few shots of vodka this afternoon." In view of the fact—in view of the finding that I had, namely odor of alcohol, suggestive odor of alcohol on the Sergeant's breath, and the fact that he admitted having had something to drink, I concluded—which is a moot question—he may have possibly been under the influence of alcohol to a sub-clinical degree which no one, of course can determine. Clinically he was not intoxicated.

Just to ensure that the point was clear to the court, Berman hammered one more nail into the coffin of the hapless doctor.

BERMAN: In other words, your conclusion, then and now, in the best opinion you have with a reasonable degree of certainty, is that this man was not intoxicated or under the influence of liquor or anything else on any basis that you could discover, isn't that so?

ATCHESON: Sergeant McKeon was not clinically under the influence of alcohol as far as I could determine.

Colonel Hutchinson then interjected himself into the examination to administer the coup de grace.

HUTCHINSON: We should assume then, doctor, that in view of your answers to the questions that you have been asked that the question No. 7 here,

which says "clinical evidence of intoxication" and the word "yes" and "no"
follow and you circled "yes." You should have circled "no." Is that correct?
ATCHESON: Yes, I would say no.

One cannot help but wonder how much different the findings of the court
of inquiry would have been, how much inflammatory media coverage
would have been squelched, and how much unfavorable publicity of the
Marine Corps would have been averted if Dr. Atcheson had answered the
question about clinical evidence of intoxication correctly on the night of
April 8.

After a thirty-five-minute morning recess, Counselor Berman was again
on his feet with another dramatic announcement:

> Mr. President, Mr. Law Officer, and members, it is with greatest reluctance
> that I am compelled to address myself to you regarding an adjournment at
> the conclusion of today's session at four o'clock until Monday morning. I
> am under an obligation to undertake a mission which I regard as of the
> highest importance connected with this case, and it cannot be done in any
> other way. By that I mean that I could not possibly do it at a time when the
> court would ordinarily not be in session. This is the only opportunity in
> which I could perform this particular mission. You have my assurance that
> I regard it as a matter of importance in connection with this trial so regret-
> ful as I am, I respectfully request, Mr. President, that when court adjourns
> today it adjourn until Monday morning at 9 A.M.

Colonel Hutchinson approved on behalf of the court, and Major Sevier
graciously concurred. Berman was still making the headlines, and this latest
intriguing rendezvous generated its share of speculation.

When the court got back down to business, Captain Weddel was again
recalled to authenticate orders that McKeon had previously received precluding extra instruction by drill instructors "approached from a disciplinary or
harassing point of view." The same order also precluded mass punishment and
"extra instruction" on Sundays except during the evening period in preparation for the following day.

Berman countered this testimony with other arguably conflicting orders,
which mandated that one of the primary objectives of recruit training was
discipline, that the drill instructor was charged with teaching and maintaining discipline. Further, nowhere among the many examples of maltreatment
in the orders was there a reference to swamp marches.

The prosecution's thirty-seventh and final witness would be Lt. Col. David Silvey, the assistant chief of staff at Parris Island, who at the court of inquiry had denied that drill instructors had any discretion to do anything in shaping their recruit platoons other than activities specified in the daily training schedules. Silvey, who was primarily responsible for recruit supervision, had been very defensive at the court of inquiry, no doubt motivated in part by the fact that the Ribbon Creek incident had demonstrated rather conspicuously the absence of any degree of effective supervision.

Silvey told the court that no night marches had been scheduled behind the butts or in the waters of Ribbon Creek. Berman objected that the prosecution's questions to Silvey were vague. He and Captain Klein then engaged in a three- or four-minute exchange. This tactical move not only interrupted Sevier's orderly exchange, it also forced him to frame his questions with greater specificity. Silvey referred to the order precluding entering the marshes and waters in the Elliott's Beach area.

Berman knew that his cross-examination of Silvey had to be tightly structured, with narrow questions designed to preclude the type of semantic obfuscation at which Silvey was adept. Like two wrestlers they confronted one another, each vying for control, Berman reaching out with a question and Silvey evading a direct answer while trying to put his own spin on the response. Finally, Berman's tenacity and inherent ability to control the dialogue pinned Silvey down. He had to admit that there was no order putting any swamp area other than Elliott's Beach out-of-bounds and that one of the primary objectives of recruit training is to teach discipline. Silvey was finally rescued by Major Sevier, who launched a barrage of spirited objections when Berman sought to force Silvey to agree to a number of general propositions about the importance of the drill instructor in the training of recruits. Sevier was ultimately successful in persuading Klein that Berman's questions were vague and hypothetical. Berman sat down having accomplished what he could. Silvey himself had been disciplined. He was not going to suggest to the court as he had in the court of inquiry that a DI had no authority to take disciplinary action.

At 3:55 P.M. on Thursday, July 26, 1956, Major Sevier announced that the prosecution had completed its case. A number of marines, both retired and active, were waiting under subpoena to testify for the defense. On Monday morning, after Berman's mysterious weekend trip, the defense would have the opportunity to present its own witnesses.

# T W E L V E

# The Defendant's Version

T he third week of the trial began promptly at 9:00 A.M. on Monday, July 30, 1956. The first order of business, which Captain Klein had anticipated at the end of the day on Thursday, was a hearing on motions to dismiss by the defense. Berman was hoping to obtain what in civilian courts would be termed a "directed verdict" or a "required finding of not guilty" by the law officer. In effect, the defense would argue that the evidence at the conclusion of the prosecution's case was not sufficient even to present the case to the seven-member jury for deliberation.

Unless the prosecution had introduced substantial evidence that together with all proper inferences to be drawn from it tended to establish every essential element of each charge, the defense was entitled to a finding of not guilty without proceeding further. There was no downside to bringing the motions. If Captain Klein could be persuaded that the prosecution had failed to introduce substantial evidence on any essential element of any of the alleged offenses, he would enter a finding of not guilty on that charge or those charges. The defendant would then have to face whatever charges remained. If the law officer was not so persuaded, the defense was no worse off than if the motions had not been made.

Berman argued that the charge of oppression should fail for lack of any clear definition of the crime. Further, he said, the term in other contexts connoted cruelty or tyranny. He cited the conduct of such colorful historical and literary figures as Nero and Captain Bligh as examples of oppression. McKeon's conduct, by contrast, was the antithesis of cruelty or tyranny. "No man, it seems to me, can be accused of oppressing troops under his command who undertakes to lead them and to subject himself to whatever are the consequences and the rigors; if need be, even the hardships of what has been commanded."

The second motion sought a directed finding on the charge of death by culpable negligence. Berman argued that culpable negligence is a gross and wanton disregard for life and limb almost rising to the level of intent to cause the harm resulting. Berman claimed that McKeon's act of leading his troops into the water "negates any notion of culpability in connection with what subsequently turned out to be tragedy."

The prosecution responded by arguing that "oppression" is a relatively minor offense, essentially excessive use of authority causing harm or injury. Culpable negligence, according to Sevier, simply denotes a higher degree of blameworthy negligence than simple negligence. Sevier then argued that the two field days and the taking of recruits whom the defendant knew to be nonswimmers into dangerous tidal waters at night amounted to both oppression and such a high degree of negligence as to be culpable.

Klein, it seems, had already made his decision because he immediately denied all of Berman's motions. As the court members were present during the argument, each was polled to determine if he objected to the ruling. Inasmuch as the motions raised essentially questions of law, and the primary responsibility of the court was to find the facts, the seven judges deferred to the law officer's ruling. None had any objection to Captain Klein's decision.

The denial of the motions meant that the question of McKeon's guilt or innocence would be decided by the seven-member court. As the prosecution's case was complete, the defense now had an opportunity to call its own witnesses and offer whatever additional evidence might be available to counter the charges or at least attempt to mitigate the punishment.

Berman's first witness was S.Sgt. Elwyn B. Scarborough. He had been a technical sergeant on April 8 but had since lost a stripe for drinking in the barracks with King and McKeon. Scarborough, who was clearly a heavy drinker, was not likely to make a particularly favorable impression on the court; nevertheless, he had firsthand information about the amount of vodka that McKeon had consumed. In response to Berman's questioning, Scarborough related that he had brought a half-full bottle of eighty-proof vodka to McKeon's room at about 11:30 on Sunday morning. He and the accused had remained in the room for about an hour and twenty minutes before leaving together in McKeon's car to go to Mainside.

Berman used Scarborough to establish that he had personally seen some of the platoon members lying down in back of the building. Scarborough testified that after he and McKeon returned to the drill instructor's room, he poured himself two drinks mixed with water. At some point Sergeant King joined them and had one or two drinks. McKeon got a bottle of Coca-Cola and had two drinks. McKeon left at about 12:50 P.M., intending to pick up the platoon's mail. Scarborough joined him, planning to continue his social activities at the Staff NCO Club.

Scarborough's testimony confirmed that the defendant was guilty of drinking in the enlisted men's barracks. However, Berman knew that he had no defense to that relatively minor charge. Instead he focused on showing that McKeon was not inebriated or under the influence on the evening of April 8. If the court members believed that McKeon had led six men to their deaths while even mildly intoxicated, it would be much easier for them to find him guilty of oppression and/or culpable negligence, the two most serious charges. Furthermore, a finding that his actions were influenced by the vodka would likely lead to more severe punishment for whatever charges might ultimately be proved.

The better part of Monday, July 30, was devoted to the testimony of the defense's second witness, WO Leslie E. Volle. Warrant Officer Volle was a survey officer and topographer assigned to Camp Lejeune who had been sent by the Marine Corps to perform a hydrographic survey of Ribbon Creek in the area where the drownings occurred. Berman's primary purpose in calling Volle was to try to corroborate the anticipated testimony of Matthew McKeon that if the platoon had followed his route, the water would never have been over their heads. The defense, that is, was seeking to establish that the drownings occurred because some of the recruits behind McKeon wandered off course and out into deeper water, causing unanticipated panic and chaos.

Volle and his crew had spent ten days in June measuring the depth of the water in the creek and adjoining mudflats at various tide levels and from various vantage points. It appears that Howard Lester conducted the direct examination as at one point Berman briefly left the courtroom while the interrogation was in progress. According to Volle, a man would have had to be near the center of the creek two hours after high tide to get into water over his head. Using the earlier testimony of the former recruits to try to establish the distances marched in each direction, the defense tried to show that McKeon and the men directly following him were never in water more than four or five feet deep. Volle also related that he found no evidence of the trout hole, despite the testimony of numerous former recruits at the court of inquiry and trial that the bottom had suddenly dropped off.

The transcript of the testimony is difficult to follow as the questions and answers were often framed in reference to points on a survey, map, or photograph on display in the courtroom. As the platoon's precise entry point into the creek was unknown, the witness was asked to determine the depth of the water assuming that the column had entered the water at various points.

The prosecution's cross-examination blunted much of the proof that the defense was trying to establish through Volle's neat measurements. Sevier or Haden simply took another arbitrary point where the platoon might have entered the water. Using that hypothesis, Volle's contour map showed that the men could have been in water as deep as 8.3 feet while marching downstream after making the turn. However scientific and accurate the measurements were, they could show conclusively how deep the water was on the men in the stream only if the precise point where the platoon entered the water and its route were known. Because McKeon and all the men he led into the creek were unfamiliar with the area, which was already shrouded in darkness, no one could locate the precise point where the men left dry ground, much less their exact direction and distance once in the water. Without that information, the measurements had little meaning. Volle spent most of a day on the witness stand. Because his findings were based on such a tenuous foundation, it is unlikely that anything except confusion was accomplished by his lengthy testimony.

During the balance of the day the court heard from Lt. Benjamin Kraynick, an orthopedic surgeon attached to the Beaufort Naval Hospital. Kraynick had first examined Matthew McKeon on June 18. Based on the history he gave to the doctor, McKeon apparently sustained a ruptured intervertebral disc on March 12, 1956, while bending over and reaching for his trouser leg. By the time of Dr. Kraynick's examination, McKeon had been relieved of much of his former pain after two months of sleeping on a hard bunk in the brig.

Berman displayed his erudition in the field of anatomy in examining the doctor. Other than that and perhaps generating some sympathy for the defendant, the doctor's testimony added nothing material to the charges pending before the court.

Before calling McKeon to the stand, Berman introduced records from the DI school that confirmed that he had done well, finishing fourteenth out of fifty-five men who completed the four-and-one-half-week course. McKeon's psychiatric screening revealed a man who was unusually stable, with an average amount of hostility, appropriately controlled, and a better than average service record. Again, the evidence had no bearing on the charges before the court. Berman was getting everything he could into the record to persuade the court members, or ultimately the secretary of the navy on appeal, to avoid a harsh punishment.

For more than two weeks, the central character in the drama being played out in the depot schoolhouse had sat tall, slim, and erect, dressed in his neatly pressed summer tropical uniform. His assignment from his lawyer was one of the most physically difficult of his military career. He was to sit at attention throughout the trial except when testifying. He was not to slump, slouch, or move about. Like a sphinx, he sat before his jurors, maintaining a rigid posture, the perfect embodiment of a marine's marine.

After nearly four months of anguished waiting, of guilt and remorse, of separation from his family, of being the target of public vituperation whipped up by relentless media accusations ranging from truthful to slanderous, Matthew McKeon was finally to be allowed to speak. At last he could tell the spectators and reporters in the sweltering courtroom as well as the rest of the world just what happened as he remembered it on April 8, 1956.

Other than his initial statement to Technical Sergeant Cummings, McKeon, on the advice of his lawyers, had made no public statements about the events leading up to the drownings. However, a chance encounter with Maggie Meeks, the mother of Thomas Hardeman, at the outset of the trial provided a moment of high emotion and an opportunity for McKeon to express his remorse. According to a United Press account,

> Mrs. Meeks was pointed out to McKeon who then approached her. "Your son was one of the finest boys in my platoon," he said. "He never gave me any trouble. I am truly sorry for what happened."
>
> Mrs. Meeks replied quietly, "The Master tells us we shouldn't hate anybody. Whether you are guilty or not, your conscience will show you the way."
>
> Tears welled in the eyes of the usually impassive McKeon as he told her: "If I have to be punished, I would rather be punished here than up there." Later Mrs. Meeks consented, at the request of photographers, to shake McKeon's hand.

At mid-morning on Tuesday, July 31, Emile Zola Berman arose to announce: "If it please you all, the defense desires to call the accused." Captain Klein was prepared for this moment. He looked directly at McKeon and advised him of his constitutional right to remain silent. He informed McKeon that if he chose not to testify it would not count against him, nor would it be considered an admission of guilt. Furthermore, if he chose to testify he would be subject to cross-examination by the prosecutors. For the record, the law officer recommended that the accused take the time to consult with his lawyer and then advise the court.

Such a suggestion was, of course, a formality, as a decision so critical had undoubtedly been thoroughly discussed, evaluated, and long since decided. Berman, ever skilled at milking any situation for a few drops of drama, arose and announced: "Mr. President, Officers of the Court, Mr. Law Officer, we have consulted. It is the Sergeant's desire to take the stand and testify fully and truthfully."

Berman gently guided his client through a series of preliminary questions designed to allow McKeon to work off some of his anxiety before getting to the critical testimony pertaining to the issues before the court. Equally important, Berman wanted to ensure that the seven men who would pass judgment in the case were aware that the accused was neither a sadist nor a criminal.

Responding to his attorney's questions, McKeon described his family and the ages of his children. He told of joining the navy at age 17 in 1942 and serving aboard the carrier *Essex,* which participated in operations "around Bougainville, Rabaul, the Gilberts, Marshalls, Mariannas, Iwo Jima, up through Okinawa"— glorious names that linked the witness with the Marine Corps heroes who fought in the Pacific theater during World War II.

McKeon told the court that he received an honorable discharge from the navy in 1946 and enlisted in the Marine Corps in 1948. Berman used McKeon's own experiences at Parris Island to begin laying the foundation for one of the major prongs of his defense strategy—that swamp marches had long been an accepted practice in boot camp.

BERMAN: During the course of your boot training here at Parris Island in 1948 was your platoon taken into the marshes and boondocks, swamp and marshes of Parris Island?

MCKEON: Yes, sir, they were.

BERMAN: Once, or more than once?

MCKEON: On several occasions, sir.

BERMAN: And were you taken in by a superior?

MCKEON: Yes, sir.

BERMAN: Who?

MCKEON: The drill instructor, sir.

BERMAN: In connection with the swamps, marshes or waters you were taken into, where was it?

MCKEON: The first time I got acquainted with the swamps or marshes was with the platoon in the Elliott's Beach area, and the second occasion was behind the barracks at the rifle range.

BERMAN: How high was the water . . . into which you were taken as a recruit?

MCKEON: Just a little above my knees, sir.

BERMAN: Was there anything done in connection with you being in that area at that time?

MCKEON: Yes, sir. There was a blast on this whistle, squad leader's whistle, which would indicate an air raid, and we all had to hit the deck.

BERMAN: In this water and mud?

MCKEON: Yes, sir.

McKeon went on to describe his marine service record. After boot camp and a tour of duty at sea, he taught fire team tactics and squad tactics at basic officer's school in Quantico, Virginia, until his enlistment expired. Promptly reenlisting, he served briefly at Camp Lejeune before being sent to Korea in December 1952 for a combat assignment as sergeant of a machine-gun platoon.

After the Korean War and a brief tour at Quantico, McKeon reenlisted and volunteered for DI school, which he completed in February 1956. Following a brief observation period with another platoon, he and Sergeant King were assigned as junior drill instructors to work under Staff Sergeant Huff in training a group of raw recruits who had just arrived at the receiving barracks and would be joined together to form Platoon 71.

BERMAN: And in the early phase, the early weeks of the training of Platoon 71, did they go through what you had been taught at Drill Instructor's School as a stage known as the "shock and fear" stage?

MCKEON: They certainly did, sir.

BERMAN: What was the state of discipline of these raw recruits during the early period when they were going through the shock and fear stage?

MCKEON: They were an outstanding platoon.

BERMAN: Tell us about this platoon as you observed it from that point on until this tragic April 8.

MCKEON: Well, when we first picked this platoon up, we immediately put them in the shock and fear stage. That is usually not any violence or anything, but we keep them moving all the time. Up until about a week before we went to the range, maybe a few days before we went to the range, you could see the platoon kind of slacking off. They had spirit, they had good morale in it, but I noticed the platoon was more or less working in groups. I suppose you could call it a buddy-buddy system. They weren't working as a unit, and they were told about it. . . .

BERMAN: What did you notice about the discipline of the platoon during this period from right before you got on the range, and as it was developing while you were on the range?

MCKEON: . . . Tell them to fall out, and they would fall out but their manner was slow. In shock and fear if a man was slow you could walk over him, but then they came out of the shock and fear stage, and maybe started coming out too slow. . . . They would fall out and when they got out there maybe a quarter would be scratching their buttocks or looking up at the airplanes, or whatever they might be doing when they all knew they had to fall in at attention. I would go up and correct them. I might ask if it was necessary to tell them the position of attention, and maybe give them a slight slap to put them in the position of attention. . . . Anyway, little things like that was adding up and adding up. . . . Sgt. Scarborough brought [it to] my attention, I didn't think it was that bad, but he said that he had had quite a few platoons out there on the range, and he said this was without a doubt the poorest disciplined platoon he ever had.

McKeon related the efforts he had used to try to restore the platoon's ebbing team spirit. Traditional forms of discipline or punishment such as push-ups, stationary double-time drill, and getting in and out of the rack worked only for brief intervals.

BERMAN: Well now, with that situation brewing . . . , the platoon lacking in both discipline and spirit, was that a matter of concern to you?

MCKEON: It certainly was, sir.

BERMAN: What was your desire? That is, what was it you wanted to make of these men?

MCKEON: Well, I liked to have an honor platoon like any other drill instructor would, I suppose, but I always thought if they went off this island knowing something about discipline then they would go off the island with something.

BERMAN: You mean you figured that was a foundation they would have?

MCKEON: I always believed without discipline you have no foundation regardless. What you may put on top of that foundation in later years, the kid may become the best technician the Marine Corps ever laid eyes on, but when the chips were down if they didn't have that discipline, the thing would crumble.

After the morning recess, Berman led McKeon through a detailed recitation of the significant events of April 8. In response to his lawyer's questions, McKeon outlined to the court the events that led up to the moment of panic in Ribbon Creek.

For reasons he never explained, McKeon had reported for duty at the rifle range at 5:00 A.M. on Saturday, April 7. He was scheduled to work the weekend but was not required to go on duty until approximately 11:30 A.M. when the platoon returned from the rifle range. Saturday afternoon was devoted to cleaning shooting gear and weapons and washing clothes on the cement wash racks behind the barracks.

On Saturday evening the Catholic boys had the option to attend confession. The platoon was then marched a short distance down Wake Boulevard to the Lyceum to watch the evening movie. McKeon spent the night in the drill instructor's room adjacent to the squad bay where his recruits were quartered during their brief stay at the rifle range.

He related the details of the events of Sunday, April 8, including the visit by Scarborough; the embarrassment at seeing many of his platoon crapped out behind the barracks; the two field days; the drinks from Scarborough's half-empty vodka bottle; the brief stop at the Staff NCO Club while picking up the mail; and the frustrated interactions with Langone, Wood, Maloof, and McPherson that ultimately led to his decision to try to restore the platoon's spirit with a march into the chilly waters of Ribbon Creek.

As he described it, the platoon left the front of Building 761 and crossed Wake Boulevard on a diagonal and headed across Baker range near the five hundred yard line. Immediately in front of the column was a water sprinkler. McKeon "gave an order not to go around it but to go through it," knowing that the men were going to be far wetter before the evening was over. Marching in route step with the drill instructor at the head of the formation, the platoon continued on to the Baker range butts, turned ninety degrees to the right, and marched behind the butts. On arriving behind the adjoining Charlie range butts, McKeon ordered a ninety-degree turn to the left. The column was now approximately one hundred feet from Ribbon Creek and headed directly toward it.

McKeon led the platoon over the bank and down two to two and a half feet into the water. After a couple of steps he was in water up to his knees with mud over his ankles. He then turned the column right ninety degrees so that it was marching parallel to the bank at the edge of the stream, five or six feet out from shore. Gerald Langone was dispatched to the rear to ensure that everyone followed. The column followed a course parallel to the bank for a distance McKeon estimated to the court to be twenty-five to thirty feet upstream. He then made a sweeping curve to his left and began leading the formation back in the direction from which they had come but ten or fifteen feet farther out into the stream.

As the men headed downstream, the water became continually deeper, until it reached chest height. He asked if everyone was all right and asked where the nonswimmers were, to which he heard several men respond, "Here, sir." McKeon testified that there was moonlight reflected on the water, prompting him to tell the recruits around him that if they were crossing a body of water to keep close to the shoreline and in the shadows. He then saw two men carrying a petrified Lewis Leake. He tried to calm Leake but to no avail, so he "told the two guys that had him to take Leake in the back and watch [him]."

After resuming his position at the head of the column, McKeon was looking toward the bank, intending to come out at a drainage ditch near where they had originally entered, when he suddenly heard a "big, mad commotion" to his right rear. He saw figures "thrashing in the water." After ordering everyone out, he swam toward the group splashing in the water. He pulled one young man in about ten feet toward the shore and started back out toward a boy who appeared to be under water except for the top of his head; three or four other recruits were splashing in the water beside him. Just then,

this other boy, this other man, he latched onto me—well, I can't just say—it surprised me—and when I did realize what happened the man had hold of my neck. I tried to break his hold, and every time I started treading water the both of us went down. We went down, and as we came up I told the guy to keep his head and I'd get him in . . . he wouldn't leave go, . . . and he wasn't saying anything, wasn't saying a thing. He went down a second time, and the second time he [we?] went down it seemed to me like he [we?] went down further than the first time. While down there all I was thinking of was getting to the top. I was pulling toward the top and this kid let go; this kid let go and that's the last I seen of him.

When he resurfaced for the second time, McKeon told the court, the water was still. His composure now shaken, tears streaming down his cheeks, McKeon continued recounting the painful details.

I swam around awhile, and I knew then that I lost some men and I remember saying: "Oh my God, what have I done?" I swam in towards shore, and I was met by two men. I believe one of them was Private Martinez. He wanted to go back and start diving for them, and I told him, "No, there is no use. We will never be able to find them."

. . . I knew when I was out there struggling with this boy that there was a current. There was a current, and at the time there was no light. There was no light, and I figured if I did get a detail together and start to go out there diving for them, there was a possibility I may have lost another one.

While McKeon was gathering his strength and his wits, he told the court, Technical Sergeant Taylor appeared. McKeon identified himself to Taylor and then returned to the barracks with the bedraggled remnants of his platoon. Moments later he was placed under arrest by Captain Patrick and ordered into the drill instructor's room. As he dropped his jacket on the floor he noticed the vodka bottle, which he picked up and placed beside the commode in the adjacent head. Moments later the bottle was retrieved by Corporal Lyons.

After the sobriety tests were performed at the dispensary, McKeon was taken to the brig and from there to the provost marshal. After advising McKeon of his right to remain silent because of a potential charge involving homicide, Provost Marshal McLeod asked if McKeon would go out to the area where he thought the people went under. "I told him if it would help I would go out, and we did go out." At approximately 2:00 A.M. on April 9, "we went out and I pointed in the vicinity where I thought they went down."

Often a witness has made prior statements that are not fully truthful or are inconsistent with his trial testimony. Good trial lawyers bring out and explain such inconsistencies during the direct examination. In that manner, the witness can be asked to explain his inconsistency while appearing forthright and honest in acknowledging any error in what was previously said. That approach also preempts the opposing lawyer from portraying the witness as a liar by extracting the admission of inconsistent statements on cross-examination.

Berman knew that certain portions of the statement given by McKeon to Technical Sergeant Cummings pertaining to events that occurred on April 8 were not fully candid. Here is how he handled the inconsistencies:

BERMAN: And now it says here that "Shortly after they had started, that is, started the morning field day, I had to stop them and take them to chow." Did you secure the field day?

MCKEON: No, sir, I didn't secure the field day.

BERMAN: Did you take them to chow?

MCKEON: No, sir, I didn't take them to chow.

BERMAN: Is there any doubt about that at all that it was Sgt. King who took them over?

MCKEON: No sir. It was Sgt. King who took them to chow, and I told him to secure the field day, and take them to chow.

BERMAN: Have you got any explanation of how that got into that statement?

MCKEON: Well, I didn't want to involve anyone else's name regarding the activities during the day.

BERMAN: You mean the drinking?

MCKEON: The drinking.

Berman had succinctly flushed out the potentially damaging inconsistencies between McKeon's statement and his testimony and allowed his client to explain that he was willing to shoulder more than his share of the blame for the drinking in order not to injure his companions. Such a forthright admission could hardly harm him in the eyes of the court.

Having disposed of the problem of the inconsistent statements, counsel immediately shifted the subject to allow the accused to address the central issues in the case.

BERMAN: Well, were you at any time that day, morning, noon, night or evening, either drunk, intoxicated, or even slightly under the influence of any liquor whatsoever?

MCKEON: No, sir, I wasn't.

BERMAN: And what was your purpose in taking the men on this exercise that night?

MCKEON: Well, as I said before, sir, we tried several different varieties of teaching discipline and nothing seemed to work. It was just a mass [sic], a big cycle over and over and over, and I figured we would take them down to the swamps and show them[;] that way if they went down and got a little wet and muddy it may put a little more spirit in the platoon also, and I believed it would build up morale in that platoon if they did something different. The main thing though was to take them down there, and the next time I would tell them to do something or anyone told them to do something they would have done it.

BERMAN: Had any officer ... or anybody ... ever told you or instructed you that you were not to take men into the boondocks?

MCKEON: No, sir, no one ever instructed me on it.

Berman then moved on to introduce further evidence of prior swamp marches. He asked McKeon a number of questions about his conversations with other drill instructors about different ways of teaching discipline and "what the practice or practices were that were discussed." In the absence of an objection to this question, which called for inadmissible hearsay evidence, McKeon responded, "Well, it was discussed as regards taking the platoon into the swamps and marshes, around different battalion areas."

After the next question, Sevier objected and was sustained. He then moved to strike "the testimony pertaining to any such practice." Captain Klein permitted the testimony to stand "subject to some connection," a curious ruling that seems irrelevant to the admissibility of hearsay statements. Needless to say, the issue of "connection" was soon lost in the shuffle. Berman had succeeded in getting evidence into the record that McKeon knew of discussions about prior swamp marches. (Ironically, the evidence would probably have been admissible for the purpose of establishing McKeon's state of mind; that is, whether he had heard of prior swamp marches, whether or not they had actually occurred. His subjective belief that such a practice existed and may even have been condoned would have some bearing on whether or not he was culpably negligent. But Berman never pressed the point because he had what he wanted when the law officer allowed the testimony to stand.)

The direct examination closed with a measurement from the floor to the point on the witness's chest that he claimed was the maximum height of the water on him before the panic broke out. The tape measure indicated that the water depth was never more than four feet, eight inches.

At 3:45 P.M., Sergeant McKeon stepped down from the witness stand. He had spent nearly a full day telling his version of the events. Tomorrow morning the prosecution would find out how well that story held up on cross-examination.

\* \* \*

Court opened at 8:40 A.M. on Wednesday, August 1, with Sergeant McKeon seated in the witness chair facing Major Sevier. To the extent that the arid print of the transcript reveals, McKeon had performed well on direct examination. His answers were candid and forthright as he explained what had occurred and why he acted as he did, without seeking to evade responsibility for his conduct. The defense team seems to have accomplished all they could have hoped for in pursuing their overall strategy: to show that despite the disastrous outcome of the swamp march, the accused was neither a sadist nor a brute, but rather a decent human being who had made a terrible error of judgment that warranted convictions only on substantially lesser charges.

Major Sevier's cross-examination tended to be repetitious and argumentative at times, but he was effective in drawing out a number of admissions and statements that bolstered the prosecution's case. McKeon acknowledged that he had slapped a number of recruits for disciplinary reasons, that drinking in front of a recruit was a bad gesture (although he had earlier claimed that the cap was on the bottle when he raised it to his lips in David McPherson's presence), and that he had never previously been in Ribbon Creek or made any prior reconnaissance of it. He conceded that once in the water he never ordered the platoon to remain in a column and that he asked where the nonswimmers were after the men were in the water, figuring that if anything happened there would be enough men around them to prevent any difficulties.

Despite the confrontational nature of Sevier's examination and the damaging facts McKeon was forced to acknowledge, his responses were unevasive and without a hint of duplicity. In one very telling exchange during which the prosecutor was attempting to show inconsistencies between the statement given to Technical Sergeant Cummings on April 9 and the court testimony, McKeon denied recalling just what he had said in his earlier statement. Sevier continued to press:

SEVIER: But you signed all that?
MCKEON: I would have signed anything, sir. I would have walked to the gallows—

Shortly thereafter the record reflects that "the accused withdrew from the witness stand and took his seat at counsel table." He had told his story for better or worse. Some of what he had testified to would strengthen the prosecution's case and would be used in the closing argument to seek convictions on the charges. On balance, however, it seems that McKeon's day and a half on the witness stand worked to his benefit. Most of his self-damaging testimony already was or would have been established by other evidence. Despite the gravity of the offenses, the members of the court had a full opportunity to make a personal evaluation of this combat veteran with an exemplary record, who must have impressed them as a decent and remorseful man speaking to them with candor and humility.

In modern trial practice there are few surprises. Relevant documents and witness lists are exchanged and witnesses are deposed before the opening statements are ever made. In the 1950s, however, very little pretrial discovery was permitted. Consequently, neither side knew just what evidence would be offered and who would be testifying. Such secrecy prevented either party from being fully prepared to cross-examine the opponent's witnesses, particularly if these witnesses were not known to them. On the other hand, the secrecy often produced suspense, and suspense makes for good drama. Suspense and drama were among Emile Zola Berman's strong suits. Throughout the trial he had alluded to mysterious trips, calls from the commandant, and other events that were being played out behind the scenes.

When McKeon concluded his testimony and resumed his seat, Colonel Hutchinson asked the defense team when they preferred to take the morning recess. Berman immediately set the reporters and courtroom abuzz with another dramatic announcement: "I believe there will be a phone call that will set our schedule a little better. That will be between quarter of 11:00 and 11:00 o'clock. Thank you." Colonel Hutchinson concurred, and Berman let the matter hang in the air without further explanation.

Having a few minutes left before the recess, the defense recalled Warrant Officer Volle. Volle established that other creeks and streams about Parris Island were similar to Ribbon Creek in tidal conditions, depth, and vegetation. The testimony had no value in and of itself; its purpose was to lay a foundation for further anticipated testimony that swamp marches into other waters similar to Ribbon Creek were common practices by Parris Island drill instructors.

Before Sevier could cross-examine Volle, the anticipated morning recess was called. Berman's request that court not reconvene until 1:15 was granted without objection. Apparently the defense counsel, Captain Klein, and Colonel Hutchinson had been tipped off as to what was about to occur.

# THIRTEEN

# Pulling Out All the Stops

W hen court resumed at 1:15 P.M. on Wednesday, August 1, Emile
Zola Berman rose to announce,

If it please you, Mr. President and members of the court, Mr. Law
Officer, I ask leave to interrupt the proposed cross-examination of the last
witness, Mr. Warrant Officer Volle, and I state now the defense desires at this
time to call General Pate, Commandant of the United States Marine Corps,
to stand as a witness for the defense.

Randolph McCall Pate was born in Port Royal, South Carolina, only a
fifteen-minute boat ride from Parris Island. He was commissioned a second
lieutenant in the Marine Corps in 1921 and rose through the ranks in the ensuing years. His experience was largely in staff positions; he had only limited
combat experience in his long career. In January 1956, President Dwight D.
Eisenhower appointed Pate commandant of the Marine Corps.

General Pate was not held in high regard by those who served under him.
Allan R. Millett, whose authoritative *Semper Fidelis* surveys more than two
hundred years of Marine Corps history, offered the following critique of
Pate's qualifications for the Corps's top position:

To guide the Marine Corps through the "M" series reorganization and to
absorb the helicopter into all aspects of Corps operations were tasks that
called for leadership of the highest order, but in General Randolph McCall
Pate, its twenty-first Commandant, the Corps did not have such a leader.
Sponsored for the commandancy by General Shepard, a fellow VMI graduate

and distant cousin, Pate had rich experience in staff jobs but little of the military stature and moral authority necessary to command the Corps. . . . The Corps fell heir to a Commandant who combined the worst habits of garrison traditionalism and the new managerial-bureaucratic style. Unlike his predecessors, Pate had not run the risks of command in extended combat. . . . Being a part of the "1st Division club" . . . gave Pate an aura of strength he did not fully deserve.

In all likelihood, the mysterious telephone call that Berman was expecting between 10:45 and 11:00 A.M. that morning was to confirm that the commandant was en route to Parris Island and his estimated arrival time. When General Pate arrived, he was promptly escorted into Berman's makeshift office. Sergeant McKeon was waiting in a corner, and an array of press photographers was in another corner. Berman introduced the commandant to his awestruck client, the very same man Pate had promised would be punished to the fullest extent of the law only a few months earlier.

General Pate extended his hand and greeted McKeon. "Hello, Sergeant. I'm glad to see you. I'm sorry we meet under such circumstances. How are you?"

"I'm fine, sir."

"I'm glad to help you in any way I can to see that the interests of justice are met."

"Thank you, sir."

"Best of luck to you and I hope everything turns out all right."

General Pate, by proclaiming that the Marine Corps was on trial, may have skillfully averted a congressional investigation. But those very words enmeshed him in an inescapable dilemma when it came to the trial of Matthew McKeon. Emile Berman had met secretly on several occasions with the commandant and had forced him to recognize the unpalatable alternatives before him. He must either testify on behalf of McKeon or suffer the negative publicity the Marine Corps would face if Berman were forced to take Pate at his word and really put the Marine Corps on trial for its long-accepted practices in recruit training. Against the advice of many of his staff, Pate finally consented to appear at the trial on McKeon's behalf.

Pate sought to mask the impotence of his position as well as his embarrassment with a feigned air of jocularity. He arrived in the courtroom sporting sunglasses, which he never removed during his testimony. The low esteem in which he was held by many of his subordinates was reflected in the faces of the six marine officers on the court, who sat impassively and looked elsewhere as their commandant entered the courtroom.

Berman, obviously relishing his coup in pressuring the Corps's top brass and one of his client's most outspoken accusers to appear for the defense, fawned over his star witness. The following exchange illustrates the feigned attempts at casual humor, which only detracted from the seriousness and dignity of the proceedings.

BERMAN: I show you this paper, General, and ask you whether or not this brochure was put out as the official document of a policy by your command by you, as Commandant.

PATE: I published and signed that, yes.

BERMAN: Will you sign that for me, and I will take it home as my autograph?

PATE: I will be glad to. Do you have a pen?

BERMAN: I will take it in pencil—as this may have to be preserved for posterity, we'd better have it in ink, General.

(The witness signs document referred to and hands to defense counsel.)

Berman (Returning to counsel table): Excuse my back, General.

PATE: The best looking part. Touché?

BERMAN: Touché.

PATE: He will probably get back at me before he gets through with me.

After that initial spate of foolishness, Berman and his witness got down to business. Pate outlined his career from his early years as a "rat" at Virginia Military Institute through his thirty-five-year service in the Marine Corps, rising from a second lieutenant to its top officer. He acknowledged that the mission of the Marine Corps is to prepare for war, that discipline is the single most important factor in training, and that methods of training may vary depending on the individuals and platoons being trained.

Because General Pate was a witness called by the defense, Berman was not permitted to ask leading questions—questions, that is, that contained within them the desired answer. On direct examination, properly framed questions should be of the "who," "what," "where," "when" variety that do not suggest the answer to the witness. If the opposing lawyer made no objection when objectionable questions were asked, however, the law officer was not going to intervene.

After General Pate had outlined his military background and responded to the questions about general concepts of training, Berman audaciously began to ask a series of highly improper questions. The first was a lengthy hypothetical inquiry.

> Now, if you as Commandant, or the commanding officer at any level, were asked to assume that a junior drill instructor, on a week-end, that is having a week-end duty with his platoon, in his view, finding the platoon undisciplined, lacking spirit, with an opinion that perhaps the best way is to get through with Parris Island without regard to other members of the platoon—speaking now of recruits, not the drill instructor—and where various methods of attempting to instill discipline had been tried, such as lecturing and talking about the purpose of training, calisthenics, field days and measures of that type, and all had proved signally unsuccessful, so that this drill instructor, in an attempt to teach discipline and instill spirit and develop an esprit de corps, on an unscheduled march, marched his men on a Sunday night from a barracks possibly less than a thousand yards across a rifle range to a swamp and marsh and creek, quite apart from the result, would you equate such a march led by him as being oppression of troops?

The question was objectionable on multiple grounds. First and foremost, witnesses may ordinarily testify only as to facts of which they have firsthand knowledge. If the facts are of a technical nature, such as engineering principles, accounting practices, or medical procedures, a properly qualified expert may assist the jury (in this case the seven-member court) in reaching a decision by offering expert opinions based on the facts in evidence. In order for an expert's opinion to be admissible, however, the subject must be one about which ordinary laypeople would not have knowledge and would need assistance in making their ultimate determination. In the present case there was no complex factual situation requiring the assistance of an expert witness. The question of whether or not the accused was guilty of oppression was the very decision the court was charged with determining. Berman wasn't attempting to offer expert testimony to assist the court in explaining or understanding a complex fact pattern; he was trying to usurp from the court the very decision it was uniquely responsible for making. There was neither need nor lawful basis for expert opinion on that ultimate function.

The harm in allowing the commandant to answer such a hypothetical question in the context of a court-martial was compounded by the very nature of the military structure. In civilian life, if an "expert" is permitted to offer his or her opinion on an issue reserved for the jury, the jury members can give the opinion the weight they believe it deserves with impunity. In a military context, however, the word of a commanding officer is not easily rejected. For men such as those sitting on the court, whose careers hung on the reports of their superior officers, an opinion expressed by the highest-ranking officer of the entire military unit might well be deemed little short of an order.

Sevier should have been on his feet to object the instant the lengthy hypothetical question was finished. Instead, he sat on his hands, allowing Pate to respond, "I wouldn't call that oppression, no."

After a number of leading questions, to which there was still no objection, Berman decided to gamble that he could get away with asking the ultimate question for which had had enlisted the commandant's assistance. Sevier finally made a move.

BERMAN: I want to ask you, sir, in your official capacity as Commandant of the United States Marine Corps, had you been permitted to deal with Sergeant McKeon, what, in your considered view, would have been the action you would have taken?

SEVIER: I object. That goes to the ultimate issue, and that is in the province of these gentlemen sitting over here in the court and not of this witness.

KLEIN: Objection sustained.

Berman, who had labored for weeks to bring the commandant around to his side, was not about to quit. He tried rephrasing the same question any number of ways, but each time the objection was sustained. However, Sevier's objections, which related only to the witness testifying to the ultimate issue, never addressed the fundamental objection that should have disposed of the entire line of inquiry—that there was no need in this case for any expert opinion because the facts the court would weigh in reaching its decision were neither technical nor complex.

Captain Klein hinted that a hypothetical question might be in order as the commandant obviously could not base an opinion on evidence he had not heard. Sevier fell into the inadvertently laid trap. He objected and claimed that the initial form of the hypothetical question was improper, while acquiescing in permitting the witness to offer an opinion once the question was properly stated. Berman jumped at the opportunity and framed a lengthy hypothetical question based on many of the salient facts in evidence. He concluded with, "Now assuming those facts . . . what action, sir, in your opinion, stated with a reasonable degree of certainty, would you have taken?"

Sevier again objected on the ground that the answer would invade the province of the court on the ultimate issue in the case. This time Klein overruled him but offered him the opportunity to pose a hypothetical question based on the evidence he considered most significant to the prosecution. Sevier took his defeat in stride, perhaps not even recognizing it as such, by declaring, "There's no argument about the opinion evidence being acceptable." There was not, but there should have been.

Pate, who three months earlier had expressly adopted the findings of the court of inquiry and had promised that McKeon would be punished to the fullest extent allowed under the Uniform Code of Military Justice, squirmed and equivocated before suggesting to the court what he now thought should be done.

In my opinion I probably—of course there's no final say as to what an individual would do under all circumstances and, of course, I have not had the evidence that has been introduced in this court. I think you have to take into consideration. It's evident this platoon, this drill sergeant did drink some vodka and I assume that it was against the regulations, the conditions under which he did it, I don't know. I think maybe I would take a stripe away from him for a thing like that. It's a fairly serious thing, of course, particularly when you are dealing with recruits.

As to the remaining part of it, that's a little fuzzy and hazy to me as to just what transpired but I suspect I would have transferred him away for stupidity, or, if you want to be a little more polite, for lack of judgment. I would have probably written in his service record book that under no conditions would this Sergeant ever drill recruits again. I think I would let it go at that. That's not a final answer I know, that's about what my judgment would be.

In his cross-examination Major Sevier devoted about ten minutes to rather innocuous questions. He established only that the commandant thought taking untrained troops into unfamiliar territory where there was a possibility of serious personal harm showed a lack of good judgment.

One of the most powerful weapons to undercut the effectiveness of a witness on cross-examination is to impeach his credibility by showing that he made prior statements inconsistent with his testimony under oath. General Pate had previously stated to the Committee on Armed Services of the House of Representatives, as well as to the public, that the accused should be punished "to the fullest extent allowed by our Uniform Code of Military Justice."

He had expressly adopted the findings of the court of inquiry, which recommended that McKeon be charged with oppression and culpable negligence resulting in death as well as the lesser charges. He concurred with the court of inquiry that the accused should face a general court-martial, a procedure reserved only for the most serious offenses under the code.

The prosecution could have gone through each of these prior statements, established that the commandant had uttered them as well as the basis for each, and then shown the degree to which Pate equivocated or completely reversed himself with his comments and recommendation that McKeon lose one stripe. (Sergeants Scarborough and King had already lost one stripe in earlier proceedings simply for drinking in the barracks, the least significant of the charges faced by McKeon.)

Captain Haden, who was assisting Major Sevier with the prosecution, wanted to subject Pate to a vigorous cross-examination. As he later described it, "My theory was if they change their testimony burn them like any other witness." According to Haden, Sevier was not afraid to cross-examine the commandant but had made a strategic decision that doing so would further damage the Marine Corps by embarrassing its top officer in a manner that would receive national attention.

Captain Klein must have realized that the commandant was being allowed to escape from prior rhetoric that was entirely at odds with his courtroom testimony. He must also have known that as a naval officer, the consequences he might face for challenging the head of the Marine Corps would be far less than they would be for one of the commandant's own subordinates. Further, Klein may have realized his error in allowing the latitude he had given Berman in his direct examination. Consequently, Klein began asking the questions the prosecutor might normally have been expected to ask.

Berman immediately realized that his valuable witness might have to face an unpleasant examination. He muddied up the waters sufficiently to distract Klein and cause him to back off and allow the commandant to leave the courtroom virtually unscathed.

KLEIN: General, did you take any action on a court of inquiry which inquired into the circumstances of the drowning of six men at Parris Island on April 8, 1956?

PATE: I did, I reviewed the court of inquiry.

KLEIN: And did you take any action concerning a recommendation for disciplinary action regarding the accused in this case?

PATE: I made a recommendation to the Secretary of the Navy that the recommended action of the court of inquiry be implemented by him.

KLEIN: And do you recall what the recommended action—the recommendation for discipline of the court of inquiry was concerning the accused?

BERMAN: I object to that, that's no longer opinion evidence, and that's like the matter of putting before the court the action of a grand jury on the limited basis in which they know the facts.

KLEIN: I appreciate that but I do want to know whether at a prior time the same expert made another recommendation and other than the opinion of the expert you have submitted.

BERMAN: As I understand the question to the General, it is does he know what the recommended action of the Board of Inquiry was.

KLEIN: He said it should be implemented, the testimony is that he stated it should be implemented.

BERMAN: I am suggesting to you respectfully that your question to the General is "What was the recommended action?"

KLEIN: I will withdraw the question on the basis of your—and I instruct—basis of your recommendation and I instruct the members of the court to disregard my question. I now ask you, did you recommend to the Secretary of the Navy that a recommendation for trial by general court martial of the accused be implemented?

PATE: I did, yes.

KLEIN: That's all.

Berman then mopped up whatever minor damage Captain Klein's questions may have caused.

BERMAN: In line with the questions asked of you by the Honorable Law Officer, does that in any way change the views you have expressed here in response to the questions asked of you by me?

PATE: Not at all, no.

General Pate left the courtroom at the afternoon recess, fifty minutes after he had entered. It would remain to be seen what effect his dramatic turnabout and recommendation that Matthew McKeon receive a relatively innocuous punishment would have on the seven inscrutable men sitting in judgment.

Berman had yet another ace up his sleeve, but before that witness would be available he had to fill up some time and try to make some further points with the court. He began with Cdr. Maurus Cook, the Catholic chaplain.

After McKeon had been released from the Parris Island brig on May 23 and allowed to return home to his family, he was assigned to serve as an assistant to Father Cook during the day. He had turned to Cook for spiritual help in facing his anguish and depression after his arrest. Forty years later, still choked with emotion, McKeon recalls those dark days. "If it weren't for the people and their support, I wouldn't have made it. . . . I had a very good man down in Parris Island. The chaplain, Cook, Father Cook, he was very supportive."

Father Cook was called as a character witness. He testified that he had found McKeon to be "truthful . . . dependable . . . kind and gentle and deeply religious. He is a family man. Very much devoted to his family, his wife, and children, and secondarily, devoted to the Marine Corps."

On the Tuesday of the second week of trial, Berman had requested that 108 former marines be subpoenaed to testify. By that afternoon he had reduced his demand to 82 and was willing to pare the list to just 18 provided he had the option of calling more witnesses after the 18 had testified. Eight days later, after Father Cook was excused, Berman again addressed the court. He asked for an adjournment for the day at 2:50 P.M. and announced that he anticipated concluding his case the following day.

Obviously Berman was not going to call eighteen witnesses in one day. It is impossible to know whether he ever intended to call the eighteen witnesses he wanted subpoenaed; it may have been just a grandstand play. The most likely explanation seems to be that he wanted the eighteen people available, leaving him with the option to call them if they were needed. His own client had held up well on the stand, and the commandant had given Berman everything he wanted with his testimony. His defense was going as well as he could have hoped, so perhaps the time had come to start wrapping up his case.

As court opened on Thursday, August 2, Berman called on Sgt. Leland Blanding, a twenty-two-year-old former drill instructor who had trained eight recruit platoons at Parris Island in the preceding twenty-eight months. Blanding testified that he took at least two platoons into the swamps and marshes in 1954, in water from knee to neck deep, in both day and night in order to instill discipline. Sevier tried to intimidate him by suggesting that Blanding's admission might make him liable for prosecution. The witness was unmoved, despite knowing that his career may have been on the line. Whatever his judgment may have been as a drill instructor, he was a courageous man.

James Flaherty, a former drill instructor for fifteen months in 1953 and 1954, followed Blanding to the witness stand. Flaherty claimed to have taken all ten of his platoons on disciplinary marches into the swamps in the early evening behind the rifle range barracks, behind the Third Battalion training grounds, on the road to Elliott's Beach, and behind the butts of Able range in water ranging from knee to chest deep.

When Berman attempted to introduce through this witness statements allegedly made by other drill instructors about taking their recruits into the swamps, marshes, and waters to teach discipline, Sevier properly objected. The question was improperly leading, called for inadmissible hearsay, and was indefinite as to time and place. Klein, who had earlier sustained several prosecution objections, reversed himself, suggesting that Flaherty's testimony as to what he had heard on that subject be admitted "for what it is worth."

After Blanding and Flaherty testified, Berman called his final witness. When General Chesty Puller marched through the door, a thrill of electricity ran through the courtroom.

Lt. Gen. Lewis B. "Chesty" Puller is perhaps the most colorful and valorous marine ever to have worn the uniform. A graduate of Parris Island boot training in 1918, he was commissioned shortly thereafter. Puller spent most of his military career in France, China, Nicaragua, and other hot spots around the world where marines were called to serve. Never a desk man, he was in the thick of the fighting in the South Pacific during World War II and later in Korea. Tenacious and direct, he was revered for his fearless leadership in one combat mission after another.

Puller had just retired to his farm in Virginia when news of the Ribbon Creek incident broke. In the early days, when McKeon was being eviscerated in much of the press and the Marine Corps was taking a public relations beating as well, marines from all over the country had written to Puller to express their concern about the future of the Corps. Somehow the word had filtered down to Berman that this near mythical hero might be available to help McKeon's cause. Berman delegated to Thomas Costello the task of calling Puller.

With some trepidation, Costello put through a long-distance call to Puller's home. Mrs. Puller answered. Costello identified himself and asked to speak with the general, who, he was told, was out in the backyard. Costello still remembers vividly hearing Mrs. Puller's deep Virginia drawl beckoning "Chayes-ty, Chayes-ty." When Puller came to the phone, Costello announced his reason for calling and pleaded with him to come to Parris Island. In keeping with his character, there was no hesitation in the general's response. "You tell me when and I'll be there."

After General Puller arrived at Parris Island, Berman took over and pre-pared his star witness (as much as anyone could prepare such a bulldog) for his day in court. Puller agreed to meet with the three prosecutors as well. Although the defense had enlisted Puller's assistance, the prosecution team was not worried after they heard Puller's views on McKeon and the trial. Fred Haden remembers the interview:

We got Chesty . . . in a room. And Chesty assured us. I can see him there. He was walking up and down. That was him, walking all the time, talking. . . . He said that son of a bitch [McKeon] ought to be shot. It's just absolutely terrible . . . he was just a bad apple . . . and that there was nothing wrong with the system, but it was him. And that was just what we wanted because he was a prominent guy in the Marine Corps.

At 10:15 A.M. on August 2 Berman choreographed his final act with the announcement, "The defense desires to call to the stand Lieutenant General Puller." In contrast with the commandant's courtroom entrance during the preceding afternoon, during which the court sat in stony silence, Puller's appearance immediately electrified the audience. Without hesitation Colonel Hutchinson reflexively stood and ordered the members of the court to do the same.

The following day the *New York Times* described the general's entrance:

A living legend came back to Parris Island today. He is Lieutenant General Lewis B. (Chesty) Puller, retired, the most decorated and revered of living Marines. . . .

The appearance of the stubby tenacious man with the face of an English bulldog and the chest of a pouter pigeon brought the largest crowd yet to the schoolhouse. . . .

Ramrod-straight, his uniform blouse ablaze with ribbons, the general sat in the witness chair and testified in a drill-field voice.

In Puller, Berman had a showman to match his own gifts. Bellowing loud enough to be heard at the far end of the island, the witness brought a ripple of laughter when he declared, "Now, if I don't talk loud somebody back there sound off and I'll talk louder."

The salty veteran immediately commanded center stage as Berman fed him his cues.

BERMAN: And for how long have you been in the United States Marine Corps?

PULLER: Thirty-seven years, four months and two days.
BERMAN: Where did you, sir, receive your training to become a soldier?
PULLER: Parris Island, South Carolina.
BERMAN: Can you tell us of the things that you learned while here as a recruit?
PULLER: Well, the main thing that I learned here as a recruit, that I have remembered all my life, is that I was taught the definition of esprit de corps. Now my definition, the definition that I've always believed in, is that esprit de corps means love for one's own military legion; in my case, the United States Marine Corps. It means more than self-preservation, religion, or patriotism. I've also learned that this loyalty to one's corps travels both ways, up and down.

In response to a request to "tell us briefly" about his military career, the general offered an impressive ten-minute monologue detailing every outfit in which he had served and every outpost to which he had been assigned. He had been awarded five Navy Crosses, the nation's highest award for valor short of the Congressional Medal of Honor.

BERMAN: What in your opinion is the mission of the United States Marine Corps?
PULLER: Well, I would like to say that the definition, my definition, a definition in the drill books from the time that General Von Steuben wrote the regulations for General George Washington, the definition of the object of military training is success in battle. . . . It wouldn't be any sense to have a military organization on the backs of the American taxpayers with any other definition.
BERMAN: What in your view is . . . the most important element of training?
PULLER: Well, I'll quote Napoleon. Napoleon stated that the most important thing in military training was discipline.

Having successfully enabled General Pate to tell the court whether McKeon's conduct constituted "oppression," Berman was ready to walk Puller down the same path. He framed a hypothetical question that outlined some of the most significant elements of McKeon's testimony and asked the general whether it was his opinion that such conduct constituted "oppression." Sevier objected on the same basis he had during the preceding afternoon—that the ultimate issue was strictly for the court to decide and not a subject about which the witness should be allowed to give his opinion.

Klein, however, allowed the general to offer his opinion, "as a military man," whether such conduct constituted oppression of troops. Puller told the court that in his opinion such actions were not oppression.

Berman then constructed a similar but more lengthy hypothetical question essentially assuming in greater detail the events McKeon had testified to and asking the general whether or not leading the men into the waters for the purpose of instilling discipline and morale was good or bad military practice. Sevier objected and was again overruled by the law officer.

Puller spun off on a tangent about the lack of night training during the Korean War and what would be necessary to win the next war. Berman reined him in and repeated the question, this time extracting the one-word response he had hoped for: "Good."

Once he had elicited the desired testimony Berman had the good sense to call it quits, but not without a few unctuous closing comments.

BERMAN: We have met before and discussed some of the problems of military training and practice on other occasions, have we not?

PULLER: Yes.

BERMAN: I have also had the privilege of meeting your charming wife, is that correct, sir?

PULLER: That is right.

BERMAN: Well, may I make this suggestion, if at any time you may want a break or care to refresh yourself, just indicate it, and I am sure the president of the court will entertain such a suggestion from you.

KLEIN: Do you desire a recess?

PULLER: No, not a bit.

When Major Sevier began his cross-examination he knew that he had a wily maverick to contend with. His most obvious line of cross-examination would have been to remind Puller of the comments he had made and the opinions he had expressed about McKeon only hours earlier when the prosecution lawyers had interviewed him. Captain Klein was allowing this witness broad latitude to express his opinions about military training. Puller's earlier opinion about McKeon and his reasons for it as expressed to Sevier and Haden would have been no more inadmissible than Berman's questions on direct examination.

Apparently not recognizing that the bombastic Puller was just getting warmed up, Sevier asked him a question about the propriety of night training for raw recruits. The question allowed the general to continue his earlier sermon about the deficiencies in night training.

The trouble with the average American today is that he is so used to the electric light that he has become practically night blind. Now, when you give him this training, his eyes improve under night training. As to when you give him his night training it doesn't make any difference when you give it to him. It is excellent. It is beneficial, and as I said before if we are going to win the next war, in my opinion 50 percent of the time of training should be allotted to night training.

Sevier then decided to try the Berman approach—frame a long hypothetical question, but one that assumed that the drill instructor led recruits, some of whom he knew could not swim, into waters at night with no reconnaissance, as a result of which six men drowned. Sevier asked Puller whether he thought any action should be taken against the drill instructor.

PULLER: I would say that this night march was and is a deplorable accident.
SEVIER: Would you take any action against me if I were the one who did that, if you were my commanding officer, sir?
PULLER: . . . I think from what I read in the papers yesterday of the testimony of General Randolph MacPate [*sic*] before this court, that he agrees and regrets that this man was ever ordered tried by a general court martial.

A deflated and incredulous Sevier sat down. Chesty Puller strode from the courtroom and the court recessed for half an hour. At 11:32 A.M. on Thursday, August 2, Emile Zola Berman declared: "May it please the court and you, Mr. Law Officer, the defense rests." Berman had pulled out all the stops, and now decided to quit while he was ahead. However, having pretty much run the show so far, it was for him to have the last word before final arguments and deliberations would begin.

BERMAN: Mr. President and Mr. Law Officer, I have never seen a Marine Corps review. I understand that General Puller will conduct a review tomorrow morning at eight-thirty. Could you put it [the next day's session] at nine-thirty tomorrow? I should hate to have to leave here and not have seen a review.
HUTCHINSON: Very well, we will adjourn until nine-thirty tomorrow morning.

# F O U R T E E N
# Seven Courageous Men

F or three weeks the seven court members had sat impassively while the prosecution called thirty-seven witnesses and the defense responded with eleven of its own. With the evidence phase of the proceedings concluded, the court opened at 9:45 A.M. on Friday, August 3, on the conclusion of the morning review. All that remained before final deliberations and the verdict were closing arguments by counsel and instructions as to the applicable law by Captain Klein.

Major Sevier summarized the evidence to the court, which, he argued, supported conviction on all counts. Berman's arguments followed. The prosecution was allowed a brief rebuttal. Each lawyer spoke for just over one-half hour. Sevier first addressed the alcohol-related issues:

We have shown you that there was an order [prohibiting drinking in the enlisted barracks] . . . that [McKeon] had knowledge of that order . . . that he did willfully and intentionally drink intoxicants in Barracks 761, that he knew Barracks 761 was a barracks housing single enlisted personnel.

. . . We have the testimony of Private McPherson that he saw him with the bottle, saw him raise it to his lips, and McPherson demonstrated here in this courtroom that the liquor came up into the neck of the bottle when the accused tilted it. . . . The accused's explanation that he was merely trying to demonstrate to McPherson that he being a man, and McPherson not being a man, that he was just giving the impression that he was drinking, gentlemen, that is impossible, that is unbelievable. . . . It is an offense to drink in front of a recruit, especially when the recruit is a member of your platoon. . . . The drill instructor is the one who is the pattern for the recruit. That is supposed to be the perfect Marine where this Marine patterns his entire Marine Corps career after the drill instructor.

Now, if I may skip back to charge 2, oppression. . . . The accused waited until after the movie at the Rifle Range Lyceum started before he even fell his troops out to move out across that dark range down behind the butts where there were no lights and no one in authority who would find him or could see him down there. . . . There can be no other implication, there can be no other assumption or inference that non-swimmers led into the dark tidal waters of Ribbon Creek through deep mud and unknown waters without any supervision on the part of the drill instructor who was leading them produced fears.

. . . No one could say that those men were not oppressed. Private Leake was taken to the hospital or sick bay. Four other men were taken to the sick bay with him. All with subnormal temperatures. You have heard the description of the platoon when it left that water. Naked, cold, wet, shook, scared, almost speechless with shock.

We have the testimony of the accused's activities during the day. It shows an intent, a design or plan, a scheme. There are the two additional field days given for no other purpose but punishment. There is the slapping of the recruits intended to scare them, and put them in fear, to punish them. You don't slap a man because you like him. You don't bully him. This was for punishment.

We turn then to Specification 1, which alleges violation of Article 119 in the Uniform Code of Military Justice involving manslaughter by culpable negligence. . . . Not one of those men would have been in that stream that night except for the orders of the accused. By his action he placed those men in a dangerous situation. That day, six Marines, six United States Marines, lost their lives. Gentlemen, those are six Marines who will not take their places in the Fleet Marine Force. Those are six Marines who will never get to go to sea duty. Those are six Marines who will never be riflemen or tankers. Those are six United States Marines lost to the United States Marine Corps, lost to their Service, to their country, and also lost to their families and loved ones. Placed in that stream by the acts and orders of the accused.

Now, we have the testimony that a number of those men were non-swimmers. Some of them said on the stand they couldn't swim a stroke. The accused admitted on cross-examination that he took for granted that he had non-swimmers. He admitted on the stand that he asked for the non-swimmers, and he admitted on the stand that some members of his platoon spoke up and said that they were non-swimmers. . . . After asking where the non-swimmers were he made no effort, he took no precautions whatsoever to see that they were in a safe position. . . . Let's assume that the accused was right, maybe he did have a bad platoon, maybe he was having a little trouble disciplining them, so he takes this platoon, a platoon . . . he admits he has no control over, on an unscheduled night march. He leads them out through the dark with more or less just a "follow me," no orders to close-up, no order to keep in column, and leads this mass out across the rifle range through the dark and into the stream, makes no effort whatsoever to maintain control. Gives no orders whatsoever. Does not supervise his column. Just plows on ahead through the dark. Now from the very testimony of the accused he says this was a disciplinary march. Is there any single instance shown even by the accused's own testimony where he attempted to maintain any semblance of discipline on that march? How can you teach discipline if you do not attempt to maintain it? There is only one answer. He just took his platoon out there because he was mad and he wanted to punish them. He wanted to get them wet and cold.

. . . The route which the accused took down to the area of Ribbon Creek was that route which would take him the furthest from any sentry post, that route by which he would have the least chance of discovery.

Now, at the beginning of this trial, the defense attempted to make much out of some alleged practice for unscheduled night marches. So far they have produced two witnesses out of three hundred, or out of two hundred and eight [actually 108], which in open court they first called for. . . . If there had been such custom condoned, some of the witnesses who were subpoenaed could have no doubt gotten on the stand and supported the contention of the defense, but only two witnesses were brought in front of you gentlemen. . . .

Gentlemen, based on the evidence—and I say all the evidence—that has been presented by both the prosecution and the defense, I ask you to return a verdict of guilty to each charge and each specification thereunder.

Sevier had done a professional and workmanlike job. His presentation was crisp and factual, alluding to most of the evidence, which when tied together supported conviction on each of the five charges. He never overplayed or overdramatized his hand; and, of course, he made no mention of the commandant's about-face or Chesty Puller's rambling discourse.

Emile Zola Berman rose for his final effort to persuade the court to extend to his client the leniency that had been recommended by the two illustrious witnesses of the preceding day. His polished peroration was as different in style from that of the prosecutor as were their backgrounds—one a career tank officer and part-time military lawyer, the other a seasoned professional city lawyer at the peak of his form.

> This ... affords me an opportunity, which I welcome, to thank you for what has been noticeable, your devoted attention to the evidence in this case, and at all times and frequently under circumstances which were not too comfortable. Also to thank you, Mr. President, for the many courtesies you have shown me in the granting of various requests I have made of this Court.
>
> I would be untrue to my own self-respect, gentlemen, if, at the very outset, I did not make it plain to you that no one is more aware that you, and you alone, have the sole responsibility, under your oaths and upon your consciences, to decide this case—yes to bring to it your combined intelligence, wisdom and passion for justice. I surely need not remind you of what was said long ago by a great sage: If judges—and that is what you are on these facts, judges—if judges would make their decisions just, they should behold neither the plaintiff nor the defendant nor the pleader, but only the cause itself. I am satisfied that your combined wisdom and experience will bring that view to bear upon the facts of this case.

Berman then tried to forge a more personal bond with the court. When the trial began, he had asked for their trust. He now closed in a similar vein, employing a technique he often used to gain the trust of New York juries. But this was no New York jury. It would be interesting to know the thoughts of the seven seasoned military veterans as they listened to this folksy approach.

> If I were to discuss this case with you, I would prefer to discuss it in an atmosphere of the living room of your home or mine, where I might sit down with you, both of us comfortable and neither of us formal, to tell you if I were there, what is the evidence in this case: that a fellow by the name of McKeon ... had a desire—maybe because his brothers had been Marines, maybe because he had been exposed to Marines in the Navy—a desire to become a Marine and to devote his career to it. . . .
>
> ... He had a devotion to produce Marines, basic Marines; in fact he even had a desire if it could have been accomplished to produce an honor platoon with men who were smart, well disciplined, well trained independent Marines

with that esprit de corps that makes this Service different from any other service in our country. . . . I say it's a fair intendment from the evidence that is before you, and I would say it to you in your own homes, that if McKeon had turned this platoon out in their present state as described here, to take their places on ships and stations in this Corps throughout the world and go into combat, his conscience would have hurt him to his dying day.

. . . Trial counsel still talks in terms of punishment, punishment. He wanted to get them cold and wet. What about himself? What about himself? Isn't that the key to his entire motivation? Do you punish someone by subjecting yourself to whatever rigors are to be accomplished even when you are less physically fit than those who are supposed to be punished or oppressed? This is lawyer talk, this isn't talk that's handled in life where people meet to make decisions. What about this practice that obviously other drill instructors, probably from the time that this base was established, were confronted with the necessity of doing other things not contained in the syllabi or the lesson plans, that almost every drill instructor on this base knew that there was a practice for certain kinds of circumstances in teaching men discipline to take them into the boondocks or marshes or these creek waters. . . .

. . . If these men had accomplished this exercise as so many other platoons have, they would have come out proud. They would have proclaimed that they had been able to do this. When you have pride you have spirit, and when you have spirit discipline becomes no problem whatsoever.

. . . Since this tragic event of April 8, everyone now talks about these dangerous waters, about what lurking pitfalls there were, but what did people think about this before April 8? Has there been one called to this stand, has there been a single regulation put in evidence, has there been a single statement made by anyone that up to April 8, on Parris Island, Ribbon Creek was called [anything but] a meandering little creek from which people fished? . . .

What happened? It's an unhappy thing that's really a melancholy fact, gentlemen, that even with this trial no one, no one will ever know precisely what happened. We do know that there was an accident and that there was panic, but I tell you this tragedy was not caused as a result of danger. It was not caused by any carelessness. It was not because of any wrongdoing, and it was not because of any heedlessness. The loss of these lives was due to panic.

. . . Panic can never be predicted, panic can never be foreseen, and not even by the most careful of reasoning men, because panic cannot be explained by reason.

Were I, then, maybe in your homes, sitting with you, to go on and tell you that because of this tragedy, gentlemen, because of this tragedy, in the light of the after result, because of public clamor, because of politics and high places—yes, even in the Halls of Congress—because of mistakes that were made in handling this matter, that this man whose life and career, whose devotion and dedication I have already told you about was then charged with being a criminal, would there be one amongst you who would not have exclaimed, "What a shame, what an outrage, what are they trying to say, that this man who in his whole lifetime of exemplary conduct, of devotion to duty, of religion, of protection of family, all of a sudden and unaccountably turns out to be a criminal and behave like one?" Because make no mistake about it, oppression and manslaughter are crimes, high crimes.

I have spoken to you about the injustice of the charges of oppression and manslaughter. A word about a thing called negligent homicide. That is to say, the loss of life as a result of simple negligence. You know the combination of hindsight and tragedy impose a great emotional strain on anyone called to consider it. Negligence, gentlemen, negligence is not determined in the light of the after results no matter how distressing or tragic the result may have been. Negligence has to be bottomed on and premised upon the acts of a man before the results as to whether or not those are acts that others in the same position would reasonably have done, and for that reason I have shown you what is common practice here. Negligence depends on knowledge. Was there any reason on the part of any one here on this whole base to assume that there was danger lurking in the marsh and waters of Ribbon Creek? The answer to that was not before April 9. . . .

I come now to Charge 1 [drinking in enlisted barracks]. I think it is a fair interpretation from the reading of that regulation that what was being prohibited, and there was a prohibition, was to prevent carousing in such quarters. . . . Nevertheless my self-respect and my duty to deal fairly with the court requires me to tell you that in my view there was a technical violation of that regulation. So I leave that matter for your own good judgment.

With respect to Charge 4 [drinking in the presence of a recruit]. . .ordinarily you would have an inference that if a fellow puts a bottle up to his lips there is an inference that he put it there to have a drink, but inferences always yield to the facts. Sgt. McKeon is not being tried here for the appropriateness of a gesture or the weak kind of an illustration to prove a point. . . . You have all seen Sgt. McKeon. You have had him under your observation for close to 3 weeks. You have seen him on examination and cross-examination.

You have watched his manner. You have observed the way in which he has testified. You have listened to him and you have studied him. Is there one, is there one among you who doubts his sincerity, his decency, and that the truth was told by him?

... The whole concept of justice demands that each man, each man receive his just due. We have a right, I say we have a right to expect a verdict of acquittal on Charges 2, 3 and 4, and along the specifications thereunder contained. Not because I stand here before you to ask for it, but because the evidence, the opinions of outstanding experts, the facts, and the cause itself requires it. Indeed, because justice cries out for it.

I have spent many, many weeks with my obligation and responsibility to Sgt. McKeon, and to the United States Marine Corps. I have tried to serve them both well. At least, to the best of my ability. At long last it comes to me to take this mantle of responsibility that I have carried heavily now for a long time and turn it over to you. You must now assume that burden both for McKeon and the court. I am confident you will deal well with each. You have my thanks for your patience in listening to me.

After the morning recess, Captain Klein faced the court to instruct them on the law they would have to apply to determine their verdict. The law officer had had the preceding evening to prepare his instructions, aided by briefs and proposed instructions submitted by the lawyers for the prosecution and the defense.

Among the charges the accused was facing was oppression, a term not defined in the Uniform Code of Military Justice. The issue of the proper definition of oppression had already arisen during the arguments over Berman's motion for dismissal at the conclusion of the prosecution's case. The prosecution maintained that oppression meant simply "an act of cruelty, severity, unlawful extraction, domination or excessive use of authority." The defense argued that "oppression" denoted something more severe—cruelty and the subjection of another to unjust hardships through tyranny.

In his charge to the court, Klein adopted the definition urged by Berman, Lester, and the defense team: "Oppression means the unjust or cruel exercise of authority or power, the subjection of unjust hardships through tyranny." The defense was pleased. The more stringent the standard, the less likely McKeon's conduct would be considered to have been in violation of it.

Klein spoke for nearly an hour, defining the legal elements of each of the charges. He explained to the court the meaning of "proximate cause" and "reasonable doubt," advising them that they were the ultimate arbiters of the weight of the evidence and the credibility of each of the witnesses. The court members were told in conclusion that each of them "must impartially resolve the ultimate issue as to the guilt or innocence of the accused in accordance with the law, the evidence admitted in court, and your own conscience."

Court closed at 12:45 P.M. on Friday, August 3. The fate of Matthew McKeon was now in the hands of the six marine officers and one navy doctor who had sat for three weeks in the steamy schoolhouse listening impassively to testimony from witnesses ranging from lowly privates to the most powerful man in the Marine Corps. McKeon, his pregnant wife, Betty, and his family members joined Father Cook for lunch at the base cafeteria. After that they could only wait and pray.

Colonel Hutchinson and the other court members ate lunch and immediately began their deliberations. Hutchinson, by appointment as well as through the respect he had earned during the three weeks the men were together, led the discussions.

At the outset, one issue caused great concern among the marine officers. The commandant had switched his position in the case and was advocating only minimal punishment for McKeon. To defy that "recommendation" might be considered tantamount to defying a command order. Lt. Bentley Nelson, the navy doctor, and Maj. Nicholas Sisak had been unimpressed with Pate's demeanor and his testimony. Nelson thought that Pate failed to exhibit the class that a man of his profession should have shown. Sisak found him too jocular and flippant. Perhaps their lack of respect aided them in making their decision. In the end, all seven men agreed that regardless of the possibility of retaliation and personal outcome, they were going to do what they considered right. Having made that courageous decision, they all agreed that they would not be prejudiced by the commandant's opinion.

McKeon had impressed each officer of the court as a sincere, honest, and straightforward man. Lieutenant Nelson was impressed by the difficulty the sergeant was facing in trying to train the platoon. The alcohol factor—which, other than the drownings, had been the most inflammatory aspect of the case—was discussed. Although McKeon by his own admission had drunk vodka in the barracks, none of the seven court members thought McKeon was drunk on the evening of April 8.

Ultimately, despite his exemplary prior record and the fact that this was not the first time a drill instructor had led his recruits at night into the boondocks, the consensus was that McKeon had done wrong. Leading men into unknown waters knowing there were nonswimmers among them was a seriously negligent act.

Colonel Hutchinson explained that whatever penalty the court imposed could be reviewed by the secretary of the navy, who had the authority to reduce any penalty but not to increase it. Whatever penalty they decided on would be their decision; they would not be influenced by either Chesty Puller or the commandant.

After just over six hours of deliberation, Colonel Hutchinson polled each member of the court. All agreed that the drownings had been caused by McKeon's negligence. The prosecution had not proven that the negligence was culpable—that is "gross, reckless, deliberate, or wanton disregard for the safety of others." Further, the charge of oppression had not been proved. On the final charge—that he had drunk alcohol in the presence of recruit David McPherson—the court was willing to give the accused the benefit of the doubt. Each member announced his affirmation. The decision was unanimous. At 7:25 P.M. the seven men returned to the courtroom to announce their decision in what had become probably the most celebrated court-martial in the history of the Marine Corps.

McKeon, with Berman at his side, stood at attention facing Colonel Hutchinson when court resumed. The president announced that by the required two-thirds vote (actually by unanimous vote) the accused had been found guilty of involuntary manslaughter by simple negligence and of drinking in an enlisted barracks. He had been found not guilty of the two most serious offenses—manslaughter by culpable negligence and oppression—or the lesser offense of drinking in the presence of a recruit.

Because of the lateness of the hour, sentencing was postponed until the following morning. The McKeon family and the defense team must have been pleased. Ideally, McKeon would have been acquitted on all counts except drinking in the barracks. Realistically, beating the two most serious charges left him with a good chance of achieving his two primary objectives: staying out of prison and remaining in the Marine Corps.

The sentencing hearing convened at 9:25 A.M. on Saturday, August 4. Major Sevier reported that the accused had no prior record. Berman was afforded the opportunity to address the court and used it to remind the court members of Matthew McKeon's excellent character and commendable prior military record. He implied that the reduction of one grade in rank, similar to the punishment received by Scarborough and King, would be fitting for drinking in the barracks.

As to involuntary manslaughter by simple negligence, Berman claimed that the United States military code is the only body of law that makes simple negligence a criminal offense. He asked the court to impose the sentence it considered appropriate subject to two conditions. The first was that any sentence to the brig be limited to time already served, particularly as McKeon's third child was due to be born within a week. The second request was that he be allowed to remain in the Marine Corps and assigned to a place "where his experience, and his talents and his devotion can well be used."

After Berman spoke, Captain Klein advised the court that the maximum penalty they could impose on the two guilty verdicts would be a dishonorable discharge, confinement at hard labor for three years, forfeiture of all pay and allowances, and reduction to the lowest pay grade.

The court adjourned to consider the appropriate penalty for McKeon's acts. After just over four hours, McKeon and Berman once again stood before the court. Colonel Hutchinson looked directly at the two tense faces before him and announced the sentence of the court: reduction to the rank of private, nine months of hard labor, thirty dollars per month forfeiture in pay, and the toughest blow of all, termination from the Marine Corps with the disgrace of a bad-conduct discharge.

McKeon and Berman were taken aback. After gaining acquittals on the most serious offenses, and considering the testimony of Generals Pate and Puller, it seemed to them that the court had been unduly harsh. Betty McKeon stood weeping as Berman tried to console her with a kiss on the cheek, telling her: "Go on home with Mac. See nobody and say nothing."

Because of the notoriety of the case and the commandant's involvement, there still remained a chance that the secretary of the navy would reduce the severity of the court-imposed punishment. Public passion had been quelled by the passage of time and by Berman's masterful public relations efforts prior to the trial.

Inasmuch as the secretary had convened the McKeon court-martial (the commandant having recused himself from doing so because of prior prejudicial comments), it was incumbent on him to review the entire record. The power granted to the secretary of the navy in this regard goes far beyond typical appellate review, which is confined to the narrow question of whether there was an error of law requiring reversal. Court-martial convening authorities may review the entire record, including the sentence, although they may modify the court's decision only in favor of the accused, never against him or her.

The office of the judge advocate general was charged with the responsibility of reviewing the trial record for the secretary of the navy. Although there was ample evidence to support the findings and sentence of the court-martial, any conviction resulting in confinement of six months or more or a punitive discharge required a review by the Naval Board of Review. There were strong indications that Captain Klein had made so many errors prejudicial to McKeon (leaving aside errors in his favor) that the case would have to be remanded for a new trial, although only on the charges on which he had been convicted. Further, if he were again convicted, the sentence could not exceed that imposed after the first trial.

The last thing the commandant and the Marine Corps wanted at that juncture was to retry McKeon. The crisis was finally over. Their objective was to find a means to keep the case from the Naval Board of Review. Berman now had the leverage he needed to negotiate a reduction in McKeon's sentence and achieve his primary objective of allowing McKeon to remain in the Marine Corps. In order to avoid a retrial, the Marine Corps agreed to a reduced sentence—one more in keeping with the crimes of which McKeon had been found guilty—that would not necessitate intervention by the Naval Review Board. Those negotiations resulted in the ultimate decision by Secretary Thomas.

On October 5, 1956, the secretary issued a fifteen-page report outlining his findings and decision. He concluded that "the accused received a fair trial in every respect." That left only the issue of the sentence. Thomas related that he had reviewed Sergeant McKeon's prior military history and found an excellent service record in both World War II and the Korean War. He then turned his focus to an appraisal of the sentence handed down by the court.

> In dealing with this sentence I would not, of course, reduce it in any way which would in my opinion condone misconduct, reduce the deterrent effect against possible future misconduct by others, or cut the sentence below the level of adequate punishment for the accused under the circumstances of this particular case. I believe, however, that . . . some reduction can be made in this sentence without injustice or danger to the discipline or morale of the service.
>
> . . . This case presents to me the problem of adjudging an appropriate sentence for "simple" negligence, which is not generally regarded by the law or society as nearly so blameworthy as the much more serious types of misconduct classified as culpable negligence or intentional misconduct.

The principal question in connection with the sentence is whether or not the bad conduct discharge should be allowed to stand. A bad conduct discharge will affect his entire future life and rehabilitation.

Thomas questioned whether a punitive separation from the service was necessary, particularly as such a discharge would wipe out virtually all veteran's benefits for McKeon and his family as well as severely limit his future employment opportunities. In reviewing the testimony, Thomas commented on how impressed he was that so many of the recruits who had followed Sergeant McKeon on the fatal night march testified positively about his character.

I am convinced that a punitive separation from the service is not necessary as punishment for this man, nor would the interests of the Marine Corps be served by such a separation. For him I believe that the real punishment will always be the memory of Ribbon Creek on Sunday night, April 8, 1956. Remorse will never leave him. Further, he is the father now of three children. He may be expected to appreciate the feelings of those whose sons were lost that fateful night. His conduct immediately following the loss, and the spontaneous statements he made at the time, speak eloquently of remorse.

For all of the foregoing reasons, I have determined that the bad conduct discharge should be remitted.

The secretary was also inclined to grant some leniency on the sentence of nine months of hard labor. Noting that McKeon had already served six and one-half weeks in the Parris Island brig and more than four months of confinement thereafter, Thomas reduced the punishment to a total of three months' hard labor.

Having extended himself this far, however, Thomas was unwilling to modify the reduction in rank to private imposed by the court-martial. He observed that by McKeon's own testimony he had ordered the recruits into tidal waters in an area unfamiliar to him while knowing that his platoon included nonswimmers. Retaining McKeon in a position of trust after such a fatal breach of it by him would tend to weaken the confidence marines must have in their noncommissioned officers.

The court reached the decision that Staff Sergeant McKeon should be reduced to private, a grade which does not carry with it command authority over men. I concur, and I will approve the court's sentence of reduction from staff sergeant to private.

By remitting the bad conduct discharge, I have restored to Sergeant McKeon the opportunity to build for himself a useful and honorable career. I hope and believe that he will avail himself of this opportunity. I am convinced of his fundamental dedication to the Marine Corps and to his country. I recognize that the road back will be a hard one for Sergeant McKeon. I am giving him his chance.

With McKeon's sentence reduced below the level requiring further review, the Marine Corps could put the case to rest and begin to heal the wounds it had caused. Matthew McKeon would have an opportunity to rebuild his career in the military unit he had served so well but for the fateful decisions he made on April 8, 1956.

# F I F T E E N

# Closing the Book

The events at Parris Island during the weekend of April 7 and 8, 1956, illustrate the latitude given to drill instructors in controlling and disciplining the recruits under their supervision. Sergeant McKeon had been left free to drink in the barracks with his two companions, to leave his platoon while on duty to order a drink at the Staff NCO Club, to sleep for the better part of the afternoon while still on duty, and to lead a platoon of seventy-five men across the heavily traveled main road at the rifle range and off toward the marsh and waters beyond without any interference from his superiors. At no time until Sunday night, when Captain Patrick discovered the shivering survivors straggling back from Ribbon Creek, was there any hint of officer supervision of the weekend's activities. The drill instructor was the boss—answerable only to himself except in the rare circumstances when he happened to be caught in flagrant misconduct.

Drill instructors had long been given a free hand to accomplish the enormously difficult task of making proud, disciplined basic marines out of raw recruits in ten weeks. Strenuous physical activity, classroom sessions, rifle training, and hours of marching drill were all part of the daily routine. Each platoon marched wherever it went and never left Parris Island from the beginning to the end of boot camp. An integral part of the "instruction" method long in use involved occasional application of physical force known as "thumping." Pushing and shoving, a rap on the back of the head, a kick in the seat of the pants were commonly accepted means of "motivation" designed to instill discipline. Only if a recruit received serious injuries, and then only if there were ample witnesses ready to testify, would a drill instructor be court-martialed for maltreatment.

Richard Hudson, a 1948 Parris Island recruit and later a drill instructor in the mid-1950s, remembers,

> During the time I was in boot camp there were incidents of "thumping." . . . A lot of the DIs were veterans of the Pacific and seemed to be an unforgiving group. I received a hard kick in the butt when I moved my foot a couple of inches after the platoon was called to a halt.
>
> One senior DI had a routine that he felt was good for instilling discipline. He would place a very young looking DI in his platoon with new dungarees, hat pulled down to his ears, and blend him in with the others; this would be in the first couple of days before they knew each other. Once on the drill field the "shill" would start screwing up. The DI would then go into his act of beating and screaming at the individual causing him so much grief. After a period of time the PLANT would start yelling that he could not take any more and leave ranks. When ordered to fall in he would yell more, "No, I can't take it, I can't take it," drop his rifle and start running across the drill field. In the meantime the DI had picked up his rifle and was yelling, "Get back here you son-of-a-bitch." The PLANT, yelling, "No, sir," continued to run, whereupon the DI chambered a round (blank, of course) in the rifle and fired.
>
> The planted recruit would scream and fall. The DI would then turn toward a couple of other DIs awaiting their cue and [say,] "Carry that worthless bastard off my drill field." "O.K. Sarge, we'll take care of it."

The plant was carted off the field, and the awestruck recruits' terror and fear of their drill instructor were instantly elevated to a new plateau. The routine continued with other platoons in their formative stages until an officer happened to spot the charade and, suppressing his mirth, suggested that it not be repeated.

Eugene Alvarez, who served two tours as a Parris Island drill instructor in the mid-to late 1950s and later wrote a detailed history of Parris Island, documented the pervasiveness of at least some degree of thumping since the inception of recruit training.

> Prior to the mid-1950s, a miniscule amount of published material existed on harsher methods used by DIs. Hazing and maltreatment were simply accepted as part of becoming a Marine—something the uninitiated cannot understand. . . . Forms of hazing and maltreatment have been evident at

Parris Island since 1917, although maltreatment was never "officially" sanctioned by the Corps.

Although thumping and hazing in varying degrees have always been an integral element of recruit training, such practices have never been without controversy. Rather ironically, those marines and former marines who have suffered through the rigors of boot camp are the strongest defenders of traditional forms of training. In a survey of former recruits conducted immediately after the Ribbon Creek incident, 83 percent of Parris Island graduates believed they had been treated as marines should be treated. Only 7 percent of former recruits thought their senior DIs were "poor." Officer supervision was reported as "relatively infrequent." Dr. Alvarez reports that the survey "overwhelmingly revealed that the former boots approved of a continuation of the tough training, and some stated it should be more intense." In a letter to *Time* magazine in May 1956 responding to the initial report of the fatal march, a reader noted, "If the U.S. Marine Corps had not used the type of training program employed, your magazine would be limited to a Japanese edition."

While most marines who had successfully completed boot camp prior to 1956 endorsed the thumping, hazing, profanity, and tough training methods, which were left largely to the imagination and discretion of the individual drill instructor, that view was by no means shared by members of other branches of the service or by many civilians. A retired army colonel wrote to *Time* shortly after the drownings, "Where were the lieutenants, captains, majors and colonels who were McKeon's superiors? They are the real culprits. General Pate should have been above placing the blame on a four-stripe sergeant."

A retired air force lieutenant colonel wrote to the *Washington Post* in August 1956:

> But in the vicious system McKeon was at the bottom of the stack. More culpable than McKeon are the officers appointed over him who deliberately and purposely closed their eyes to what they knew was going on. Their condemnation should be more severe. It is plain that the Marine Corps' hierarchy will not condemn these officers. It remains a job to be done by the United States Congress.

Brig. Gen. Wallace Greene, who was the presiding officer at the court of inquiry, described the situation as he found it shortly after arriving at Parris Island in the spring of 1956.

What we had at Parris Island in 1956 was an establishment using outworn, discredited methods (in a large part)—e.g. "Hazing" which was introduced by young inexperienced DIs in and after WWII—to handle—to train an entirely different type (in many ways) of American boy or girl. The material was there—the methods were wrong. . . . In P.I. the time for change was long before the catastrophe of 1956.

Old time Marines had been and were still in command positions at Parris Island in 1956 and the years immediately preceding. They failed the Marine Corps through their unwillingness to carefully and constantly monitor and supervise the training. SUPERVISION—24 hours daily—continual examination of planning programming, training and the accurate perception of [the] kind of individual arriving as a recruit was absolutely essential—the keystone to a successful depot. Instead, most of the old-time officers devoted their energies and time to golf, fishing, drinking and womanizing—leaving training principally to the NCOs. . . .

Immediately after his report to Congress on May 1, 1956, General Pate authorized the sweeping changes in the command structure at Parris Island that he had promised on Capitol Hill. General Greene was selected to head the newly created Recruit Training Command. Maj. Gen. David Shoup, a World War II Medal of Honor winner, was chosen as inspector general for recruit training. Both men would later serve as commandants of the Marine Corps.

Time was of the essence in the spring of 1956 as Congress was holding in abeyance the final decision on whether or not to authorize a full investigation of recruit training practices. Within forty-eight hours of General Pate's report to Congress, Greene and Shoup were in place and had selected their top staffs. Greene knew that not only he but also the entire Marine Corps was under the gun.

If things had not improved—*and quickly*—at Parris Island, there was certainly a real danger of traditional recruit training being abolished.

Among other changes in program was the introduction of a new and better balanced competitive physical training program involving DIs, officers as well as recruits. In changing the administration, a Recruit Training Regiment was established *separate from* and supported by the Recruit Depot command and facilities. In people—those who would not or failed in supporting new ideas, actions and programs were *summarily fired* and in most cases both officers and men transferred out of the Depot within 24 hours.

General Greene immediately met with all the DIs and NCOs under his command. He outlined to the six hundred or so men present what he planned to do and asked whether they wished to help him or opposed the changes. Despite a strong undercurrent of opposition, particularly from the younger NCOs, the senior men who were generally supportive of the changes prevailed. When he finally received assurances of support from the assembled group, Greene promised two things: "(1) no lowering of standards in recruit training and (2) a betterment of conditions under which DIs worked."

To implement the improvements he was determined to make, Greene

demanded money, personnel and fast logistical support from Headquarters, Marine Corps and, when it was slow in coming, immediately contacted General Shoup at Hqtrs. . . . *who always helped me—to the hilt!* The Commandant (Pate) and his staff (e.g., personnel, training and QM) often objected and deleted my requests but with Shoup's support "in house" and the ever-present threats of a congressional investigation and public image as clubs over their heads—I always got what I needed.

The changes instituted by Greene were both substantive and symbolic. Drill instructors, who often were on duty in excess of one hundred hours a week, were given more off-duty time with the addition of more DIs. New housing was built to alleviate serious shortages of suitable quarters for drill instructors and their families. Each DI received free laundry service, no small benefit in a climate where uniforms became quickly soiled and wilted in the heat and humidity. Some drill instructors were given special preference in assignments after their tour of duty on the drill field ended. In deference to the uniquely prestigious position of the drill instructor as well as to symbolize the new regime, the traditional broad-brimmed campaign hats were reintroduced.

In addition to the improvements designed to enhance the status and relieve pressure on the drill instructors, two other changes were instituted. A vigorous physical training program was implemented to ensure that recruits left Parris Island in top condition, and officer supervision of the daily training program was significantly increased.

The changes at Parris Island were real and visible. Thumping had not ended, but there was a new awareness that maltreatment would be taken more seriously than in the past, particularly with the increase in oversight. The essential features of recruit training—drill, marksmanship, and vigorous physical exercise—remained largely unchanged. The DI's traditional role as the molder of the basic marine was unaffected. By the time the McKeon trial was under way, there was already a new vitality in the Corps that ran all the way down the chain of command. Drill instructors, past and present, may have resented the way Sergeant McKeon was being treated, but they could hardly complain that the conditions under which they worked had not improved. Perhaps most significantly for them and for the rest of the Marine Corps, the changes brought about under the leadership of Generals Greene and Shoup persuaded Congress that the Corps had, in fact, put its own house in order as promised, thereby alleviating any need for further congressional action.

The turmoil at Parris Island that began on April 8 lasted through the conclusion of the trial. By August, when McKeon had been sentenced, the reporters had finally left and the new training regimen was firmly in place. The DIs and other personnel at Parris Island could finally resume uninterrupted their fundamental mission of developing good basic marines.

As normality returned, Matthew McKeon waited patiently for his final sentence from Secretary Thomas. He recalls being in Chaplain Cook's office just after the verdict, watching Don Larsen pitch his perfect game in the 1956 World Series and being returned to the brig without knowing the outcome of the game. His third child had just been born. McKeon remained in confinement until October when Thomas's report came out.

Thomas's decision to permit McKeon to remain in the Marine Corps and to limit his sentence to time already served was the outcome he had hoped for at the conclusion of the trial. Shortly after the secretary's determination, Private McKeon was transferred to Cherry Point, North Carolina, in an attempt to rebuild his shattered career. Arrangements were made for him to arrive unobtrusively at the vast marine air station under cover of darkness to avoid further notoriety. When he received word of Thomas's decision, McKeon vowed to "try to be the very best private in the Marine Corps." He immediately set about accomplishing that task, applying himself by day to his duties with an all-weather fighter squadron and working evenings in the kitchen of the enlisted men's club to augment his private's pay. In January 1959, his diligence and likable manner earned him the "Marine of the Month" award from his squadron. It soon became apparent, however, that McKeon was unlikely ever to regain his status as a noncommissioned officer and the command authority that went with it. Still bothered by his ailing back, he was found medically disabled and received an honorable discharge in 1959.

Today, Matthew McKeon lives with his wife, Betty, in a large brick former farmhouse in a suburb of Worcester, Massachusetts, near the spot where he grew up. His five children are all grown and on their own. His hair is thinner now and gray, but still close-cropped in the style of an ex-marine. At seventy-three he is a bit lame, but otherwise he looks fitter than most men of his age.

After forty years he recounts the events of April 8, 1956, haltingly while choking back tears. The memories still haunt him, and as Secretary Thomas predicted, remorse will always be a part of his life. He speaks of his forty-year burden with heartfelt honesty.

> If it wasn't for those people, I wouldn't have made it. If it wasn't for my family, I wouldn't have made it. I say it's religion, whether you believe it or not, it's a comfort, it's a comfort. You go down to the church and just sit there and meditate, pray for those kids. It's the only thing I can do for them. I hope they're much better off than you or I. I feel it. Some days you never think of it; other days it just hits you.

The ghosts who haunt Matthew McKeon will keep Ribbon Creek off-limits for as long as marines are trained at Parris Island. The memory lives on in every old-timer who ever went through boot camp. And as for the DIs too young to have heard of the tumultuous events of 1956, none will make the mistake of stepping into the tidal waters behind the rifle range. Every student at the Parris Island drill instructor's school must master a lesson entitled "Ribbon Creek" before he or she is allowed to graduate.

# SIXTEEN

# Retrospect

## THE COMMANDANT'S ROLE

By all accounts, Randolph McCall Pate was a decent man. He had held a series of staff positions as he rose in rank from second lieutenant to top general of the Marine Corps. However, his lack of charisma and limited combat experience in the branch of the service that most prided itself on valorous performance under enemy fire had earned him little respect from his subordinates, officers and enlisted men alike.

Pate's most pressing problem when he became the commandant was to ameliorate as much as possible the budgetary and manpower reductions imposed by the president and Congress in the aftermath of the Korean War. The news of the Ribbon Creek drownings only exacerbated the fears of the marine top brass that increasing political pressure would result in further damage to the Corps. Against that backdrop, General Pate decided to go to Parris Island immediately after receiving the report of the drownings to assess the situation.

The commandant has been roundly criticized by much of the Marine Corps for that decision. Fred Haden believes that

> there's no question . . . he should never have gone down there. That was a big mistake. That got the press down there. They announced that he was going down there and they [the press] got there before he did. Because they thought there must be something horribly wrong if the Commandant is going to leave Washington to go down there to look at this training accident.

Gen. Wallace Greene was also of the opinion that the commandant should not have rushed to Parris Island, a decision that Greene believed created unnecessary media attention. In Greene's view,

> General Burger, as Depot Commander, should have been directed to conduct a thorough investigation of the incident and to have expedited an early report to CMC [the commandant]. CMC would then have announced this to the media and stated that further action on his part would await the results of this initial investigation.
>
> In rushing personally to P.I., Gen. Pate's precipitant action mirrored his lack of judgment and his fear of public clamor (which was actually acerbated and intensified by his appearance at P.I.).

Such criticism of the commandant seems somewhat unfair. Certainly his appearance at Parris Island increased the publicity stemming from the calamitous events surrounding the drownings. On the other hand, Pate must have known that an incident of this sort could not be wished away or even minimized by essentially ignoring it or downplaying its importance. Only by taking prompt and decisive action could the commandant, as leader of and spokesman for the Marine Corps, gain some control of the public's perception of the events at Ribbon Creek and, in a larger context, of recruit training in general. The wolves were always there, and a hostile or mistrustful press would only feed their appetites. Furthermore, it was an election year, and Congress was very likely to begin a full-scale investigation unless immediate steps were taken to demonstrate that the Marine Corps recognized the seriousness of what had occurred and was prepared to do whatever was necessary to correct the situation.

Thus, General Pate and his advisers believed that unless a rapid response was implemented, the situation at Parris Island would soon metastasize and place the well-being of the entire Marine Corps in jeopardy. The strategy devised to blunt the potential disaster was two-pronged: to contact key congressmen sympathetic to the Marine Corps and promise them that there would be a full investigation and disclosure of the facts and that systematic training abuses would be eradicated, and to have the top officer of the Marine Corps show that he was personally taking control of the situation.

That strategy, including the commandant's Parris Island trip, was intelligent and insightful. In fact, the quick and forthright actions accomplished the ultimate goal by persuading both branches of Congress that no investigation was necessary. The real difficulty lay not so much in the strategy as in the man who implemented it. The commandant was not a sufficiently secure and decisive leader to oversee such a strategy. His intimation that McKeon was guilty before the investigation was concluded was extremely demoralizing to most active marines, particularly to staff NCOs, who sensed that one of their own was being summarily thrown overboard. Pate's subsequent declaration that the entire Marine Corps was on trial for the Ribbon Creek incident only served to exacerbate the bitterness. Furthermore, it gave Emile Zola Berman the tools he needed to mitigate his client's guilt and the leverage to persuade the commandant to appear at the trial as a defense witness. Pate's embarrassing performance there must have confirmed the perception in the minds of many marines, active and retired, that the captain of the ship was a lightweight. Ironically, while the commandant accomplished his primary goals of warding off a congressional investigation and implementing improvements in recruit training, his own lack of stature became painfully apparent during his pathetic performance at the Parris Island schoolhouse courtroom.

## ALCOHOL

The court of inquiry's determination that Matthew McKeon was under the influence of alcohol to an unknown degree when he led his platoon into Ribbon Creek was probably its single most damning finding. The popular press seized on the issue to paint McKeon as a callous drunkard indifferent to the safety and lives of the young men entrusted to his care. The prejudicial effect was enormous and only partially offset by the skillful public relations effort orchestrated by Emile Zola Berman in the weeks preceding the court-martial.

That McKeon drank vodka in the barracks on April 8 was not disputed. That he took a swig of vodka in the presence of recruit David McPherson was disputed but not persuasively. But the court's conclusion that he was under the influence of alcohol when he waded into the tidal stream and marched six of his men to their deaths deserves further scrutiny.

As previously noted, Dr. Atcheson had overseen a Bogens, or blood alcohol, test on the night of the drownings. Atcheson drew the blood from McKeon and read the results of the test. However, he was occupied with another patient part of the time the test was being performed, and certain mechanical aspects of the test were performed by either Corpsman Fox or Corpsman Redmond. Although the test result apparently indicated the presence of some alcohol in the sergeant's blood, Dr. Atcheson noted that he had little experience or familiarity with the test, that it had been discredited, and therefore that he could not determine the amount of alcohol in McKeon's blood. For those reasons, he stated, he did not lend any credence to the Bogens test results.

In addition to the Bogens procedure, Dr. Atcheson conducted several clinical sobriety tests. None of the tests so much as hinted that McKeon was in any way under the influence of alcohol; in fact, Dr. Atcheson found him to be "in complete control of himself." Then, however, despite his own observations, the doctor concluded that there was clinical evidence of intoxication—based only on a suggestive odor of alcohol on McKeon's breath and his acknowledgment that at some unspecified time during the day he had had a few shots of vodka. The doctor's report made no mention of when McKeon may have had his few shots of vodka—information that was essential in view of the series of negative field sobriety tests—in determining whether there was any reasonable basis for reaching that extremely damaging conclusion.

At the trial, Berman skillfully led Dr. Atcheson through an enumeration of the various sobriety tests he had performed on McKeon. Atcheson admitted that he knew next to nothing about the Bogens procedure. The doctor attempted to sustain his damning opinion that McKeon was under the influence by limply suggesting that he may have been under the influence of alcohol to a subclinical degree, but clinically he was not intoxicated. Having nowhere to turn, he had to acknowledge that when he circled "yes" on the question asking if there was clinical evidence of intoxication, he should have circled "no."

There is another point to be considered here. Despite Dr. Atcheson's turnabout, his tests were performed at least two hours after McKeon had immersed himself in the chilly waters of Ribbon Creek. Even if he was sober when Atcheson examined him, what is the likelihood that he was under the influence of alcohol at the time the march and drownings occurred?

Unfortunately, and for reasons difficult to fathom, many of the recruits who testified at the court of inquiry were not asked about McKeon's behavior or appearance, testimony that would have been of considerable assistance to the court in weighing the evidence on this critical issue. Fifteen of the twenty-three recruits were asked no questions bearing on the issue of McKeon's sobriety. Privates Porter, McGuire, Mulligan, McPherson, Butler, and Langone all stated that there was nothing abnormal about McKeon on the evening of the march.

Other than Dr. Atcheson, no witness, including the twenty-three recruits who testified, offered any evidence of conduct that was suggestive of any degree of intoxication. The only ambiguous testimony on this issue came from recruits Earl Grabowski, Lew Ray Brewer, and Richard Drown. Brewer noted that McKeon seemed unsteady on his feet and appeared to be tired. However, Brewer did not see McKeon take a drink, nor did he smell alcohol on him. Drown also remembered that McKeon had been somewhat unsteady on his feet, but this unsteadiness was similar to the limp McKeon had had for quite some time. When he returned from church, Grabowski "smelled a little liquor on" McKeon but saw nothing in his behavior that hinted at intoxication.

In addition to the medical and lay testimony, reasonable inferences can be drawn from the amount of vodka in Sergeant Scarborough's bottle from the time it was brought into the barracks until the march began. By all accounts, the bottle when full contained a "fifth," or 25.6 ounces of vodka. When Scarborough retrieved it from his automobile late Sunday morning it was just over half full according to his account at the court of inquiry. At the court-martial he testified that the bottle was approximately half full. Sergeant King joined Scarborough and McKeon shortly after they brought the bottle into the drill instructor's room. King claimed that the bottle was about half full when he entered the room. It was not clear whether Scarborough or McKeon or both had poured a drink when King arrived. There is no other evidence as to how full the bottle was before the first drink was taken.

If the bottle was exactly half full, it would have contained 12.8 ounces. Assuming that there are approximately eight inches of alcohol in a fifth, and that the bottle was slightly more than half full when Scarborough brought it into the drill instructor's room, in all likelihood there would have been no more than 14 ounces in the bottle.

Elwin Scarborough admitted to the court of inquiry that he had "a couple of drinks" with McKeon. King saw Scarborough take two or three drinks. King testified that he had one drink. Scarborough claimed King had one or two drinks. Keeping in mind that both Scarborough and King were facing courts-martial for drinking in the barracks, it is unlikely that they overestimated the amount each of them consumed.

Let's assume further that an average drink consists of about 1.5 ounces of vodka. If Scarborough had no more than two drinks and King had only one, between them they would have consumed about 4.5 of the 14 ounces available. We now know that McPherson took a "swig," which would probably account for the depletion of another ounce.

When Pfc. Fred Magruder arrested McKeon, the bottle was about one-fourth full, or so Magruder recollected at the court of inquiry. He later hedged his testimony at the trial and said about one-fourth or less. Corporal Lyons retrieved the bottle from behind the commode in the drill instructor's bathroom. Lyons recalled that there was about an inch and a half of fluid in the bottle, which would make it slightly less than one quarter full. Staff Sergeant Overpeck, the sergeant of the guard, was given the bottle by Magruder. He recalled that there was about one and a half to two inches of fluid in the bottle. The depot officer of the day, Lieutenant Oral Newman, was next in the chain of custody. When the vodka bottle was turned over to him, it contained about an inch and a half to two inches of vodka. McKeon testified that about three inches remained in the bottle. Sergeant Huff estimated that when he saw the bottle at about 10:00 P.M. there was about two and a half to three inches of liquid in it.

If the 25.6 ounces of vodka filled a bottle to a height of about eight inches, each inch would represent just over 3 ounces. If one and a half inches of fluid remained in the bottle when it was confiscated by Private Magruder, there would have been about 4.5 ounces of unconsumed vodka. Other estimates would indicate that an even greater amount remained.

If the bottle contained about 14 ounces of vodka to begin with, and 4.5 ounces remained when the bottle was confiscated, there are 9.5 ounces to be accounted for. Scarborough, King, and McPherson drank at least 5.5 ounces; McKeon, in turn, could not have drunk more than 4 ounces. If Scarborough had a third drink and King had a second drink, or if more than 4.5 ounces remained in the bottle when it was confiscated, McKeon would have consumed even less than 4 ounces. Scarborough's testimony that McKeon had a couple of drinks; King's uncertainty as to whether McKeon had had one, two, or three drinks; McKeon's trial testimony that he had two drinks which he chased with a Coke; and his earlier statement that during the course of the day he had at the most three or four drinks are all consistent with McKeon having consumed no more than 4 ounces of vodka.

At the Staff NCO Club in the early afternoon, McKeon had a sip of whiskey and a few "swallows" of beer. He was there for only a short time, part of which was spent admiring an acquaintance's automobile. The acquaintance never testified, nor was he ever identified. There is no evidence suggesting that his testimony regarding his activities or alcohol consumption at the club was untruthful. In fact, his testimony seems quite candid, as there was no one who would have testified to any alcohol consumption at the NCO Club if McKeon had not admitted it.

In sum, McKeon's alcohol consumption was no more than—and perhaps less than—about three ounces of vodka near midday, a sip of whiskey and a few swallows of beer at about 1:30 P.M., and probably a swig of vodka near

8:00 P.M. In the meantime, he slept for about two hours in the afternoon and ate a full meal shortly before 6:00 P.M. It may be that McKeon had an odor of alcohol on his breath. It defies common experience to conclude that such a modest amount of alcohol, nearly all of which was consumed seven hours or more before he first set foot in Ribbon Creek, would have had the slightest influence on his judgment or conduct on the evening of April 8.

## CHARACTER

What kind of man could callously lead seventy-five men entrusted to his care into treacherous waters knowing some could not swim and allow six of those men to drown? It was not difficult for the public to conjure up the image of McKeon as a drunken sadist exemplifying the worst characteristics of a brutal training program run amok. The commandant's declaration that certain unacceptable practices had crept into the training programs, as a result of which the Marine Corps itself was on trial, seemed to confirm in diplomatic terms the public's suspicions that McKeon was one of a primitive species that was debasing young American boys at Parris Island.

Only through the strenuous efforts of Emile Zola Berman and the testimony of the very recruits McKeon had commanded was the image of McKeon the heartless brute dispelled. One after another, the men he was supposed to have oppressed and maltreated took the witness stand at the court of inquiry, and later at the trial, to speak of their DI. Almost to a man they spoke well of him. The accolades were similar: "a good drill instructor," "lot of patience," "helped you if you needed help," "not violent or abusive," "best drill instructor on the island," "a good teacher," and so forth in a similar vein.

There was probably no single event that prompted Matthew McKeon to take his men into the unfamiliar creek on the night march. Certainly frustration must have been one of the most significant causes. His assessment that the platoon had lost its cohesiveness and spirit was confirmed by many of the recruits who testified. McKeon's colorful assessment that 25 percent of the platoon were "foul balls" may not have been far off the mark based on the testimony of several members of the platoon at the trial and in later interviews. Staff Sergeant Huff, the crusty senior DI, claimed at the court-martial that Platoon 71 was the worst disciplined of the five platoons he had trained since becoming a drill instructor.

The quality of some of the men under McKeon's tutelage may also be measured by their behavior after completing boot camp. At the time of the court-martial, two men were AWOL from Parris Island, one was AWOL from Camp

Lejeune, one had deserted, one was in the brig, and one was awaiting punishment by his commanding officer. Although there are no statistics available to compare these infractions with those of other platoons, such conduct suggests that McKeon certainly had to contend with a number of recruits who posed serious disciplinary problems.

To compound the difficulties in dealing with a platoon of dubious overall quality, McKeon had been left to carry an inordinate share of the training burden. Staff Sergeant Huff had basically washed his hands of the young men under him. A World War II veteran, he was nearing the end of his tour on the drill field and had largely detached himself from any efforts to work with or motivate this disparate assemblage. Sergeant King, on the other hand, was hardly more than a recruit himself. Although he was earnest and well meaning, he lacked McKeon's maturity and experience. His willingness to allow the platoon to have a secret smoke when Huff had given orders to the contrary illustrates his inability to generate respect and discipline by example. The upshot of it all was that Sergeant McKeon became the man in the middle—a combat-savvy but inexperienced drill instructor trying to mold a quality platoon from extremely raw material with only limited help from his two colleagues.

At some time on Sunday, April 8, the myriad pressures working on Sergeant McKeon prompted his fateful decision to try a night swamp march in a desperate attempt to generate the spirit and teamwork that would be necessary for the platoon to complete the final inspections and drill leading to graduation. Whatever may have been its causes, the decision itself can never be justified. It was an egregious lack of judgment to undertake such a foolhardy exercise at night knowing that nonswimmers would be entering waters of unknown depths. That he did not intend the consequences does not excuse McKeon's negligence in exposing seventy-five young men, many of them there precisely because they were undisciplined, to a number of foreseeable hazards.

Judgment is one thing; character is quite another. Whatever personal shortcomings Matthew McKeon may have exhibited during the weekend that culminated in the fatal march should be viewed as only one dimension of the man's character. When the time came to face responsibility, he never wavered. Moments after emerging from the deadly stream, in all likelihood in some degree of shock, he was confronted by Sergeant Taylor, who demanded to know who was in charge. McKeon's response: "Sergeant, I am, I'm responsible for this." When a weaker man would have equivocated, evaded, or sought refuge in half-truths, he stood up and took the full blame for his own actions.

Later that night, when asked to give a statement as to what occurred at Ribbon Creek, he did so. He was less than candid about some minor details, but only to shield King and Scarborough. He admitted to taking several drinks. His statement was forthright and truthful in all material respects. When he was testifying at his trial he acknowledged going to the Staff NCO Club and having a few sips of beer and a sip of whiskey while on duty. Had he not volunteered that information, it is unlikely that it would ever have come out through any other witness.

McKeon's character was exemplified in other ways as well. Morton Janklow, the young lawyer who had accompanied Berman and Lester to Parris Island ostensibly as part of the defense team, had actually come along for another purpose. During one of the trial weekends while Berman was away on one of his secret missions, Janklow approached McKeon and offered him approximately $1,000 to sign over his rights to the story of the Ribbon Creek incident to a television or movie production company. At the time McKeon was earning $270.60 per month, which included a housing allowance, and was expecting his third child. That kind of money must have been an enormous temptation to a man in his financial position. To accept the offer, however, would have compromised him personally as well as Berman, Lester, Costello, and the other people who were fighting in his defense. To Matthew McKeon the $1,000 was a form of blood money, and he would have no part of it. After discussing the offer with his brother-in-law, Thomas Costello, who fortuitously had remained at Parris Island over the weekend, McKeon told Janklow that he was not interested. When Berman returned on Sunday evening and heard about the surreptitious proposal, he was furious. By that time, however, Janklow had vanished. He had no further interest in the trial after his proposal was rejected.

In August 1970, fourteen years after his conviction, a reporter from *Newsweek* interviewed McKeon at his home. When asked about the outcome of his trial, he was as forthright as ever: "I deserved what they gave me." His opinion has never wavered. By fateful coincidence, only a few years ago Matthew McKeon was a patient at the University of Massachusetts Medical Center in Worcester, Massachusetts. His nurse was a woman named Peg Michalak, whose father, she revealed, was Nicholas Sisak, one of the seven members of the court that had passed judgment on McKeon in the summer of 1956. McKeon looked at her from his hospital bed and told her that he bore no grudges. As he put it then and always has: "I got a fair trial."

Let the reader judge the man's character.

## WHERE ARE THEY NOW?

Gen. Randolph McCall Pate retired from the Marine Corps at the end of 1959 when his four-year tenure as commandant expired. No sooner had he entered civilian life then he was diagnosed with intestinal cancer. A preretirement physical examination also revealed that he was suffering from a brain tumor. He lived for a year and a half after completing a thirty-eight-year military career. He died in 1961 and is buried at Arlington National Cemetery.

Charles Sevier, the lead prosecutor at the McKeon court-martial, remained on active duty for another thirteen years after prosecuting his most celebrated case. Although he was an officer in a tank battalion, his court-martial experience was extensive both as prosecutor and as defense counsel. Sevier had great respect for Emile Zola Berman, particularly for his ability to orchestrate favorable publicity. He remembered Chesty Puller being "as elusive as an eel in a barrel." Sevier died of congestive heart failure on March 9, 1997.

Fred Haden, Sevier's assistant, was an artillery officer who also was called on to both prosecute and defend marines in courts-martial. He remained on active duty until 1970 and now practices law in Fairfax, Virginia.

Emile Zola Berman was at the peak of his career in the mid-1950s. Although an outstanding and successful trial lawyer, the two cases for which he received the greatest notoriety were both undertaken without compensation. In addition to the McKeon case, Berman was a prominent member of the team that defended Sirhan Sirhan for the murder of Robert Kennedy. In fact, Berman's role in the latter case was indirectly connected to his performance in the former.

After Robert Kennedy's murder, an effort was made to retain the renowned criminal lawyer E. Bennett Williams, part owner of the Washington Redskins and counsel to Jimmy Hoffa among others, to defend Sirhan. Bennett could not accept the case because he was a personal friend of members of the Kennedy family. However, Jeremiah Collins, the young lieutenant who had initially defended McKeon at the court of inquiry and assisted at the court-martial, was an associate in Bennett's law firm. Remembering Berman's stellar performance, Collins recommended him to the Sirhan defense team.

Berman's personal life was filled with considerable anguish. He was married three times. Both of his parents had experienced early senile dementia.

In 1956 he was a heavy drinker but was still functioning well. By the time of the Sirhan trial in 1969, Berman was clearly headed downhill and was probably suffering from early dementia. He retired from active practice in 1972 and died a resident of a New York City nursing home in 1981.

Howard Lester, the young lawyer who served as one of Berman's primary assistants, was responsible for researching and arguing several of the legal issues that arose during and after the trial. Lester continued in a civil practice in New York similar to that of Berman, his mentor. Today he is the senior partner of the firm of Lester Schwab Katz & Dwyer in downtown Manhattan.

Matthew McKeon's brother-in-law, Thomas Costello, continues to practice law in New York. Now in his early seventies, he remembers well the efforts by the highly respected Judge McNally to ensure that the Marine Corps would not grind up and spit out McKeon without a fight. Costello's office walls are covered with photographs memorializing this most prominent case of his career.

Capt. Irving Klein remains something of a mystery figure. Klein had never presided over a case tried under the Uniform Code of Military Justice. His lack of confidence in his role and lack of experience became obvious during the course of the trial, culminating with the near circus atmosphere by the time Chesty Puller took the stand. Klein committed suicide not long after the dust had settled at Parris Island.

Gen. Wallace Greene, who presided over the court of inquiry and spent a year implementing the reforms at Parris Island in the wake of the drownings, enjoyed his ninetieth birthday in 1997. A man of intelligence and high standards, Greene fought hard for the funds to improve the lax practices he believed had become entrenched in the Parris Island culture before he assumed command. Greene outlasted many of his enemies and was named the twenty-third commandant of the Marine Corps in 1964.

Duane Faw, the depot legal officer at the time of the McKeon trial, ultimately became the staff judge advocate for Commandant Leonard F. Chapman Jr. He retired in 1971 as a brigadier general. Following retirement, he taught for fifteen years at Pepperdine Law School.

The members of the ill-fated Platoon 71 are scattered about the country. I located and requested interviews with twenty-eight of them in preparation for this writing. All but one willingly cooperated. With one exception, all of the men interviewed forty years later spoke as highly of their former drill instructor as they had at the trial.

The lives of these men have taken different directions. David McPherson, the recruit in whose presence McKeon lifted the vodka bottle to his lips, became a marine flight instructor and later flew for thirty-five years for United Airlines, retiring recently as its number-one pilot in seniority out of Chicago.

Leonard Banashefski changed his surname to Bantel and became a rehabilitation counselor. Lew Brewer is retired from Chevron. Willard Brooks became a carpenter. Mims Brower still lives on his Georgia farm. Robert Dombo retired to Florida from the New York fire department in 1980. Richard Ferkel became a crew chief with an auto racing team. Walter Nehrenz is a retired police officer. Walter Sygman is a Spanish teacher in Miami, Florida. Many others are retired or pursuing disparate occupations. Bert Brown, Reginald Butler, Clarence Bruner, Soren Daniel, and Earl Grabowski are all reported to be dead. Fate has joined them with the young comrades they left behind in the murky waters of Ribbon Creek.

# Bibliography

## GOVERNMENT DOCUMENTS AND TRANSCRIPTS

Record of Proceedings of a Court of Inquiry, "To inquire into the circumstances surrounding the marching of Platoon 71, Third Recruit Training Battalion, into the swamps adjacent to the Weapons Training Battalion on 8 April 1956 and the disappearance of Private Thomas Curtis Hardeman, 1587021, USMC; Private First Class Donald Francis O'Shea, 1550900, USMC; Private Charles Francis Reilly, 1566628, USMC; Private Jerry Lamonte Thomas, 1585496, USMC; Private Leroy Thompson, 1590031, USMC; and Private Norman Alfred Wood, 1590034, USMC." Department of the Navy, Office of the Judge Advocate General, Alexandria, Virginia.

*Report of Commandant of Marine Corps on Parris Island Incident.* House of Representatives, Committee on Armed Services, May 1, 1956. Obtained from the Superintendant of Documents, Boston Public Library.

Verbatim Record of Trial of Matthew C. McKeon by General Court-Martial, Appointed by Secretary of the Navy, July 16–August 4, 1956. Department of the Navy, Office of the Judge Advocate General, Washington Navy Yard, Washington, D.C.

## LETTERS

Letters from General Wallace Greene, USMC (Ret.) to Eugene Alvarez, Ph.D., dated January 13, 1982; February 4, 1982; March 23, 1982; December 11, 1982; December 24, 1982; March 10, 1983; March 28, 1983; May 4, 1984.

## ORAL INTERVIEWS

*Platoon 71*

Richard Acker, telephone interview, June 3, 1996.

Eugene Ashby, telephone interview, June 1, 1996.

Leonard Bantel, telephone interviews, June 1 and 8, 1996.

Marvin Blair, telephone interview, July 23, 1996.

Lew Ray Brewer, telephone interview, May 28, 1996.

Willard Brooks, telephone interview, July 14, 1996.

Mims Brower, personal interview at Sylvania, Georgia, April 6, 1996; telephone interview, April 21, 1997.

Clarence E. Cox, telephone interview, May 25, 1998.

Jerome Daszo, telephone interview, May 28, 1996.

John Delahunty, telephone interview, May 28, 1996.

Robert Dombo, telephone interview, June 5, 1996.

Richard Drown, telephone interview, May 30, 1996.

Richard Ferkel, telephone interview, June 2, 1996.

Frederick Golden, telephone interview, July 7, 1996.

John Kochis, telephone interview, June 9, 1996.

Gerald Langone, telephone interview, August 17, 1998.

Lawrence Mann, telephone interview, June 6, 1996.

Matthew McKeon, personal interviews at West Boylston, Massachusetts, May 13, 1996, and July 14, 1997.

David McPherson, telephone interview, July 17, 1996; personal interview at Newburyport, Massachusetts, November 10, 1996.

Stephen McGuire, telephone interview, June 3, 1996.

Stephen Mihalcsik, telephone interview, June 5, 1996.

John Mitchell, telephone interview, August 19, 1996.

Hugh Mulligan, telephone interview, May 30, 1996.

Walter Nehrenz, telephone interview, August 19, 1996.

Daniel Sulitka, telephone interview, June 2, 1996.

Walter Sygman, telephone interview, May 30, 1996.

Ronald Tyre, telephone interview, June 1, 1996.

Thomas Vaughn, telephone interview, June 6, 1996.

Robert Veney, telephone interview, June 1, 1996.

*Other Persons*

Leland Blanding, telephone interview, December 14, 1997.

Rose Bond, telephone interview, September 24, 1996.

Plato Cacheris, telephone interview, October 1, 1996.

Jeremiah Collins, telephone interview, September 30, 1996.

Thomas Costello, telephone interview, May 14, 1996; personal interview at New York City, September 12, 1997.

Robert Sinclair Daniel, telephone interview, July 14, 1996.

John DeBarr, telephone interview, June 9, 1996.

Brig. Gen. Duane Faw, USMC (Ret.), telephone interviews, September 24, 1996 and June 25, 1997.

Fred M. Haden, personal interview at Fairfax, Virginia, August 13, 1996.

Richard Hudson, electronic interview, June 6, 1997; letter, June 13, 1997.

Hugh G. Jones, personal interview at Hepzibah, Georgia, April 3, 1996.

Nadine Stover LeBlanc, telephone interview, June 3, 1996.

Howard Lester, personal interview at New York City, August 12, 1996.

Richard Mample, telephone interview, April 27, 1997.

Bentley A. Nelson, M.D., telephone interview, January 21, 1997.

Charles Sevier, telephone interview, June 9, 1996.

Nicholas A. Sisak, telephone interview, January 21, 1997.

Charles R. Weddel, telephone interview, September 24, 1996.

## BOOKS AND ARTICLES

Alvarez, Eugene. *Parris Island: The Cradle of the Corps.* Macon, Ga.: privately published, 1984.

Davis, Burke. *Marine! The Life of Lt. Gen. Lewis B. (Chesty) Puller, USMC (Ret.).* Boston: Little, Brown, 1962.

"Death in Ribbon Creek." *Time,* April 23, 1956.

di Mona, Joseph. *Great Court-Martial Cases.* New York: Grosset and Dunlap, 1972.

Fleming, Keith. *The U.S. Marine Corps in Crisis.* Columbia: University of South Carolina Press, 1990.

Halberstam, David. *The Fifties.* New York: Fawcett Columbine, 1993.

Jeffers, H. Paul, and Dick Levitan. *See Parris and Die: Brutality in the U.S. Marines.* New York: Hawthorne, 1971.

"Making of Marines." *Newsweek,* July 30, 1956.

Manchester, William. *Goodbye Darkness: A Memoir of the Pacific War.* Boston: Little, Brown, 1980.

McCarthy, Joe. "The Man Who Helped the Sergeant." *Life,* August 13, 1956.

McKean, William B. *Ribbon Creek: The Marine Corps on Trial.* New York: Dial, 1958.

Millett, Allan R. *Semper Fidelis: The History of the United States Marine Corps.* New York: Macmillan, 1980.

Moore, Herb. *Rows of Corn: A True Account of a Parris Island Recruit.* Orangeburg, S.C.: Sandlapper, 1983.

"Official Report: The 'Death March' At Parris Island." *U.S. News & World Report,* May 11, 1956.

"A Right Guy." *Newsweek,* August 6, 1956.

"Too Tough for Soldiers?" *Newsweek,* May 14, 1956.

"The Tragic Ordeal of Platoon 71 Puts Marine Training under Fire." *Life,* August 23, 1956.

"The Trial of Sergeant McKeon." *Time,* July 30, 1956.

"The Trial of the Corps." *Life,* July 30, 1956.

"Where Are They Now." *Newsweek,* August 17, 1970.

## Newspapers

*Beaufort Gazette,* April 12, 1956–July 1956.

*Boston Globe,* November 2, 1989.

*Charleston News and Courier,* August 5, 1956.

*Evening Star,* July 26, 1956–January 29, 1959.

*Long Island Press,* May 1, 1956–August 8, 1956.

*Navy Times,* August 11, 1956.

*Newark News,* July 15, 1956–August 1956.

*Newsday,* July 19, 1956.

*New York Daily Mirror,* April 10, 1956–August 4, 1956.

*New York Daily News,* April 11, 1956–August 3, 1956.

*New York Journal-American,* July 8–28, 1956.

*New York Post,* April 10, 1956–July 25, 1956.

*New York Sunday News,* April 22, 1956.

*New York Times,* April 10, 1956–August 5, 1956.

*New York World-Telegram and Sun,* July 20, 1956.

*Parris Island Boot,* July 20, 1956.

*Washington Post,* August 20, 1956, July 5, 1981.

*Washington Star,* August 5–9, 1956.

# Index

Acker, Richard, 2, 4, 5, 9, 16
alcohol: analysis of vodka consumption, 166–68; charges concerning,
   57, 142, 147, 149, 150; consumption of, 90, 115, 170; McKeon
   under influence of, 56, 63, 80, 81,
   100, 102, 105, 109–10, 149; regulations against, 83, 84, 106; summary
   discussion, 164–68; testimony concerning, 90, 97, 100, 102, 103–4,
   105, 107, 109–10, 114, 115, 123,
   124. *See also* Bogens test
Alvarez, Eugene, 156, 157
Archer's Creek Bridge, 11
Armed Forces Committee, 61, 113
Armed Forces Information Office, 64
Army Air Corps, 68
Atcheson, Robert J., 105, 164–65; testimony of, 30, 48, 109–11

Baker, Hershel, 50
Banashefski, Leonard, 173
Barber, Melvin, 7, 98
Barrett, James Lee, 64
*Beaufort Gazette,* 72
Berman, Emile Zola: background of,
   67, 68, 69, 71; closing argument,
   144–48; examination of McKeon,
   118–25; examination of Pate,

129–33; examination of Puller,
   138–44; examination of Thompson,
   85–86; military service, 68; opening
   statement, 81–83; public relations,
   76, 77–78; today, 171–72; trial
   preparation, 69, 73, 75, 76, 79; trial
   strategy, 70, 74, 126; verdict, 150;
   voir dire, 79, 80
Bishop, James, 75–76
Blair, Marvin, 2, 4, 16
Blanding, Leland, 136
Bogens test, 29–30, 105, 106, 109–10,
   164–65. *See also* alcohol; Atcheson,
   Robert J.
boondocks. *See* swamps
Brennan, 104
Brewer, Lew Ray, 44, 165–66, 173
Brooks, Willard, 7, 173
Brower, Mims, 2, 4, 6, 9, 16, 28, 173
Brown, John R., 64, 173
Bruner, Clarence, 9, 173
Burger, Joseph C., 14, 31, 36, 37, 40,
   61, 163; court of inquiry order, 41,
   56; report, 59–60
Buse, William, 35, 57
Butler, Reginald, 165, 173

Camp Lejeune, 71, 73, 97, 119
Carlton, Edwin T., 70, 71, 80

Carneal, Wyatt, 64
charges against McKeon: Berman
strategy, 74, 83, 115; discussion of,
93–94, 106, 113–14; specified, 57.
*See also* alcohol
Clement, John E., 87–89
Collins, Jeremiah, 41, 71, 76, 171
commandant of the Marine Corps. *See*
Pate, Randolph McCall
Congress: investigation, 38, 60, 61;
and Marine Corps budget, 38,
162–64
Cook, Maurus, 135, 136, 160
Costello, Thomas C., 47, 48, 76, 79,
99, 170; closing argument in inquiry,
53–54; and McNally, 66, 67; and
Puller, 137; today, 171
court-martial: charges, 57; closing
arguments, 142–48; convened, 79;
deliberation, 149–50; directed verdict,
113–14; evidence of prior marches,
88, 89, 93, 94, 98, 118–19, 125,
144, 146, 149; hearing schedule,
72–73; hearsay, 105–6, 124, 137;
law officer, 71, 72; members of
court, 70–71; opening statements,
80–81; protocol concerning examination, 83–84, 85, 89, 92–93; recommendation of, 56; sentencing,
150, 151, 153; subpoenas, 102–3,
136; verdict, 150; voir dire, 79–80
court of inquiry: and alcohol, 165,
166; closing argument, 51–52, 54;
findings, 55–56; findings announced,
61; investigation of recruits, 45; and
Pate, 134–35; recommendations, 57
Cox, Clarence E., 28, 86
culpable negligence, 93–94, 104, 114,
124, 134, 143, 150, 152
Cummings, Samuel, 46, 117, 124,
126; testimony of, 106, 108–9

Daniel, Robert Sinclair, 173
Daszo, Jerome, 7
DeBarr, John, 63, 71, 76

Delahunty, John, 15
Demas, John, 70, 71
depot commander. *See* Burger, Joseph C.
Depot Order 348: 53. *See also* drill
instructors
Depot Order 5000.1: 83, 94. *See also*
alcohol
depot orders: against alcohol, 83, 94;
against swimming, 83. *See also* alcohol
*D.I., The,* 64, 65
discipline: enforcement of, 103, 107,
120, 124–25, 143, 146; McKeon's
orders concerning, 111, 112; Pate
on, 130; Puller on, 139, 140;
recruits' lack of, 82, 99, 100, 101,
102, 119, 120, 168–69; Silvey on,
49–50, 112; "thumping," 155, 156
Dombo, Robert, 15, 173
Dreyfus, Alfred, 68
drill instructors: generally, 64–65,
159–60; and hazing, 85, 111, 156,
159; McKeon's background as, 119;
Silvey on, 49–50, 111–12; supervision of, 61, 112, 155, 158; and
swamp marches, 94–95, 111, 112,
124, 146
drinking. *See* alcohol
Drown, Richard, 44, 104, 165–66
drownings of recruits. *See* march into
Ribbon Creek

Elliot's Beach, 112, 119
Ervin, Eugene, 9, 44, 102
*Essex,* 118

Faw, Duane, 37, 57, 60, 73; and Klein,
72; McKeon's confession to, 41;
today, 172
Ferkel, Richard, 97, 173
field day, 21, 23, 90, 99, 107, 114,
124. *See also* discipline
Flaherty, James, 136–37
Fleet Marine Force, 143
Fleming, Keith, 36
Fox, 105, 164

Fultz, Duane, 70

Gaines, Alice Rose, 69
Gall, Walter, 70
Geckle, Ronald, 9, 104
Golden Eagle Hotel, 76
Grabowski, Earl, 7, 8, 15, 165–66,
 173; assessment of McKeon, 45; tes-
 timony of, 97–98
Greene, Wallace M., Jr., 74; background
 of, 48; findings of court inquiry,
 55–56; instituting change, 159–60; on
 Pate, 163; recruit training command,
 61, 157, 158; today, 172
Grey, Richard, 50

Haden, Frederick M.: background of,
 71; on Pate, 162–63; on Puller, 138;
 today, 171; trial preparation, 73–74,
 76; trial strategy, 74
Hardeman, Thomas, 2, 4, 9, 16, 28,
 33, 89, 117
hazing. *See* discipline; "thumping"
hearsay. *See* court-martial
Heles, John B., 40
Hendrix, Lester, 2, 7, 16, 101
Herlihy, Charles B., 47
Hittle, James, 36
Holben, Donald J., 40, 41, 49, 51–52, 54
Holtzman, Lester, 38
House Armed Services Committee. *See*
 Armed Forces Committee
Hubbard, Hampton, 70
Huff, Edward A., 104, 119, 167, 168;
 background of, 16–17; testimony of,
 28–29, 91, 92–93, 95
Hutchinson, Edward L.: background
 of, 71; at court-martial, 70, 85, 98,
 108, 110–11; deliberations, 149,
 150; sentencing, 151

intoxication. *See* alcohol
involuntary manslaughter, 150, 151

Janklow, Morton, 99, 170

Jones, Edward, 15
Judge Advocate General, office of, 152

Kennedy, John F., 67
Kennedy, Robert, 171
King, Richard J.: and alcohol, 22, 166;
 background of, 16, 17, 119; McKeon
 testimony concerning, 124, 167, 170;
 and Pate, 75; sentence, 134; statement
 of, 46; testimony of, 90
Kinson, Carl, 38–39
Klein, Irving N.: background of, 71–72;
 concerning swamp marches, 94; and
 Faw, 72; instructions to court,
 148–49; likelihood of new trial, 152;
 McKean criticism of, 72; today, 171.
 *See also* Berman, Emile Zola; court-
 martial; Sevier, Charles B.
Korean War, 119, 162
Kraynick, Benjamin, 116

Langone, Gerald, 5, 122, 165; alterca-
 tion with McKeon, 23–24; testimony
 of, 44, 102
Lawless, Richard, 15
Leake, Lewis, 4, 6, 15, 28, 122; testi-
 mony of, 100–101, 122
Leonard, Edwin, 45, 104
Lester, Howard, 71, 76, 79, 172
*Life* magazine, 33, 69, 76
Lyceum, 121, 143
Lynch, Walter A., 68
Lyons, 29, 104, 123, 166–67

Magruder, Fred, 29, 50, 104–5, 166
Maloof, John, 7, 24–25, 99–100
Mample, Richard, 64
manslaughter. *See* culpable negligence
Manthey, Hans, 50, 84
march into Ribbon Creek: charge concerning, 56, 57; drownings, 7–10;
 McKeon's familiarity with, 56, 57;
 McKeon's testimony concerning,
 107–8, 118–19, 121–23; orders prohibiting, 59, 83, 85, 94, 111, 112;

march into Ribbon Creek (*continued*)
  prior swamp marches, 88–89, 93, 94,
  95, 98, 118–19, 125, 136–37, 144,
  146, 149; recruit testimony concerning, 98, 100, 102; recovery of bodies,
  32–33; route of, 2, 4–6, 98, 99, 100,
  107–8, 115–16, 144; water depth,
  124. *See also* swamps
marshes. *See* swamps
Martinez, John, 8, 123
McCarthy, Joe, 69, 76
McGarry, James, 48
McGuire, Stephen, 8, 44, 165
McIntyre, Gerald B., 40
McKean, William, 28, 32, 36; background of, 31; criticism of Klein, 72;
  order of arrest, 29, 31; testimony of,
  50
McKeon, Betty, 76, 77
McKeon, Matthew: and alcohol, 25,
  29, 30, 43–44, 63, 164, 165,
  166–68; altercation with Langone,
  23–24; altercation with McPherson,
  25–26; in Berman's opening statement, 81–83; Berman's trial strategy
  for, 70, 74; Burger's report on,
  59–60; character of, 1, 5, 17–18,
  109, 117, 119, 145, 147, 149, 168;
  character summary of, 168–71;
  charges against, 57, 74; confession
  of, 41; and court verdict, 150; cross-
  examination of, 126; direct examination of, 118–25; discharge of,
  153, 154, 160; experience of, 1, 5,
  56, 57, 169; and findings of court of
  inquiry, 56; official statement of, 46;
  opinion of recruits concerning,
  45–46, 168; Pate's report on, 60–61;
  and preparation for trial, 69–70, 76;
  on prior marches, 118–19; prosecution's trial strategy for, 74; sentencing of, 150, 151, 160; statement of,
  106–8; today, 161
McKeon family, 67, 75, 149, 150, 151,
  161

McLeod, Stanley, 31, 86
McNally, James B. M., 66, 67, 109,
  171
McPherson, David, 15, 57, 63, 100;
  altercation with McKeon, 25–26,
  164; assessment of McKeon, 45,
  165; testimony of, 25, 26, 44,
  103–4; today, 173
McTeer, J. E., 32
media. *See* press
Meeks, Maggie, 117–18
Michalak, Peg, 170
Millett, Allan R., 128–29
Moran, Joseph A., 8, 42–43, 45
Muckler, 21
Mulligan, Hugh, 8, 15, 165
"Murder of a Sandflea, The," 64

national mood, 12, 156
Naval Board of Review, 152
Navy Medical Corps, 70
Navy, secretary of the, 150, 151, 152
negligent homicide. *See* simple negligence
Nehrenz, Walter, 173
Nelson, Bentley A., 70, 149
Newman, Oral, 29, 51, 167
*Newsweek,* 170
*New York Daily News,* 62
*New York Journal-American,* 75
*New York Post,* 62
New York Supreme Court, 67, 68. *See
  also* McNally, James B. M.
*New York Times,* 63, 138
night training, 140–41. *See also* Puller,
  Lewis B.
Nolan, Algin, 48–49, 89–90

Opotowsky, Stan, 61
oppression: and Berman, 113–14;
  charge of, 57; defined, 148; Pate
  opinion, 131–32, 133; Puller opinion, 139–40; and Sevier, 143. *See
  also* charges against McKeon
O'Shea, Donald, 7, 8, 15, 28, 97
Otten, William L., Jr., 71, 87

Overpeck, Malcolm, 51, 167

*Parris Island Boot,* 72
Pate, Randolph McCall, 14, 35, 36, 59, 77, 84; background of, 128–29, 130, 162; and Bishop articles, 75; charges, 158; and Congress, 60, 61; criticism of, 157, 158, 163–64; disqualification of, 57; effect in court, 149–50; press conference, 37–38; report of, 60–61, 63, 72; response strategy, 163–64; testimony of, 130–33, 134, 135; today, 171
Patrick, Charles E., 2, 28, 29, 31, 104, 155; testimony of, 50, 95–96
Perdeas, John, 50
Platoon 71: 91, 95, 97, 119, 168; description of, 16, 19; during marksmanship training, 18–19; today, 172. *See also* recruits
Platoon 351: 64
Porter, Donald J., 8, 165; assessment of McKeon, 45; testimony of, 43–44
press: accommodations for, 72–73; generally, 111, 163; and Pate, 37, 38, 129; and public relations, 75–76, 77, 95, 117, 151, 164; reports of, 36, 62, 63, 75–76
Public Information Office, 72
publicity. *See* press
Puller, Lewis B.: background of, 137, 138; on night training, 140–41; on oppression, 139–40; and prosecution, 138, 171; testimony of, 138–41

Raddatz, Loren, 51
Rambo, William, 44, 45
recovery of bodies, 32–33. *See also* march into Ribbon Creek
Recruit Depot, 158
recruits: Berman's opening statement, 81–83; court-martial testimony of, 165–66, 168; drownings, 8; during march, 98, 100, 101; as inquiry witnesses, 45–46; nonswimmers, 114, 143, 144, 153, 169; official questioning of, 45; opinion concerning McKeon, 45–46; quality of, 12–13
recruit training: generally, 11, 12; Greene's changes, 159–60; lack of discipline, 82, 99, 100, 101, 102, 119, 120, 168–69; Pate's changes, 61, 158, 164; and thumping, 156–57
Recruit Training Command, 61, 158
Recruit Training Regiment, 158
Redmond, Billy, 105, 106, 164
Regan, Daniel J., 70, 71
Reilly, Charles Francis, 28; background of, 2–4, 116; during march, 5, 7, 9
Ribbon Creek, 71; description of, 7; drownings, 7–10; hydrographic survey, 115; location of, 2; march to, 2; McKeon's familiarity with, 56, 57; mud, 89, 102; tides, 87–89, 90, 102; topographical features, 87; trout hole, 33, 116; visibility, 90, 98; water depth, 115, 116. *See also* march into Ribbon Creek
Rivers, Mendel L., 38
Roberts, 35

Scarborough, Elwyn B., 21, 28, 75, 90, 104, 120, 134, 166, 170; official statement of, 47; testimony of, 114–15, 134
*Semper Fidelis,* 128–29
Serantes, 104
Sevier, Charles B., 79; background of, 71; examination of McKeon, 126; opening statement, 80–81; order concerning marches, 94; today, 171; trial preparation, 73–74, 76; trial strategy, 74; voir dire, 79. *See also* court-martial
Seybold, Gerald, 33, 89
Shaffer, Robert D., 70
Shoup, David, 158, 159
Silvey, David, 49–50, 112

simple negligence, 147, 150, 151, 152. *See also* culpable negligence

Simpson, 84

Sisak, Nicholas A., 70, 71, 149, 170

Sisak, Peg, 170

Sixth Marine Regiment, 71

Smythe, Lowell, 51

sobriety tests. *See* Bogens test

Spann, William J., 40

Sparks, George W., 31

Specification 1: 57, 94, 143. *See also* charges against McKeon

Specification 2: 57. *See also* charges against McKeon

Staff NCO Club, 115, 155, 167, 170

subpoenas, 102–3, 136. *See also* court-martial

supervision. *See* drill instructors; recruits

swamps: and McKeon, 100, 101, 103, 107; orders prohibiting marches into, 59, 83, 85, 94, 111, 112; prior marches into, 98, 118–19, 125, 136–37, 144, 146, 149. *See also* Ribbon Creek

Sygman, Walter, 6, 15

Taylor, John B., 27, 96, 123, 169

"T.Sgt. Jim Moore," 64–65

Third Battalion, 84, 85, 88

Third Naval District, 71

Thomas, Charles S.: court-martial order, 57, 70; decision of, 152–54, 160, 161; Pate's report to, 60–61; and questionnaire, 77

Thomas, Jerry, 7, 9, 28

Thompson, Robert A., 7, 8, 15, 28; testimony of, 50, 85–86

"thumping," 155–57, 158. *See also* discipline

*Time,* 157

*Today Show,* 75

trial counsel. *See* Berman, Emile Zola; Sevier, Charles B.

trial strategy: defense, 70, 74; prosecution, 74. *See also* court-martial

"trout hole," 33, 116. *See also* Ribbon Creek

Truitt, Thomas O., 104

Uniform Code of Military Justice, 56, 71, 143, 151; disqualifying Pate, 38; and Klein, 72, 85; and oppression, 148

United Press, 117

Valentin, Alaric, 71, 76

Vaughn, Thomas, 15

Veney, Robert, 7

verdict, on court-martial, 150. *See also* court-martial

Vinson, Carl, 33–39, 62

Volle, Leslie E., 115–16, 127, 128

voluntary manslaughter. *See* culpable negligence

Wake Boulevard, 2, 18, 121

*Washington Post,* 157

Weapons Training Battalion, 3, 11, 31, 87, 88, 95

Webb, Jack, 64

Weddel, Charles R., 83, 85, 95, 111

Whalen, James E., 66

Whitmore, Carl, 6–7, 9, 28

Wood, Norman, 7, 8, 15, 28, 99, 100; altercation with McKeon, 24–25

Wood, Ralph, 36

Zola, Emile, 68

# About the Author

John C. Stevens III, now a Massachusetts trial court judge, was a practicing trial attorney for more than twenty-five years. Long before starting his legal career, he spent the summer of 1957 as a Parris Island recruit. During those three months he experienced firsthand some of the aftershocks from the Ribbon Creek drownings and the McKeon court-martial of the previous year.

A graduate of Brown University, Judge Stevens also did graduate work in American studies at Washington State University. Since obtaining his doctorate in law from Suffolk University Law School, he has served as a contributing author for the *Massachusetts Family Law Manual* and has lectured extensively on family law and trial practice. He and his wife, Pamela, live in Massachusetts.